John Johnson is one of the clearest, humblest, and most loving voices for shepherds, leaders, and pastors. In a world where so many have been run over by the big bus of the American church, Johnson offers us a more lamb-like way of leadership—through care, insight, humility, brokenness, and meekness. It is always a joy to endorse John as a human—to say nothing of his writing. Read this. Slowly. And hear the voice of our Great Shepherd, Jesus.

A. J. Swoboda, PhD, assistant professor of Bible, theology, and world Christianity at Bushnell University and author of *After Doubt*

John Johnson develops a biblically informed theology of leadership. His central thesis is that authentic Christian leadership must be *God-centered*, finding its definition, priorities, and patterns in the nature, character, and purpose of God. Without ignoring secular theory (which often draws its ideas from biblical truth!), Johnson keeps his focus on this theocentric model of leadership. This book is highly recommended for those wishing to go beyond leadership fads and slogans to sound biblical principles.

Mark L. Strauss, university professor of New Testament at Bethel Seminary and coauthor of *Leadership in Christian Perspective*

Leadership and theology. Typically it is assumed these are two separate fields. However, into the storm of leadership material, Johnson offers a book that roots leadership in God himself. God defines leadership. I'm thankful for a leadership book that leans so heavily into the doctrine of God, Christ, and his Word.

Patrick Schreiner, associate professor at Midwestern Baptist Theological Seminary and author of *The Visual Word*

At last, a book on Christian leadership built on a theological foundation buttressed by careful biblical interpretation. It is neither an exercise in theory nor a pragmatic how-to book. It is a serious book about a critical issue for the church. John Johnson's rich experience as a leader, pastor, and teacher enlivens his biblical thinking at every turn. This book should be shelved in every pastor's library and used in every Christian seminary.

David Fisher, former pastor of Park Street Church in Boston and author of *The 21ˢᵗ Century Pastor*

When I was in my late twenties, I was put in a leadership position in a large nonprofit. I was in over my head. I took a leadership class at seminary from Dr. Johnson, and he (and the class) was a literal godsend. With warmth, wisdom, and kindness, Dr. Johnson helped me center myself in Christ and grow as a leader. *Rooted Leadership* is an amazing book that will help you—wherever you are in your leadership journey—to grow in character, competence, and wisdom as a leader. Highly recommended.

Matt Mikalatos, author of *Journey to Love*

Einstein is reputed to have said that if he had only one hour to solve a problem on which his life depended, he would spend the first fifty-five minutes determining the proper question to ask. Why? Because if he could put his finger on the right question, he would be able to solve the problem itself in less than five minutes. If Einstein is correct, then author John Johnson has done a great service by posing eleven penetrating questions to the subject of leadership. More significantly, Johnson draws on the wisdom of Scripture to identify the most helpful answers. And the answers are surprising, turning conventional "leadership wisdom" on its head. This book is a must-read for those who yearn for a deeper understanding of biblical leadership . . . and for all would-be skeptics who are tired of worn-out clichés and one-size-fits-all formulas.

Charles J. Conniry Jr., president of Western Seminary

Dr. John Johnson not only teaches leadership and writes on the subject but also has experience in global leadership in the church and in parachurch ministry. As a mentor to leaders, Johnson knows the questions that leaders are asking and the ones that they don't know to ask. He understands the challenges that leaders face in today's world. The book you are holding in your hands is a fresh spring of water in the dry desert. More than ever, our culture needs rooted, sound leadership that is grounded on a solid foundation, leadership that will inspire and give vision and hope. This book is a must-read for any student of leadership in the church who wishes to emulate Jesus as our leader par excellence.

Dr. Dan Sered, chief operation officer of Jews for Jesus and president of Lausanne Consultation on Jewish Evangelism

A refreshing and fascinating book on leadership! *Rooted Leadership* is both profound and easy to read. John Johnson does an amazing job in giving his readers a balanced scriptural view compared and contrasted with world leaders' misunderstanding and misusing leadership for their own gain. For those of us living in the Middle East, what struck me most is the redefining of power in chapter 9: an eye-opening theology of power, where power is "God-centered" and should be assumed for the good of the world. It is best described as such: the power of God is less about prideful achievements and more about acts of humility. This is a must-read for everyone assuming a leadership role and desires to advance the work of the kingdom!

Camille Melki, CEO of Heart for Lebanon

ROOTED
LEADERSHIP

*Seeking God's Answers
to the Eleven Core Questions
Every Leader Faces*

ROOTED
LEADERSHIP

JOHN E. JOHNSON

ZONDERVAN REFLECTIVE

Rooted Leadership
Copyright © 2022 by John E. Johnson

Requests for information should be addressed to:
Zondervan, *3900 Sparks Dr. SE, Grand Rapids, Michigan 49546*

Zondervan titles may be purchased in bulk for educational, business, fundraising, or sales promotional use. For information, please email SpecialMarkets@Zondervan.com.

ISBN 978-0-310-12089-6 (audio)

Library of Congress Cataloging-in-Publication Data
Names: Johnson, John E., (Professor of pastoral theology and leadership) author.
Title: Rooted leadership : seeking God's answers to the eleven core questions every leader faces / John E. Johnson.
Description: Grand Rapids : Zondervan, 2022. | Includes bibliographical references and index.
Identifiers: LCCN 2021050853 (print) | LCCN 2021050854 (ebook) | ISBN 9780310120872 (hardcover) | ISBN 9780310120889 (ebook)
Subjects: LCSH: Leadership—Religious aspects—Christianity. | Leadership.
Classification: LCC BV4597.53.L43 J64 2022 (print) | LCC BV4597.53.L43 (ebook) | DDC 253—dc23/eng/20220207
LC record available at https://lccn.loc.gov/2021050853
LC ebook record available at https://lccn.loc.gov/2021050854

Cover design: Darren Welch Design
Cover photo: © enterphoto / Shutterstock
Interior design: Sara Colley

Printed in the United States of America

22 23 24 25 26 27 28 29 30 31 32 /TRM/ 14 13 12 11 10 9 8 7 6 5 4 3 2 1

To my wife, Heather
Behind my teaching and preaching and writing
has been her steady and unending support

Tell me who your admired leaders are,
and you have bared your soul.
—GARRY WILLS

CONTENTS

FOREWORD

When I was a young leader, I spoke like a young leader, I thought like a young leader, I reasoned like a young leader. But when I became a man, I put away young-leader-ish things.

And then the trouble began. I had nothing much to replace it with. My youthful brashness, my know-it-all-ism, my pluck and hubris and shooting-in-all-directions energy gave way, slowly, to bewilderment, hesitancy, weariness. While before I ran where angels feared to tread, now I plodded and dithered and kept to well-worn paths.

I could blame it on getting old. But really, I had fallen into scarcity thinking—believing that I wasn't enough and didn't have enough. Underneath that, though, was a deeper problem: believing that it all depended on me. That the rising and falling of the church was in my hands. I had, at root, a stunted view of God. My God was too small, too dull, too safe.

My inmost conviction, it turned out, was that a failure of leadership could always be traced to a deficiency in the leader—his or her knowledge or skill or passion or virtue or vision or strategy. I thought this even though I read a book most days, and preached from it most weeks, that measures a leader by a completely different touchstone. In the Bible, a leader's greatness, or not, always comes down to how he or she sees God.

Herein lies the genius of John Johnson's *Rooted Leadership*. He takes three hundred pages to make one point—that a leader's theology is the most important thing about him or her. Johnson is not advocating for any particular brand of theology. He means theology in its root—and rooted—sense: how we see God.

Really? Our leadership rests on that? Not on our training? Or our visionary capacities? Or our character? Or our speaking ability?

Well, Johnson gets to all that, but not first. First, he speaks of God.

Dorothy Sayers said that the drama of faith is in the doctrine. The life is in the theology. If we learn to *think with God about God*, all else comes clear. Ask Moses. Or David. Or Nehemiah. Or Paul. Or for that matter, ask a bad leader, a leader who's failed spectacularly—Pharoah or Saul or Rehoboam or Herod. Pharoah's taunt to Moses more or less sums up the creed of the whole lot: "Who is the LORD, that I should obey him? ... I do not know the LORD" (Ex. 5:2).

That boast became his epitaph.

Yet the question haunts: "Who is the Lord, that I should obey him?" Johnson goes to great lengths to help us answer that. His book is no plodding catechism, though. It is no arid survey of divine attributes. It is a lively adventure in good theology—*thinking with God about God*. It is a compelling argument for how good theology makes us better leaders. And it is a masterful demonstration of how good theology opens out into everything else we might ask or wonder about leadership—the skills we must acquire, the tasks we must do, the virtues we must cultivate, the power we must steward. It's all here, and much else besides.

Our greatness, or not, comes down to how we see God. Eventually, in my own life and leadership, I began to grasp this, though through a glass darkly. But more and more, I have devoted myself to seeking the face of God. It is my first and last and best act of being a leader— indeed, of being a human.

I have rooted my leadership, and all else, in this.

But, oh, how I wish I had this book twenty years ago. And, oh, how thankful I am—for you, for me, for all of us—that we have it now.

Mark Buchanan,

associate professor of pastoral theology, Ambrose Seminary, author of *God Walk: Moving at the Speed of Your Soul*

AN INVITATION TO BEGIN

Leadership is an obsession—a national obsession,
arguably even a global one.
—BARBARA KELLERMAN

As I write this, few would deny that a dullness has taken hold. Masks have not been able to hide it. I have seen the fatigue in the posture and in the eyes of my students. The world has been through the coronavirus pandemic. Lives, as well as jobs, have been lost. It has felt endless. The movie *Groundhog Day* has symbolized our times. COVID-19 has put us in our own Punxsutawney, fated to relive the same day over and over.

We will look back and recall the monotony of lockdowns, not to mention the disruption in relationships. Lots of things got out of place. Churches were unable to gather—or scatter. Favorite restaurants put up closed signs. Planes that once landed just long enough to unload and reload were parked at the end of runways like useless cars in a junkyard. Dress shoes that once put the exclamation point on one's wardrobe sat idle in the closet, collecting dust.

Something else has also been stuck, trapped in its own crisis. Leadership. Describing our age as one devoid of great leadership is not a hard sell. Hardly a day goes by without some commentary on how a president, a governor, a mayor, a business leader, or some religious leader is failing us. "That press conference was incoherent." "It's appalling how she suddenly switched positions!" "It is hard to know what is true, with leaders spreading so much misinformation!" "When are they going to replace him?" "When is he going to stand up and lead!" "Why is there so much incompetence, so much absence of leadership?" Lackluster and unimpressive performances are making many leaders worthy of abject mockery. We find ourselves asking the same question Warren Bennis asked at the beginning of his seminal work on leadership, "Where have all the leaders gone?"[1]

Most people listen to the news, and it leaves them more outraged than informed. We hear of yet another moral failure of a ministry leader, and it grieves our hearts. Something seems off. What explains this? There are lots of reasons. Lack of sound training. Propensity to please. Self-interest. Failure to dream. The conviction of this book is that at a more fundamental level it is spiritual. More and more leaders imagine themselves as "individuals, ideally sovereign owners of themselves and their actions."[2] A leadership marked by godliness is the exception rather than the rule. Even rarer is a leadership grounded in sound theology—leadership as God sees it. The aim of this book is to present one.

God is the radix, the essential definition of leadership. *Leadership is rooted in him and therefore sacred in its essence.* What God has revealed provides both the foundation for and practice of leading. Without this theological grounding, much of present leadership shifts with the winds and collapses in the storms. Ignoring God and his design is behind much of our havoc.

With self-leadership in vogue, few are willing to admit that our internal markers are off. Motivational conferences tell prospective leaders to take charge of their destiny, be masters of their fate, but are we ever in control? Isn't that Someone Else's job? Isn't it time we acknowledge that God alone is the rock from which we have been cut, the quarry from which all leadership is shaped (Isa. 51:1)?

---

1. Warren Bennis, *On Becoming a Leader* (New York: Addison-Wesley, 1989), 13.

2. Miroslav Volf and Matthew Croasmun, *For the Life of the World: Theology That Makes a Difference* (Grand Rapids: Brazos, 2019), 21.

A number of leadership books approach the subject from a Christian perspective.[3] In some cases it is boilerplate language drawing from the same humanistic, evolutionary assumptions. They take existing human-centered frameworks and make them applicable to Christian leaders.[4] Rules developed for business are uncritically embraced by the church. Missing is a fuller leadership analysis, one from a more theocentric perspective. Without a solid theological foundation, Christians will continue to buy into a sociological basis for human leadership, one that can become a functional heresy.

It's time for such an analysis. A generation of leaders is emerging, one in search of a better structure and one that imagines a better way, a *sui generis* leadership sourced in God to carry the day.

OUR WAY FORWARD

The aim of this book is to develop a theology of leadership, bringing together both biblical and secular scholarship. It is a formidable but necessary task. There is much to learn from both, though theology is the principal resource and final voice. Even some of the best secular material has uncredited foundations in the Bible. Reading from both, I have attempted a comprehensive work of discovery and narrowed it down to the core questions and the key principles critical to leadership theory and practice.

In looking at the theological assertions, I am not seeking to match

---

3. Helpful works include books like Bernice M. Ledbetter, Robert J. Banks, and David C. Greenhalgh, *Reviewing Leadership: A Christian Evaluation of Current Approaches* (Grand Rapids: Baker, 2016), as well as Rick Langer's "Toward a Biblical Theology of Leadership," in *Organizational Leadership: Foundations & Practices for Christians*, ed. John S. Burns, John R. Shoup, and Donald C. Simmons Jr. (Downers Grove, IL: InterVarsity Press, 2014). In the latter work, the authors begin by noting there is a significant need in the leadership literature for a systematic theology of leadership (p. 8). In a more recent book, Justin A. Irving and Mark L. Strauss, *Leadership in Christian Perspective: Biblical Foundations and Contemporary Practices for Servant Leaders* (Grand Rapids: Baker, 2019), the authors seek to integrate current practices with biblical reflections.

4. Note, for example, James M. Kouzes and Barry Z. Posner, *Christian Reflections on the Leadership Challenge* (San Francisco: Jossey-Bass, 2006), 3.

scriptural verses with preconceived groupings. I want to draw categories out of careful biblical exegesis, in every case seeking to discover what God has to say about leaders and leadership. Think of it as a theological commentary on our present state of leadership. The intent is to both complement and contrast, recognizing that some ideas will conflict with prevailing assumptions. The book will reframe many of our present notions, ones that embody many of our contemporary models of leading.

It will fall short if this work is only about leadership theory. I'm not interested in filling heads apart from calling for action. Like other disciplines, theology does not serve to coddle. It makes demands.[5] As theologian Donald Bloesch notes, understanding God's will and purpose must eventuate in obedience.[6] Hence I will move from the more abstract to the concrete. I intend to demonstrate how a theocentric approach will lead to greater leadership responsibility and effectiveness, while I also warn of the consequences of ignoring leadership as God sees it.

THE BOOK'S LAYOUT

The book is divided into eleven chapters, each one answering a pivotal question every leader faces. In the first chapter the book will argue that theology serves as the logical framework for approaching leadership. From here the remaining chapters will reveal God's view on these core leadership questions and demonstrate how it provides the proper framework.

In chapter 2 the question of leadership definition is addressed. There are hundreds of meanings out there. We explore how theology reframes the prevailing definitions of leadership, pointing to an unlikely concept as the essential meaning—one that is surprisingly simple yet profound.

Chapter 3 focuses on leadership and necessity. It's an ongoing debate. In our current climate there is a growing pushback against the conviction

---

5. Eric Weiner, *The Socrates Express* (New York: Simon & Shuster, 2020), 120.

6. Donald G. Bloesch, *A Theology of Word & Spirit* (Downers Grove, IL: InterVarsity Press, 1992), 39.

that we need leaders. Is leadership essential to the world's progress? The bigger question is whether leaders are necessary to God. Is a lack of effective leadership an impediment to God's will?

In chapter 4 we explore the question of acquisition. How does one become a leader? There is no one answer. Are some born to be leaders? Is it simply a matter of reading the right books? Theology challenges current assumptions, teaching us that leadership begins with God and his predetermined will.

In chapter 5 we address leadership credibility. I will examine the subject of character, a word that is not so easy to define. We desperately want leaders who exhibit admirable character, but is it a necessary requirement for effective leading? If so, can we gain character on our own? Theology forces us to think far deeper than most books—and egos—are willing to go.

Chapter 6 studies the wisdom necessary to lead. Everyone agrees on the need for prudence, but earthly and divine wisdom are not the same. Only one will lead to true success. Central to the wisdom from above is the fear of God, but what does this mean for leaders?

Chapter 7 tackles the question of competence. What are the necessary skill sets? Character and wisdom are essential to leadership credibility but are not of much use if a leader is poor at implementation. What skills matter most to God?

Chapter 8 delves into the necessary tasks of leadership. Having the required character, wisdom, and skills is one thing, but what is it leaders actually do? What is the work they are called to carry out? Does theology confirm? Reframe? Is leadership simply about performance? We will unpack the missional, visionary, strategic, and tactical roles of a leader.

In chapter 9 we will investigate the issue of power and authority and how theology defines their roles in leadership. So much of leadership has been—and is—about gaining influence through personal power and control. Theology will again turn things upside down, placing power in rightful perspective, and reposition a leader's approach.

Chapter 10 covers the issue of leadership and its challenges. Leaders, in light of their role, face trials and sufferings. Failure is a necessary part of their experience. How does a leader navigate the inevitable crises? Theology takes us to both the cause and the purpose and guides us in how we should respond.

In chapter 11 the book steps back and raises such questions as, Does leadership have a future? Does it end with time? If leadership moves into eternity, what will leaders be doing? The answers might surprise you.

At the end of each chapter, beginning with chapter 2, we will look at a working model from Scripture. Stories are foundational to human reason. "Storytelling," as James Wilson puts it, "is a kind of philosophical argument that cooperates with abstract reason to help us arrive at truth."[7] The intent is to provide a visual for the theological truths the chapter unpacks.

I will seek to bring to this book my thirty years of study and teaching, distilling the wisdom of notable books, journals, and articles on leadership into a well-ordered approach. Critical reasoning, however, is not enough; it must be embodied in personal experience.[8] This research also comes from the field. I have led ministries here and abroad, midsize and large. I have worked with remarkable leaders in Europe, Asia, the Middle East, Africa, and India.

Writing a book on leading is in itself an act of leadership. It should be.[9] Even though I write as a follower of Jesus, my hope is that this book will be valued by those who lead in both Christian and non-Christian settings. I will aim for scrutiny as opposed to superficial skimming. I will organize, synthesize, and contrast theological knowledge with credible secular sources. The conviction here is that all truth comes from and leads back to God.[10]

I am assuming the reader comes with a passion for leading well. This book is written for those who are training for leadership, as well as for

---

7. James Matthew Wilson, "A Guide for Recovering the Wisdom of the Past," *National Review*, June 10, 2021, https://www.nationalreview.com/magazine/2021/07/01/a-guide-for-recovering-the-wisdom-of-the-past/.

8. Thomas C. Oden, *Pastoral Theology: Essentials of Ministry* (New York: HarperOne, 1993), 311.

9. Barbara Kellerman, *Leadership: Essential Selections on Power, Authority, and Influence* (New York: McGraw-Hill, 2010), 165.

10. Ellen Charry, *By the Renewing of Your Minds: The Pastoral Function of Christian Doctrine* (Oxford: Oxford University Press, 1999), 230.

leaders who are in the thick of it. My intent is to take my research and experience from multiple sources and challenge serious minds to bring their leadership to another level. While I hope to gain a hearing from those not so theologically inclined, my main audience is leaders with a Christian worldview. I will challenge a perception that theology is abstract, theoretical, and irrelevant to the subject. The truth is, it is relevant, practical, essential, and life changing.

Writing a theology of leadership requires careful reflection upon the self-disclosure of God that is witnessed by Scripture and mediated through tradition. This is a formidable task. God, his thoughts, and his ways are too vast for us to grasp, and yet we are invited to explore and get some grip. Mark Galli, in his biography of Karl Barth, describes the paradox this way: "The entire theological enterprise, all God talk, is finally an impossibility. Yet theologians are required to speak about that which is ultimately unknowable."[11]

God is radically incomprehensible. We can know only what he chooses to reveal. We are dealing with eternal questions, questions that are less about us (Why am I here? What is the good life?) and more about God (Who is he? What is his plan and purpose for leadership?).

This demands careful study of biblical and systematic theologies, ones that honor the Scriptures and focus on God. Throughout the writing of this book, I have asked, Is this consistent with the authority of Scripture and the designs of God? Is this how God sees leadership?

There is no theology without the Bible. Apart from God's written revelation, theology cannot even begin to discharge its office.[12] Theology is literally speech about God, and Scripture is the text that gives an account of God and his work. Though not the sole source (we also have creeds and confessions, tradition, and ecclesial history), Scripture is the primary source. It is the ground, the criterion, and the final authority for theology, as well as for leadership.

The aim is to read the Bible on its own terms, avoiding the tendency to

---

11. Mark Galli, *Karl Barth: An Introductory Biography for Evangelicals* (Grand Rapids: Eerdmans, 2017), 53.

12. John Webster, *Holiness* (Grand Rapids: Eerdmans, 2003), 3.

conform it to our preconceived leadership assumptions. After all, Scripture is "the revelation of a world that is vast, far larger than the sin-stunted, self-constricted world that we construct for ourselves out of a garage sale assemblage of texts."[13] It is unified by a common author and a common message (2 Tim. 3:16).

Given these convictions, the leadership discussed in this book will be grounded in the proper exegesis of the biblical texts (the use of a grammatical, historical method of interpretation). Such a rigorous discipline is an attempt to hear what the Spirit says.

What we will find is a story of leadership, set in history and told as a grand narrative. Though God is not mentioned in every case, he is there. We are dealing with a highly self-conscious theological literature that observes the undercurrent of divine governance at every turn.[14] The terrain is immense. Before us stands a sprawling, capacious account, one we come to ponder, theologize, and enter into its unpredictable, unanticipated reality.[15]

It is only proper that we come together with humble reverence, in a posture of worship. Theology is a human and a sacred endeavor. It can easily morph into little more than a human rigor when God becomes merely a technical reference. In *A Little Exercise for Young Theologians*, Helmut Thielicke warns of the potential to no longer read the Word of God as a word for one's soul, "but only as the object of exegetical endeavors."[16] I will seek to steer clear of this malpractice, encouraging readers to do the same. Herman Bavinck provides centering words: "To profess theology is to do holy work. It is a priestly ministration in the house of the Lord. It is itself a service of worship, a consecration of mind and heart to the honor of his name."[17]

Thankfully, God, out of a willingness to condescend to our understanding, makes himself known, though he forever remains inscrutable. As Tozer

---

13. Ibid., 45.

14. Walter Brueggemann, *First and Second Samuel* (Louisville: John Knox, 1990), 200.

15. Eugene H. Peterson, *Eat This Book* (Grand Rapids: Eerdmans, 2005), 40.

16. Helmut Thielicke, *A Little Exercise for Young Theologians* (Grand Rapids: Eerdmans, 1962), loc. 307 of 371, Kindle.

17. Quoted in Bloesch, *A Theology of Word & Spirit*, 112.

notes, if we insist on trying to imagine him, we end up with an idol.[18] We must, together, come to the task with a certain trembling. Ben Witherington has written a number of books, including an impressive biblical theology. For anyone who chooses to work in this area, he advises a daily routine in which one gets up, takes a humility pill, and recites the Pauline doxology (Rom. 11:33–36).[19] I have taken this under careful advisement.

The good news is that we are not alone in this endeavor. The Spirit's ongoing work of illumination enables us to see what we would otherwise miss (Eph. 1:17–18). One must therefore anticipate the Spirit's moves and the Spirit's work. He teams up with the biblical text to, like an ice ax, "break the sea frozen inside us."[20] There must be sustained humility—an unpretentious openness to correction and a shifting of old ways of seeing self, discerning God, and understanding leadership.

There will be hard sayings directed to leaders, ones "recurringly odd and unaccommodating."[21] We will want to explain away certain biblical stories of leaders who were misfits and sayings that are strange. But as one put it, "You can't reduce this book to what you can handle; you can't domesticate this book to what you are comfortable with. You can't make it your toy poodle trained to respond to your commands."[22] There are mysteries that an inquiring spirit must yield to.

In the end, reformulating leadership theologically should stir us to be different kinds of leaders moved to get beyond ourselves to see from another world. The goal is not so much correlation with common leadership practices as conversion to God's transcendent purposes.[23] I do not want to add to what is known so much as overturn what is culturally accepted and rebuild.

---

18. A. W. Tozer, *The Knowledge of the Holy* (New York: HarperCollins, 1961), 16.

19. Ben Witherington III, *Who God Is: Meditations on the Character of Our God* (Bellingham: Lexham, 2020), 7.

20. Eugene H. Peterson, *Run with the Horses: The Quest for Life at Its Best* (Downers Grove, IL: InterVarsity Press, 2019), loc. 1086 of 1984, Kindle. He quotes here from Franz Kafka.

21. Walter Brueggemann, *Theology of the Old Testament: Testimony, Dispute, Advocacy* (Minneapolis: Fortress, 2005), 3.

22. Peterson, *Eat This Book*, 65–66.

23. Bloesch, *The Theology of Word & Spirit*, 262–67.

A CLOSING THOUGHT

A few years ago I was invited to climb Mount Kinabalu. It is the one of the highest mountains in Southeast Asia. The summit stands at 13,435 feet. Given driving rainstorms, it required two attempts. Once I and my guide broke through the clouds on the second day, I found myself in another world. This massive rock formation left me breathless—literally. I had never seen this kind of terrain. The thinness of the air required a disciplined step—breathe in, step, breathe out, step . . .

There will be times when we will find ourselves pausing to catch our breath and get our bearings. Theology forces us to aim for the summit, where the air is rarified, and the landscape feels foreign. Yet, ironically, we are coming back home, back to our roots. Like climbing mountains, theology can also be dangerous. We might begin by thinking we are in control, but we soon discover that the God we study is the God who studies us.[24]

---

24. Brian Harris, "What Do Theologians Do?," Brian Harris, January 8, 2019, https://brian harrisauthor.com/what-do-theologians-do/.

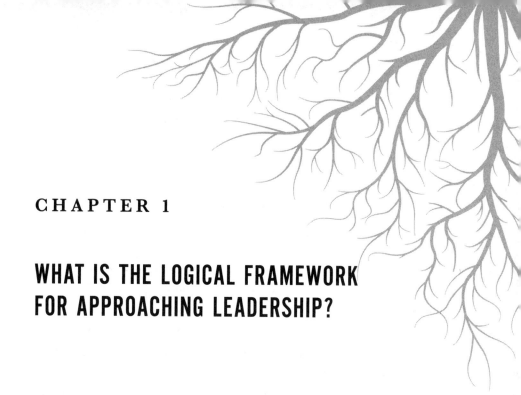

CHAPTER 1

WHAT IS THE LOGICAL FRAMEWORK FOR APPROACHING LEADERSHIP?

*Without solid theological reflection, future leaders will be little
more than pseudo-psychologists and pseudo-social workers.*
—Henri Nouwen

If you have traveled to Amsterdam, you might have missed it. Most tourists do. Facing the Damrak canal are tall iconic houses, graced with gabled facades. Impressive as they are, a closer look reveals they are tilted. Not exactly plumb and level. The Dutch call them *dansende huizen*, "dancing houses." Years ago they were built on wooden stilts. The problem is that their supports were driven into what was once swampland. Over time they have shifted in the mud.

Something similar is going on in the field of leadership. As noted in the introduction, things are off. Absent a solid foundation, leading has become crooked. Maybe *narcissistic* and *incompetent* are more appropriate terms. These are common descriptions, and they constitute a curse at multiple levels, explaining what I believe to be our cultural predicament. People are asking, "Where is the leadership that was promised?" "Why are some like puppets in a ventriloquist's act instead of leaders speaking on their own?"

Two key reasons explain the present tilt.

OUR CULTURE EMPHASIZES THE PRAGMATIC OVER THE THEORETICAL

We are enamored with what works. That which is theoretical has become secondary to that which is practical. But this goes only so far. A solid, academic framework is—has always been—essential to building a steady foundation. But fewer are making this a priority. This is the conclusion of a growing number of leadership professors like Barbara Kellerman of Harvard and Jeffrey Pfeffer of Stanford. They concede that things have changed in the training of leaders. Kellerman writes, "Overwhelmingly, twenty-first-century leadership education and development are about practice, not theory; about the present, not the past; about prose, not poetry; about education, not meditation; about the real world, not the world of the imagination."[1]

The priorities have changed. We want to know what works, and a fifty-billion-dollar leadership industry is capitalizing on this. Entrepreneurs are marketing their easy-to-read books and juicing the crowds with popular speakers. They captivate the audience, telling them that they can be whatever they dream. Wannabe leaders are urged to sign up and learn the secret to making decisions with confidence, running meetings with skill, and persuading people with words that inspire. The clear message is that one does not have to go to a university to learn leadership. One can bypass disciplines like philosophy, psychology, business, and history. If there are any books to be read, let them be how-to books.[2]

---

1. Barbara Kellerman, *The End of Leadership* (New York: Harper Business, 2012), 153. She bases her findings on Doris Gomez's article "The Leader as Learner," *International Journal of Leadership Studies* 2, no. 3 (2007).

2. A good example is found in David Rubenstein, *How to Lead* (New York: Simon & Schuster, 2020). He argues that successful leaders, like Jeff Bezos, Melinda Gates, George Bush, and Nancy

What Is the Logical Framework for Approaching Leadership?

Given the plethora of seminars and the investment of capital, all of this should bear the fruit of capable leaders. It's not happening. As Pfeffer puts it in *Leadership BS*, "The leadership industry has failed."[3] Mistrust, dysfunctional workplaces, and high turnover plague our landscape. At least half of the occupants of leadership positions are falling short. In one finding, researchers have concluded that one of every two leaders and managers is "estimated to be ineffective (that is, a disappointment, incompetent, a mishire, or a complete failure) in their current roles."[4]

The research confirms we are paying the price of pragmatic-centric leadership training. In many cases, it is conducted by popular speakers who have no credentials, have attempted no rigorous research, and demonstrate little real knowledge about the subject.

Tom Nichols has sounded a similar alarm with his *Death of Expertise*: "The foundational knowledge of the average American is now so low that it has crashed through the floor of 'uninformed,' passed 'misinformed' on the way down to 'aggressively wrong.'"[5] This is scary, but it helps explain the leadership dilemma we are in. We are obsessed with what works, what creates profit, and what draws crowds. We give less attention to reading and lesser attention to the core academic disciplines (not to mention to those with real expertise).

Even philosophers are finding themselves shoved aside. They were once viewed as the sculptors of society, providing the intellectual framework for subjects that included leadership. Today they are esoteric teachers in dwindling university departments.[6] In his book *The Socrates Express*, Eric Weiner reflects on the loss. Philosophers were once heroic, willing to die

---

Pelosi, have the following attributes: luck, a desire to succeed, a passion to create, a willingness to work hard, an ability to focus a spirit of persistence, and a willingness to learn from failure.

3. Jeffrey Pfeffer, *Leadership BS: Fixing Workplaces and Careers One Truth at a Time* (New York: Harper Business, 2015), 4.

4. Ibid., 16. Pfeffer refers to the research of Bill Gentry of the Center for Creative Leadership.

5. Tom Nichols, *The Death of Expertise: The Campaign against Established Knowledge and Why It Matters* (London: Oxford University Press, 2017), 1.

6. Jonathan T. Pennington, *Jesus the Great Philosopher: Rediscovering the Wisdom Needed for the Good Life* (Grand Rapids: Brazos, 2020), 30.

for their philosophy. "Now," he writes, "all that is heroic about philosophy is the epic struggle for academic tenure."[7]

The religious world reveals a similar trend. It's not a surprise to hear noted practitioners denigrate the seminary as a waste of time and capital. They have concluded that theology is fine for those in their ivory towers who descend on occasion to attend theological meetings and deliver papers on Trinitarian theorizing, the use of the Hebrew *lamedh* in Leviticus, or the examination of P139. Let theologians write for the guild and for the tenure review committees.[8] They have little to offer to those doing the real work out in the field.

Leadership that is sustained over time, however, requires both good methodology and sound theory. Sound academic training that includes the disciplines of history, philosophy, sociology, psychology, and business—as well as theology—is essential. Working through the lessons of each one will ensure that a leader is substantive, not superficial. Though methodology is critical, in the end nothing is as practical as good theory.[9] The right beliefs are what shape the right practices. Not the reverse.

Until the emphasis of the practical at the expense of the theoretical is corrected, leadership will remain skewed. But it will take more than this to correct the structure. Something else is amiss, and it is more troubling.

OUR SCHOOLS PRIORITIZE THE SECULAR OVER THE THEOLOGICAL

Theology is critical to establishing the lines, but leadership studies do not seem to notice its role. Theological and leadership studies rarely coexist in the same space. They remain in their own bubbles. Look inside leadership books, and you'll discover it is uncommon to find any mention of God. If

---

7. Eric Weiner, *The Socrates Express* (New York: Simon & Shuster, 2020), xv–xvi.

8. Miroslav Volf and Matthew Croasmun, *For the Life of the World: Theology That Makes a Difference* (Grand Rapids: Brazos, 2019), 41.

9. Immanuel Kant, quoted in Miroslav Volf, *Captive to the Word of God: Engaging the Scriptures for Contemporary Theological Reflection* (Grand Rapids: Eerdmans, 2010), 41.

one peruses the current offerings in leadership, management, and organizational theory, one finds that theological themes are absent in both the table of contents and the appendices.

It's an observation made by others. In his article "Toward a Theology of Leadership," Michale Ayers looks at noted leadership theorists and begins with this sentence: "With all the dynamic research in leadership over the past fifty years, the writings of Hickman, Northouse, and Yukl reveal that leadership studies do not generally embrace theology in the leadership context."[10] "Rarely" might be a better fit. He goes on to propose a common language necessary for the convergence of theology and leadership.

On the theological side there is a similar gap. The subject of leadership in most theology texts, as well as seminary curriculums, is either absent or given brief mention. In the theologies that I consulted during my research, *leadership* was found to be missing from almost every index. Though some may not find this a conclusive indicator, it is nonetheless worth noting.

Could it be that this separation explains the leadership failure in so many churches? Ministers have been equipped to preach sermons and extend soul care, but their leadership skills are found wanting. If there are leadership abilities, they are usually built on business models found outside divinity schools. In the process, the leadership skills unique to and required of ministry go missing.

Similarly, leaving God and theology out of a secular leadership curriculum has had its consequences. A significant number of leaders are graduating without a moral compass. Lacking is a solemnity of manner and purpose. This is leading to toxic workplaces, harsh environments, and questionable business practices.

Why is it that leadership studies and theology fail to intersect? What causes some to keep leadership and theology in separate silos? In the first place, theology has gradually lost its credibility in much of the academic world. Theology once had a trustworthy voice. The study of God even had precedence over research in other subjects. The modern separation of

---

10. Michale Ayers, "Toward a Theology of Leadership," *Journal of Biblical Perspectives in Leadership* 1, no. 1 (Fall 2006): 3.

theology and society, religion and politics, would have made no sense in earlier centuries.[11] Culture accorded theology wide respect. In the religious world, particularly in the first three hundred years after the church was established, ministry and theology were joined at the hip. Pastors were theologians and theologians were pastors. In the classical tradition an inseparable bond existed.[12]

The study of God and his relationship to the world was the centering voice, addressing life's most important questions. Christian theology served as the intellectual space for articulating God and his will for creation. Learning institutions revered theology as the queen of the sciences (*Regina Scientiarum*) and the crown of the curriculum. It was the authoritative voice on nearly every subject, including leadership.

Over time, values and beliefs shifted. By the age of the Enlightenment, God was perceived to be a human creation (not the other way around). Lost in a superstitious ocean, man was finally arriving at the shore of enlightened knowledge. Sophisticated minds began to deem God outdated and irrelevant. Trust in human reason supplanted trust in divine revelation. The Bible was dislodged from its role as sacred text and demoted to cultural artifact. Theologians were relegated to the margins. As one put it, "If society were one grand dinner party, the theologians were increasingly to be found in the corner, left alone to their fantastic thoughts and their pious imprecations."[13]

Eventually, other disciplines filled the void. Having deposed the queen, other sciences jockeyed for position and influence. Authority to define reality was deeded by culture to those whom they judged to have the relevant body of knowledge.[14] Theologians were no longer perceived as having any pertinent wisdom.

---

11. N. T. Wright, *Paul* (Minneapolis: Fortress, 2005), 60.

12. See Andrew Purves, *Pastoral Theology in the Classical Tradition* (Louisville: Westminster John Knox, 2001), 2–3.

13. Kevin Vanhoozer, *The Pastor as Public Theologian: Reclaiming a Lost Vision* (Grand Rapids: Baker, 2020), 88–89.

14. J. P. Moreland, "How Christian Philosophers Can Serve Systematic Theologians and Biblical Scholars," *JETS* 63, no. 2 (2020): 298.

What Is the Logical Framework for Approaching Leadership?

The erosion of theism and the rise of naturalism have affected, and continue to affect, the academic landscape. Much of historical-critical scholarship views Scripture as "bewildering archaisms, inconsistencies, questionable ethics, and a herky-jerky narrative style."[15] Secularism rejects monotheism at multiple levels, some viewing it as "the most violent form of religion."[16] This is evident on university campuses, even those with divinity schools.

Theologian Miroslav Volf, a professor at Yale Divinity School, observes, "The general sense is that theology isn't producing any genuine knowledge that accomplishes anything, that it trades with the irrationality of faith and is useless."[17] Whatever theological claims that exist are perceived by secular academia as mere expressions of feeling. The final court of appeal is man's reason. If God is given any place at the table of academia, he is there to crown the human quest for wisdom and security.[18]

Given this theological slide, most schools of leadership see little compatibility between theology and secular notions of what it means to lead. When James MacGregor Burns wrote his seminal work on leadership, he held that humanistic psychology—not theology—is what enables us to generalize about the leadership process.[19]

At Harvard, as one example, future leaders come to learn certain skills, acquire a certain awareness, develop the ability to create change, discern the difference between right and wrong, and master great leadership literature.[20] As opposed to the more popular weekend leadership seminars, Harvard requires an intellectual inquiry, one that is interdisciplinary. After all, as one leadership professor asks, "How can we know leadership, how can we know the relationship between leaders and followers without

---

15. Quoted from Kristin Swenson's *A Most Peculiar Book* by Barton Swaim in his review article "Why Read the Bible?" *Wall Street Journal*, March 17, 2021, https://www.wsj.com/articles/a-most-peculiar-book-review-why-read-the-bible-11615934322.

16. Volf and Croasmun, *For the Life of the World*, 104.

17. Ibid., 44.

18. Donald G. Bloesch, *Theology of Word & Spirit* (Downers Grove, IL: InterVarsity Press, 1992), 40.

19. James MacGregor Burns, *Leadership* (New York: Open Road Media, 2012), 3.

20. Barbara Kellerman, *Leadership: Essential Selections on Power, Authority, and Influence* (New York: McGraw-Hill, 2010), xiii.

knowing history, philosophy, psychology, politics, sociology, anthropology, literature, art, and so on?"[21] One is tempted, however, to ask, Will theology even make the "and so on"? Or will it remain in the academic attic like a discarded typewriter that has been replaced by something more in keeping with the times?

Cultural shifts are widening the gap. A loss of regard for theology coincides with the diminishing influence of Christianity. Both in academia and outside of it, some regard any leadership theory based on biblical passages as narrow and constrictive, out of date, and naive. We live in an irreligious age, one decoupled from institutions, creeds, theologies, and metaphysical truth claims about God.[22]

Like Tara Isabella Burton, Ross Douthat is a writer who has a penetrating assessment of culture. In looking at our spiritual decline, he notes that we are more attracted to "therapeutic philosophies and technologies of simulation," and less connected to ideological ambition and religious hope.[23] But it's more than this. Many in our present generation are repulsed by the loss of credibility in those religious leaders once considered to have moral character and influence. Sexual immortality and abuse of power have destabilized and destroyed institutions we once respected.[24]

Sadly, as noted above, theological institutions have returned the favor. They have exacerbated this divide by minimizing the importance of leadership and its training. This too has contributed to the tilting. Though some theological schools recognize leadership as having ministerial value, others view studies in leadership to be an anthropological and sociological discipline. Just as those in the secular university fail to see a correlation between theology and leadership, professors in a number of religious schools

---

21. Ibid., xxv.

22. Tara Isabella Burton, *Strange Rites: New Religions for a Godless World* (New York: PublicAffairs, 2020), 2. See also Ross Douthat, *The Decadent Society: How We Became the Victims of Our Own Success* (New York: Simon & Schuster, 2020).

23. Douthat, *The Decadent Society*, 4.

24. Recently a national newspaper began with the headline "Newly Leaked Letter Details Allegations That Southern Baptist Leaders Mishandled Sex Abuse Claims"; Sarah Pulliam Bailey, *Washington Post*, June 5, 2021, https://www.washingtonpost.com/religion/2021/06/05/russell-moore-southern-baptist-sex-abuse-allegations/.

find little connection between divinity and directing. Learning to lead has some advantage, they might acknowledge, but it doesn't fit into a sacred curriculum, one devoted to Bible and theology. Their conclusion is that teaching leadership is best left to the humanities departments of other institutions.

A similar attitude is found in some churches. Elders are nominated based on the character qualities defined in Scripture, but overlooked is the question of leadership gifting. Many are unsure how to assess whether one is skilled to lead. Godliness, they say, is what matters. Leadership effectiveness is secondary. The result is often a religious community void of vision, direction, and strategy. Few know how to lead a team, drive the mission, and measure outcomes.

Some justify this by reminding constituents that the church is not a business. They caution that pastors need to be less enamored with secular leadership tools and more devoted to divine calling. Voices like Eugene Peterson have served as a prophetic warning to those who spend more of their time reading management books than studying Scripture. His writings lament that too many pastors have metamorphosed into "a company of shopkeepers" more attracted to the latest leadership theories and practices. They have put metrics over evangelism and key performance indicators over relationships. The advice is that pastors put leadership books aside and get back to doing ministry.[25]

The result is that some churches have overcorrected and dismissed leadership skills altogether. Wise business practices are ignored, creating confusion and disrespect for the institution.

WHAT'S NEEDED?

We need energetic minds determined to bridge the gap, shift priorities, and make every attempt to get things back on course. Just as ministry and leadership must discover and practice a mutual respect, so theology

---

25. See Eugene H. Peterson, *Working the Angles* (Grand Rapids: Eerdmans, 1989), 1–2; and *The Unnecessary Pastor* (Grand Rapids: Eerdmans, 1999), 1–5.

and other disciplines (science, psychology, history) need to recognize their commonalities and mutual dependency. Most share a mutual commitment to seek truth. They agree on a shared system of rules for weighing evidence and building knowledge. A good number are intent to be true to the nature of things. Most submit to some authority. It may or may not be God and his revelation, but it is someone or something.

In common with other subjects, a sound theology is committed to rigorous logical thinking. As Erickson notes in his *Readings in Christian Theology*, theology is subject to the same canons of logic and the same need to be communicable. It employs similar methods and shares many of the same subjects with other disciplines.[26] In keeping with Weiner's description of philosophy, a credible theology does not look for shortcuts nor find ways to indulge . Like philosophy, the emphasis is not on palliative care. It is less spa and more gym.[27]

Also, like philosophy, theology is concerned with discerning the questions behind leadership that ultimately matter: What is the meaning of life? What could the world be? Why is there such a thing as leadership, and how did it come into being? How does one live a purposeful life? What defines a flourishing life? What is our ultimate goal? Should I get out of bed? We cannot solve life's problems without experiencing its questions.[28]

Still, with all the commonalities, it is important that we recognize and honor our differences. Christian theology speaks to a particular worldview, one that calls for an alternative way of life. There are convictions that cannot be compromised. Some of them include:

- There is an ultimate reality, and it is God—not man.
- God is knowable to some degree—as opposed to completely unknowable.
- There is no authority other than God's—no one possesses authority apart from him.

---

26. Millard J. Erickson, *Readings in Christian Theology* (Grand Rapids: Baker, 1987), 1:35–36.
27. Weiner, *The Socrates Express*, xvi.
28. Ibid., 15.

What Is the Logical Framework for Approaching Leadership?

- As with all humanity, a leader's first allegiance is to God—not self.
- Self-awareness is important for a leader—but it is incomplete apart from awareness of God.
- God knows best how humanity is designed and what will enable people to flourish—not us.
- This is a broken world of broken people who need Jesus—we cannot become whole apart from him.
- One's moral compass is found in God's revelation of himself in his Word—not in one's flawed self.
- We are not our own—we belong to God.
- Successful leadership is not a matter of fate—but of faith.

The wisdom of man and the wisdom of God are often in irrevocable conflict. The gospel (the good news that we are reconciled with God and others through the life, death, and resurrection of Jesus) is a central part of theology, and it calls into question the values and presuppositions of secular culture.[29] Human sinfulness and Christ's atonement are incompatible with human autonomy and freedom.[30] In contrast to a relativistic age, theology holds that there are absolute truths. Reason is a servant—not a master—of faith. And faith begins with God.

These beliefs do not justify the building of walls and the breaking off of dialogue. They do not excuse a secular attitude that views the tenets of Christian theology as both intellectually implausible and morally reprehensible. Nor do they tolerate the pompous pretension on the part of some theologians that assumes superior knowledge and dismisses those who disagree. All of our attempts at constructing a biblical theory of leadership will always be fallible—and provisional—even though Scripture is not.[31] A spirit of humility listens and learns, though such modesty is not to be confused with lukewarmness, pusillanimity, resignation, or

---

29. Bloesch, *Theology of Word & Spirit*, 262.

30. Carl. R. Trueman, "The Failure of Evangelical Elites," *First Things* (November 2021), 101.

31. Rick Langer, "Toward a Biblical Theology of Leadership," in *Organizational Leadership: Foundations & Practices for Christians*, ed. John S. Burns, John R. Shoup, and Donald C. Simmons Jr. (Downers Grove, IL: InterVarsity Press, 2014), 67.

confusion.[32] There has to be solidity and boldness in one's convictions, alongside respect and honor for another's scholarship and persuasions.

In the end, we must not only recognize the commonalities and differences—we need to get the priorities in their right order. Theology not only has a place at the table of leadership; it belongs at the head. This conviction is sure to be off-putting for some, but it is built on solid arguments:

First, theology frames all of life's subjects. No other discipline fashions a larger, more coherent picture. Theology is the ordered consideration or study of God.[33] He is the logical start point, the structure for everything. As Oden notes, "God minus the world is God. The world minus God is nothing."[34] Everything points to God, begins with God, and ends with God. Any other object is idolatry, an act that produces "sensory organ malfunction" (Ps. 115:4–8).[35]

Diving into the fathomless ocean of God himself, we join with Job in declaring, "The Almighty is beyond our reach" (Job 37:23). We cannot grasp the whole of God by surveying his attributes. There is no sense adding one divine quality to another until we think we have him figured out. God is radically incalculable (Rom. 11:33). Still, we pursue an ordered study of God. We can't understand leadership—let alone anything—until we have some knowledge of the divine. In this task of knowing, one finds that God frames all our being and doing. Church fathers like John Calvin affirmed this, noting that apart from a proper understanding of theology, we are without any true wisdom.[36]

A theology informed by Scripture provides a worldview that can

---

32. John G. Stackhouse, *Making the Best of It: Following Christ in the Real World* (London: Oxford University Press, 2011), 356.

33. James Leo Garrett, *Systematic Theology*, 2nd ed. (Eugene: Wipf and Stock, 2014), 2:2. Marilyn Robinson adds, "Theology is the great architecture of thought and wonder that makes religious experience a house of many mansions, open to the soul's explorations, indeed, made to invite and to accommodate them." *What Are We Doing Here? Essays* (New York: Farrar, Straus, and Giroux, 2018), 39.

34. Thomas C. Oden, *Classic Christianity: A Systematic Theology* (New York: HarperOne, 2009), 39.

35. Peter J. Leithart, *The Ten Commandments: A Guide to the Perfect Law of Liberty*, Christian Essentials (Bellingham: Lexham, 2020), 17.

36. Quoted in John R. Franke, *The Character of Theology: An Introduction to Its Nature, Task, and Purpose* (Grand Rapids: Baker, 2005), 13.

handle the complexities of life, a coherent vision that enables one to navigate life's variations.

Second, theology provides an overarching leadership theory. God is not some outside observer, a trivial contributor to leadership doctrine and practice. Any fundamental principles and manners of leadership begin with him, for leadership is *his* idea. He creates the heavens and the earth, summoning, ordering, and governing all reality, including leaders.[37] Genesis 1 tells us God made humans in his image and entrusted them with sovereignty over the rest of creation (v. 28).[38] Jesus, the self-revelation of God, is the essence, the polestar of leadership. Reading the architectural lines of what God has revealed, we discover an understanding of leadership that is seminal (versus unoriginal), timeless (versus time-bound), transcendent (versus immanent), and rooted (versus superficial).

Without this theological orientation, leaders morph into something else—something less. Catholic theologian Henri Nouwen, speaking to an audience of leaders in Washington, DC, warned that without solid theological reflection, future leaders will think of themselves as simply enablers, facilitators, role models, father or mother figures, big brothers or big sisters.[39] True leadership, rooted leadership, can be understood only in terms of a fully integrated theological vision of God and his work on earth.[40]

It's not that a theological understanding will remove all the mysteries of leading. This is not an effort to prove that theologians who theologize leadership have mastered the subject. Discerning what is actual is a lifelong work (Prov. 25:2). What theology does is move us from unconscious to conscious ignorance. We find ourselves asking more and more questions: "What is God saying?" "Is servant leadership realistic in a world impressed

---

37. Walter Brueggemann, *Theology of the Old Testament: Testimony, Dispute, Advocacy* (Minneapolis: Fortress, 2005), 145.

38. N. T. Wright, *After You Believe: Why Christian Character Matters* (New York: HarperOne, 2010), 73. In his chapter "Priests and Rulers," Wright gives an in-depth analysis of God's purpose for creating humanity.

39. Henri J. M. Nouwen, *In the Name of Jesus: Reflections on Christian Leadership* (New York: Crossroad, 2000), 66.

40. See Timothy S. Laniak, *Shepherds After My Own Heart: Pastoral Traditions and Leadership in the Bible* (Downers Grove, IL: InterVarsity Press, 2006), 249.

with power?" "Does God really need leaders?" "What makes for effectual leading?" "Why does he preserve the account of so many failed leaders?" "Is leadership forever?".

Studying biblical leadership can feel like an expedition into the dark spaces, but there are revelations that will open our eyes. Kapic encourages us to think of our task as more like a pilgrimage: "Sometimes as theologians we find ourselves climbing sun-drenched mountains or descending into dark valleys; occasionally we are rewarded with an endless vista, while at other moments fog surrounds us and obscures our path."[41] We may gain a glimpse of God, but it will be indistinct and incomplete (1 Cor. 13:12; Ex. 33:18–23). We cannot understand unless God reveals himself.

There is a third argument for honoring theology's rightful place. It serves as the needed plumbline, for theology clarifies the overarching purposes for leadership. Leaders do not lead for themselves; they lead to bring glory and honor to God. This motivates everything we do (1 Cor. 10:31). This is our overarching purpose. Leaders are not created to take charge and use their positions of power for self-enrichment; they are summoned to serve as God's priestly vice-regents for his praise.

Genesis 1:28 is the foundational statement, the key to discerning humanity's reason to be. We were created for the purpose of subduing and ruling. This gets to the origin of leadership. Leadership is, in one sense, in everyone's blood. These terms are not intended to give license to the exploitation of the heavens, land, and sea. As Brueggemann puts it, "The role of the human person is to see to it that the creation becomes fully the creation willed by God."[42] Leaders lead this effort. They rise to promote the well-being of everything and everyone. Theologically driven leaders discern, articulate, and commend a vision of how lives can flourish.[43] In contrast, leaders who deaden the hopes, oppress the spirits, and neglect

---

41. Kelly M. Kapic, *A Little Book for New Theologians: Why and How to Study Theology* (Downers Grove, IL: InterVarsity Press, 2012), 33–34.

42. Walter Brueggemann, *Genesis: Interpretation; A Bible Commentary for Teachings and Preaching* (Louisville: Westminster John Knox, 1986), 33.

43. Volf and Croasmun, *For the Life of the World*, 149–85.

the cries of their constituents are a travesty and a tragedy, the antithesis of God's mission, the reason for crooked and twisted structures.

Finally, theology is necessary, for it places leadership in its true context. Much of meaning is derived from one's setting. When Robert Caro determined to write a definitive biography of Lyndon Baines Johnson and unpack his leadership, he came to the inevitable conclusion he would have to move to the Hill Country of Texas and live there. Only by getting deeper into the circumstances could he begin to comprehend the "hardscrabble" conditions that shaped LBJ's youth and understand how it was that Johnson could be so ruthless in his leading. He writes, "If you want to understand what was behind him doing that, think of the land. Think of the *place*."[44]

Harvard Professor Barbara Kellerman makes a similar point. After tracing the stories and writings of some of the world's most influential leaders, she concludes, "Context is critical, both to learning leadership and to exercising it."[45] She adds, "For only by looking through the lens of history can we detect the all-important trajectory of power and influence."[46]

Consider this. Scripture gives us the overarching context for leadership. It is an invitation to move to Divine Country and think of the land, the place, and the times. The narrative takes us beyond the gravitational pull of the immediate, to see something far more comprehensive—the metanarrative that connects the beginning of history with its end. It tells the story of God, who alone has the "synoptic" vision of the whole of reality.[47]

What he gives us is not fiction or fable but narrative that recounts events, movements, ideas, and the lives of leaders and their followers. While the Bible contains a wide range of other genres, including poems, laws, prophecies, lyrics, proverbs, letters, and apocalypses, it is essentially a narrative with a beginning, middle, and end.[48] One finds within it a divine purpose, a theological historiography of sorts, in which God's providence

---

44. Robert A. Caro, *Working* (Visalia, CA: Vintage, 2019), 152.
45. Kellerman, *Leadership*, xviii.
46. Ibid.
47. Bloesch, *A Theology of Word & Spirit*, 116.
48. Stackhouse, *Making the Best of It*, 181.

is obvious and leadership is explained. Think of it as eternity breaking into history at a time and a place.

God sets the leadership context through a series of acts. The first act is creation. Humanity is created to lead and care (Gen. 1:28; 2:15). Made in the image of God, humanity is called into a shared leadership with the triune God. Among their leadership roles are priest, husband, father, and shepherd.

In the second act there is the story of the first Adam and the fall of humanity into self-destructive sin. It's here leadership's potential for perversion is explained.

In the third act Israel takes center stage. God chooses to make Israel his kingdom of priests and holy nation (Ex. 19:6). He comes to his people to dwell and share his presence (40:34). Israel is the alternative community, God's agent to bring light and rescue. Its leaders are the alternative leaders, and among them there is no single model of leadership. They go through various stages under different conditions: clan leaders (Gen. 10:31–32), patriarchs (Genesis 12–50), elders (Exodus 18), generals (Joshua 1), judges/warlords (Judges), priests (1 Samuel 1–8), kings (1 Kings–2 Chronicles), governors (Nehemiah), and prophets (Jeremiah).

In the fourth act Jesus the Messiah, the Leader of leaders, comes to earth. Israel's hope for a new king—the anointed Messiah who will bring salvation, reestablish worship, and bring peace—is present. He comes as the royal priest to declare God's sovereignty over the earth and cleanse the temple. Jesus brings to perfect expression what God requires of those who lead. He is the essence of character, wisdom, and leadership skills, a leader with a clear mission—to bring about our redemption. He has a focused strategy and a team to carry it out (Matt. 28:16–20).

The fifth and final act begins with the post-resurrection acts of Jesus, continues with the ascension of Jesus, and moves to the coming of the Spirit. We are now under a new covenant (Jer. 31:31–35). The church is given birth and called to humanity's original task to be a royal priesthood (Gen. 1:28; 1 Peter 2:5). Filled with the Spirit, leaders lead the work of dismantling the dominant culture (Acts 2:17–21; Eph. 4:11–16). It all culminates with a new heaven and new earth, a temple in which the saints rule (Rev. 21:1–7).

All of these stages of history serve as reference points for leading. There are ordinary leaders, but some are exceptional (Moses, Deborah, Samuel, David, Josiah, Nehemiah, Paul). A number are ineffectual at best (Jacob, Eli, Saul, Rehoboam, Manasseh). None are polished ideals, and those who tell their stories are under no compulsion to dress them up in the latest Paris silk gowns of theology.[49] It all has been preserved to provide the most comprehensive context. Entering the story, we are able to make sense of this thing called leadership.

CONCLUSION

Perhaps a day will come when misdirected leadership practices will lead to an insistence to get back to foundational theory. Otherwise, we will remain unrooted and shallow. My greater hope is for a time leadership books refer to—and use—theology as the logical starting point for approaching leadership. At the very least acknowledge that many of the stated concepts can be traced to a Judeo-Christian worldview. I am reminded of a leadership summit at Willow Creek where Ken Blanchard, author of *The One Minute Manager,* shared his coming to faith. As he studied the life of Christ, he realized that Jesus had already written his book.

Whether or not other writers of leadership ever do this, the reality is that no one gets away from the realm of theology. Theologian Karl Barth once noted, "There is no man who does not have his own god or gods as the object of his highest desire and trust, or as the basis of his deepest loyalty and commitment. There is no one who is not to this extent also a theologian."[50]

One can also hope theological faculties will come to see the essentiality of leadership as part of the curriculum. This will not be easy. As one professor of theology admitted, "We theologians sometimes do teach and

---

49. Peterson, *Eat This Book,* 43.
50. Quoted in Eberhard Busch, *The Great Passion: An Introduction to Karl Barth's Theology* (Grand Rapids: Eerdmans, 2004), 57.

write as though we have made a studied effort to avoid contact with the 'impurities' of human lives."[51] This explains some of the present ministries, their clumsy leadership, and their irrelevance to the world.

We need what novelist Marilynn Robinson calls a "theology of our time." It would, among other things, recover its old magisterial scale and confidence. Such a theology would give the world a supple, inclusive language, far more adequate to what we know. It would challenge systems and ideologies that believe they alone are sufficient to reality, "as if, in excluding all heterogenous assumptions, of religion particularly, they offered a truer representation of the world."[52] It would provide a needed reframing of current assumptions of leading.

The following ten chapters intend to do just that: challenge systems and ideologies and give centering, theological answers to core questions leaders ask. When leaders see leadership as God defines it, leaders will become the leaders God intended from the beginning. This is how revelation works. We hear the Word of God and become ourselves.[53] We discover who we are, from whence our life and leadership take their orientation, and where we need to direct our energies.[54]

We get back to the roots.

---

51. Volf, *Captive to the Word of God*, 41.

52. Ibid., 36–37.

53. Hans von Balthasar, *Prayer* (San Francisco: Ignatius, 1986), 33.

54. Ellen Charry, *By the Renewing of Your Minds: The Pastoral Function of Christian Doctrine* (Oxford: Oxford University Press, 1993), 3.

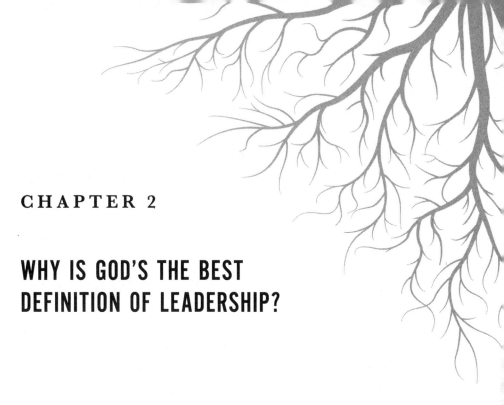

CHAPTER 2

WHY IS GOD'S THE BEST DEFINITION OF LEADERSHIP?

To an extent, leadership is like beauty; it's hard to define, but you know it when you see it.
—WARREN BENNIS

It was a heady moment. Here I was, called to lead an international church in the business center of Europe. Parishioners from some thirty-five different nations included embassy staff, corporate executives on the fast track, and even members from the international court of justice. It was my first day. But sitting at this creaky desk in what was once a Dutch Reformed Church, I found myself hopelessly lost. Confused. Questions that had demanded answers in my first pastorate caught up with me in the second.

Who am I? What am I exactly called to do? What do people expect of me? What does it mean to be a leader? Here I was, beginning a ministry yet at the same time coming to the end of myself. I was unsure of my ability to lead this amazing collection of leaders. I had to figure things out lest my tenure last as long as a Tinder date.

Maybe it was that I had said goodbye to the familiar systems in my home country and stepped into the vast unknowns of living in a foreign country. I was called to lead a diverse international community with large numbers from cultures I had little experience with—Nigerian, South African, Indonesian, and Caribbean. Reference points were harder to find here. All my belongings, including my books—especially my books—were still in transit. It was just me, the sterile walls, and the vacant shelves of this old, stately church. Traveling overseas was just the beginning of my journey. Now I was forced to go further, down to the core of myself, what David Brooks refers to as the pleroma, or substrate.[1]

I'm guessing most leaders take the same road at some point. Have you? You jump into a new venture and find yourself asking, "What am I doing?" You are drawn to pray, "God, don't let me mess this up and disappoint those I am called to lead." This is where we stop and ask a most fundamental question—What does leadership even mean? We have to get it right. As Peterson warns, "Being a leader can diminish or even destroy us and the people around us."[2]

Defining leadership is not easy. When I put my mind to examining the possible definitions, my brain begins to burn up. There are about as many descriptions of leadership as there are people who have tried to define it.[3] The subject has been stretched and pulled like taffy.

Quoting from *The Bass Handbook of Leadership*, McChrystal writes, "Often, a gathering to discuss leadership begins with a day of argument over the definition."[4] That's assuring. Little wonder Barbara Kellerman of

---

1. David Brooks, *The Second Mountain: The Quest for a Moral Life* (New York: Random House, 2019), 42.

2. Eugene H. Peterson, forward to Walter Wright's *Relational Leadership: A Biblical Model for Influence and Service* (Downers Grove, IL: InterVarsity Press, 2009), xx.

3. Peter G. Northouse, *Introduction to Leadership: Concepts and Practice* (Thousand Oaks: SAGE, 2015), 2.

4. Stanley McChrystal, *Leaders: Myth and Reality* (New York: Portfolio/Penguin, 2018), quoting from *The Bass Handbook of Leadership: Theory, Research, and Managerial Applications* (New York: Free Press, 2008), 7.

Why Is God's the Best Definition of Leadership?

Harvard admits, "I avoid like the plague definitions of leadership (of which, at last count, there were some fifteen hundred) and theories of leadership (of which there are around forty)."[5] Wait, aren't these serious leadership thinkers dedicated to establishing the lines?

James MacGregor Burns, one of America's preeminent scholars and an expert on the American presidency, acknowledges the same dilemma: "Leadership is one of the most observed and least understood phenomena on earth."[6] The definition he offers brings together a collection of observations: "Leadership is the reciprocal process of mobilizing, by persons with certain motives and values, various economic, political, and other resources, in a context of competition and conflict, in order to realize goals independently or mutually held by both leaders and followers."[7] Leadership is about achieving outcomes.

Bobby Clinton's definition is a bit more complex, though he makes the same point: "Leadership is a dynamic process over an extended period of time in various situations in which a leader utilizing leadership resources and by specific leadership behaviors, influences the thoughts and activities of followers toward accomplishment of aims usually mutually beneficial for leaders, followers, and the macro context of which they are a part."[8]

Some theorists attempt to pack a lot in their definitions. They remind me of a speechwriter who worked for a rather unbalanced governor. After some days on the job, he came to the painful conclusion, "He never says in a sentence what he can say in a long paragraph."[9]

In fairness, it might be that leadership is too multifaceted to be defined in a sentence. Some try. Consider the following examples.

---

5. Barbara Kellerman, *The End of Leadership* (New York: Harper Business, 2012), loc. 171 of 4487, Kindle.

6. James MacGregor Burns, *Leadership* (New York: Open Road Media, 2012), 1. He will later ask, "Do we really know leadership? Many of us don't have the faintest concept. Most statements are utter nonsense" (p. 451).

7. Ibid., 425.

8. J. Robert Clinton, *The Making of a Leader: Recognizing the Lessons and Stages of Leadership Development* (Colorado Springs: NavPress, 2012), 213.

9. Barton Swaim, *The Speechwriter: A Brief Education in Politics* (New York: Simon & Schuster, 2015), 111.

- "The only definition of a leader is someone who has followers."—Peter Drucker[10]
- "The essence of leadership is to create control."—Mary Parker Follett[11]
- "Leadership is the art of the future."—Leonard Sweet[12]
- "Leadership is the act of making a difference."—Michael Useem[13]
- "Leadership is focused on what can be or what must be."—Tod Bolsinger[14]
- "Leadership is the art of accomplishing more than the science of management says is possible."—Colin Powell[15]

The problem with succinct definitions is that some part of leading is left out. It may explain why some definitions wander into the abstract. What does "art of the future" mean? Here are a few that are more concrete.

- "Leadership activity is aligning people by translating vision and values into understandable and attainable acts."—Bernice Ledbetter[16]
- "Leadership is mobilizing others toward a goal shared by the leader and followers."—Garry Wills[17]
- "Leadership is the capacity to translate vision into reality."—Warren Bennis[18]

Several factors contribute to the perplexity of defining leadership. There is no simple formula. As McChrystal notes, it's nearly impossible to

---

10. Peter Drucker, "Not Enough Generals Were Killed," in *The Leader of the Future*, ed. Francis Hesselbein, Marshall Goldsmith, and Richard Beckard (San Francisco: Jossey-Bass, 1996), xii.

11. Mary Parker Follett, "The Essentials of Leadership," quoted in Barbara Kellerman, *Leadership: Essential Selections on Power, Authority, and Influence* (New York: McGraw-Hill, 2010), 92.

12. Leonard Sweet, *Summoned to Lead* (Grand Rapids: Zondervan, 2004), 11.

13. Michael Useem, *The Leadership Moment* (New York: Three Rivers, 1998), 4.

14. Tod Bolsinger, *Canoeing the Mountains: Christian Leadership in Uncharted Territory* (Downers Grove, IL: InterVarsity Press, 2018), 19.

15. Oren Harari, *The Leadership Secrets of Colin Powell* (New York: McGraw-Hill, 2002), 13.

16. Quoted in Sherwood G. Lingenfelter, *Leading Cross-Culturally: Covenant Relationships for Effective Christian Leadership* (Grand Rapids: Baker, 2008), 15.

17. Garry Wills, *Certain Trumpets: The Nature of Leadership* (New York: Simon & Schuster, 1994), 17.

18. Bennis, *On Becoming a Leader*, 192.

tame leadership into a static checklist.[19] A number of influences are at play in the difficulty of defining leadership, including but not limited to setting, seasons, traits, and myths.

Leadership does not work in a vacuum. It operates within a specific context. If you isolate leadership from its setting, an understanding of what leadership means "is limited and some would say misconstrued."[20] Garry Wills studied leaders from sixteen different contexts (e.g., military, business, church, sports). His conclusion? Leadership is not a single thing. Each "sound" of leadership differs, depending on the kind of person and kind of leadership required.[21]

Even within a given setting, there are different settings. Consider the church. Is the polity congregational or elder rule? How do I lead in a setting where different nationalities honor differing polities? In a corporate site, definitions turn on types. Profit? Nonprofit? In the political world, are we talking about executive, legislative, or judicial leadership? Each will require a different kind of leader and a different meaning of leadership.

Defining leadership also depends on the times. Are they peaceful or violent? Are people together, or are there factions creating internal disruption? Is there an external threat, or is there a season of calm? Peacetime and wartime require different kinds of leaders operating out of different definitions. In halcyon days people prefer leaders who will manage the peace and maintain the status quo. Leadership is more collaborative and less disruptive. In war a populace demands leaders who are disciplined and courageous—even disruptive. If deviance from what is popular or comfortable is required, do it![22]

Traits also play a role in defining. Is the leader a raging extrovert or a retiring introvert? Methodical or impulsive? Some leaders tend to be dynamic, like Samson toppling the pillars (Judg. 16:25–30). Others have the

---

19. McChrystal, *Leaders*, 8.

20. Bernice M. Ledbetter, Robert J. Banks, and David C. Greenhalgh, *Reviewing Leadership: A Christian Evaluation of Current Approaches* (Grand Rapids: Baker, 2016), 14.

21. Wills, *Certain Trumpets*, 267–70.

22. Judith Bardwick, "Peacetime Management and Wartime Leadership," in Hesselbein, Goldsmith, Beckhard, eds., *The Leader of the Future*, 131–39.

pulse of mannequins. Formal (four-piece suit) versus informal (polo and khakis). A leader's innate qualities will impact one's definition. Churchill's eloquence created an expectation that a leader is someone who inspires others to do what they could never do on their own. But this description of a leader does not work for people with different personalities.

Sometimes we raise leaders to mythic proportions and base our definitions on our minds' creations. Surveying a number of founders, geniuses, zealots, heroes, power brokers, and reformers, McChrystal found that we disconnect the ideal from the real. We tend to hang on to a Great Man theory of leadership, seeing leaders through rose-colored lenses. Leaders, we conclude, are those who sit atop the apex, attracting followers, influencing lives, catalyzing direction, and leading us to an envisioned outcome.[23] As a result, our definition of a leader does not always coincide with reality.

It's little wonder we have no authoritative declaration. It's no surprise I found myself mystified at the beginning of this new chapter of my life. Definitions tend to be diverse, as well as subjective. What do we mean by leadership? It depends. Some define leadership by how it happens.[24] Others find meaning in what leaders do. Definitions tend to be reduced to how leaders behave. Still others focus on the sociological context, a leader's psychological makeup, and/or what has been historic practice. Attempts at a definition can create headaches. This is where and why we need theology. We need to get back to the roots.

LEADERSHIP AS GOD DEFINES IT

A theologian must acknowledge that there is no scriptural verse that declares, "Leadership is . . ." Leadership joins many other subjects in Scripture (God, gospel, discipleship, Eucharist, church, faith, glory) that defy a simple definitional statement. Nonetheless, a step-by-step study will point to leadership's true meaning.

23. McChrystal, *Leaders*, 375.
24. Ibid., 393.

Why Is God's the Best Definition of Leadership?

Survey the biblical stories, and one might initially get lost. There seems to be as many definitions as there are leaders. Everyone's leadership is different. When we look into the narratives, we see the same multiplicity of settings, times, traits, and myths. Leaders in the Bible find the same number of ways of getting into trouble as those outside of Scripture. Some (Samson, Rehoboam, Jonah, Peter) act like incorrigible juvenile delinquents who can't stay out of pool halls.[25] Others (Daniel, Nehemiah) are extraordinary models who have figured out where they belong. Moses did not always have it together, but there was the honoring of a sacred space and a commitment to maintain a sacred rhythm.[26]

A review of Scripture's language reveals that there is no exact equivalent to the word *leader*.[27] The closest expression in the New Testament is the term *hodēgos* (from *hodos*, "way," "road"). In most passages it is translated "guide" (Matt. 23:16; Acts 1:16). Going further back to the Old Testament, humanity is called to "rule" (Gen. 1:28), but this rule takes on many forms. An assortment of words are used to describe leaders: patriarchs, civil officers, warlords, kings, generals, governors, priests, prophets, sages, apostles, elders. Male, female, godly, pagan, young, and old are all represented. God himself takes on multiple leadership roles: King, Lord, Sovereign, Head, Father.

Some leaders are transactional, in a give-and-take relationship with their followers. Think Gideon and his supporters (Judg. 8:22–24). Others are transformational, inspiring people to a higher level of living. Consider Paul's model to the leaders of Ephesus (Acts 20:18–35) and his words to Timothy: "What you heard from me, keep as the pattern of sound teaching, with faith and love in Christ Jesus" (2 Tim. 1:13).

There are impulsive models like Jehoshaphat, who seemed to decide first and pray later. Others were methodical and calculating. Faced with a crisis, Nehemiah prayed for months, planned carefully, and set out to build

---

25. A phrase borrowed from essayist Joseph Epstein, in *Gallimaufry: A Collection of Essays, Reviews, Bits* (Edinburg: Axios, 2020), 16.

26. Ruth Haley Barton, "The Old Testament Tells All," *Christianity Today*, July/August 2020, 62.

27. Ledbetter, Banks, and Greenhalgh, *Reviewing Leadership*, 23.

a wall with meticulous care. Some leaders (Elijah, John the Baptist) were austere, while others (Solomon, Herod) were ostentatious and filthy rich. Some (David, Paul) were more relational, and others (Noah, Rehoboam) were task oriented. Some (Uzziah) were vain. Others were more modest, like Moses, who was the humblest of men. Joseph was sure of himself, but Saul and Gideon lacked self-confidence. Esther preferred to keep the peace, while Jeremiah and the prophets were not afraid to confront the established order.

So much for clarity. What is leadership? Scripture so far seems to imply that there is no one-size-fits-all definition that biblical leaders were forced to squeeze into. As with all leaders, there were commonalities. Those who led had *followers*. When followers turned away from leaders, leadership all but ceased to exist (1 Kings 12:1–20). All leaders had some *influence*. They brought certain change. Under reformers like Asa and Josiah, a nation was swayed to return to God (1 Kings 15:9–22; 2 Kings 23:1–28). Early church leaders did not go unnoticed, turning the world upside down (Acts 26:26). And every leader had some *direction*, some path into the future to lead followers. We find this with biblical leaders like Abraham, Moses, and David. But we're still left without a clear and succinct definition.

Maybe Scripture's use of metaphors will help, but these images of leadership further complicate. We like metaphoric language. It connects us to workable pictures. The abstract becomes more concrete.[28] But they do not get us any closer to a singular definition of a leader. Jesus likened his leadership to multiple images (e.g., a gate that gives entry, to the way that gives direction, and to the light that gives clarity) (John 10:7; 14:6; 8:12). Paul illustrated leadership by borrowing from the images of ambassador, nurturing parent, and priest (2 Cor. 5:20; 1 Thess. 2:7; Rom. 15:15–17).

If there is a dominant metaphor for leadership in Scripture, it is the shepherd. After an exhaustive study of the term, Laniak concludes that this agrarian role serves as a frame of reference for evaluating leadership.[29] We

---

28. Eugene H. Peterson, *Tell It Slant: A Conversation on the Language of Jesus in His Stories and Prayers* (Grand Rapids: Eerdmans, 2008), 205.

29. Timothy S. Laniak, *Shepherds After My Own Heart: Pastoral Traditions and Leadership in the Bible* (Downers Grove, IL: InterVarsity Press, 2006), 37.

see this in multiple Old Testament and New Testament passages. When leaders like Jacob and David thought of God's leadership, the image of shepherd came to mind. Jacob referred to God as "the God who has been my shepherd all my life to this day" (Gen. 48:15). David declared, "The LORD is my shepherd" (Ps. 23:1; cf. 77:20; 78:52; 95:6–7).

The metaphor underscores that leaders, by definition, are not impersonal and aloof—leaving us on our own in the darkness—but those who guide, repair, and replenish. It is how the prophets saw God (Isa. 40:11; Jer. 23:1; Ezek. 34:1–31). Jesus referred to himself as a shepherd (John 10:11), and Peter extended the metaphor to human leadership, exhorting the elders to lead like shepherds (1 Peter 5:2).

Leadership is about being present with, protecting, providing, and guiding followers.[30] Like a shepherd, the leader exists for the sake of others and their well-being. Assessing its theological significance, Brueggemann concludes, "The metaphor of shepherd and sheep introduces an entire theory of governance and power."[31] This is illustrated in John 10:1–18, where Jesus pushed the metaphor to its interpretive limit in a series of parables about sheep and shepherds, climaxing in his self-identification as "the good shepherd" (v. 14).

So where are we? Have we simply exchanged one perplexity for another? Is there light at the end of this long tunnel?

Jesus Brings Leadership's Definition into Focus

The moment God took on flesh, the meaning of leadership was settled. Go back to the early narratives. We see it in God's willingness to give up a throne for a trough, the comforts of heaven for the pains of earth. He moved from the center to the periphery, leaving his glory for the shame. Rather than come to earth as a reigning monarch, he came in the tiniest form possible—an ovum, a fetus, growing cell to cell within a simple teenager from across the tracks.

The Son of God submitted himself and obeyed his earthly parents

---

30. Ibid., 111.
31. Walter Brueggemann, *First and Second Samuel* (Louisville: John Knox, 1990), 238.

(Luke 2:51), yielded to the Spirit's casting of him into the wilderness (4:1), served the needs of a grieving widow (7:11–15), went to the cross to pay the price for our failures (23:46), and was obedient to every purpose of the Father (John 17:4). These explain the words of Paul, that Jesus "made himself nothing by taking the very nature of a servant" (Phil. 2:7).

As Jesus began to teach, his words cut through the false assumptions about what leadership means, opening his listeners' eyes to what it actually was and what it should be. In the Greco-Roman world in which Jesus walked, what passed for leadership was a lie. Leadership was assumed to be about power, prestige, and honor. Wearing the right threads, having the premier occupation, and getting seated at the head of the table—these defined a leader. Leadership involved a pecking order, one designed to reinforce the values of elite society.[32] The hope was to get to the apex and be memorialized by statues, ones you can still trip over today. These cultural norms were evident in both the religious and irreligious worlds of Jesus's day, and they still mark much of leadership today—both outside and inside the church.

The disciples of Jesus bought into this definition. When Jesus announced his imminent arrest and death, his followers began to jockey for the lead position (Matt. 20:17–22). It didn't help that Jesus had just promised that the twelve would sit on twelve future thrones (19:28). This might have tripped the fear switch. It didn't seem to matter that Jesus had just taught the parable of the workers in the vineyard, concluding with the words "So the last will be first, and the first will be last" (20:16). These men were pressing to get first in the boarding line. Like passengers vying for the best seats on a plane, the disciples began arguing over seat assignments. They needed to know who had MVP status. Who of them would sit closest to Jesus?

In the race for the top, one of their mothers had words with Jesus: "Grant that one of these two sons of mine may sit at your right and the other at your left in your kingdom" (v. 21). What made this particularly offensive was that this was less a request and more of an insistence. After

---

32. John Hutchison, "Servanthood: Jesus' Countercultural Call to Christian Leaders," *Bibliotheca Sacra* 166 (January–March 2009): 66.

all, these particular disciples had been part of Jesus's inner core. They were the MVPs who went to places others were not invited to. Shouldn't they sit in first class? Isn't leadership about proximity?

Given the leadership culture they were immersed in, the disciples understood that by definition leadership is not for the passive, weak-kneed types. It is for the aggressive, those willing to shove their way to the top. They could sense that the kingdom of God was pressing forward just as Jesus had said in an earlier conversation: "From the days of John the Baptist until now, the kingdom of heaven has been forcefully advancing, and forceful men lay hold of it" (11:12 NIV 1984). The announcement that Jesus was going to be mocked and flogged was drowned out by other voices, forceful voices in their heads shouting for recognition. In their minds Jesus the revolutionary was about to overthrow the Roman order and establish himself and his followers as rulers in their place. It made perfect sense to advocate for rank and position.

Jesus warned that achieving rank comes with a cost (20:22–23). Obsessed with power, these particular sons were willing to pay the price, without hesitation, without understanding, without serious reflection, without asking for any clarity, and without any prayer. It's not surprising that the other disciples found their pursuit offensive. But then, they sought the same thing.

To use the language of McChrystal, every one of them fell for the myth of leadership—the myth that leaders are those at the top of the heap. They borrowed from the leadership playbook of the day, just as others had before them. One thinks of characters in the Old Testament like Haman, who desperately wanted a seat above all the other officials (Est. 3:1). The disciples grew up watching leaders—even the most religious—jostle their way into the spotlight and go for the seats of honor (Matt. 23:6). This is what leaders do. This is what leadership is.

It was time to expose the distortions and go back to the roots, to the original design. Jesus used this teachable moment to contrast false definitions with leadership's true definition. "You know that the rulers of the Gentiles lord it over [*katakyrieuō*] them, and their high officials exercise authority over [*katakyrieuousin*] them" (20:25). Notice here that both Greek compounds begin with the preposition *kata*, a word meaning "down."[33] In the world the disciples had known, leadership's meaning was top down. Roman rule was all about being over others, dominating and oppressing by pushing downward. Unfortunately, the likes of James and John and Peter were embracing a faulty leadership hypothesis. Life had taught them that a leader is someone with authority and power, the one out in front, steering the ship and determining the outcomes.

Suddenly Jesus flipped entrenched assumptions, turning the organizational chart upside down. He pierced through their misperceptions and egocentricities and said, "Not so with you" (v. 26). God's kingdom works on inverted principles. Those who follow Jesus operate with a leadership definition radically different than the world's: "Instead, whoever wants to become great among you must be your servant, and whoever wants to be first must be your slave" (vv. 26–27). Leadership is a matter of service.

This was profound and paradoxical. Such a definition violated cultural norms, especially those of a society steeped in fear and power, honor and shame.[34] Achieving status and recognition framed every facet of life. To serve implied subjection. It was to lose face. It could mean exclusion and rejection. Who wanted that? Israel had had its fill of taking a back seat. Its history was the story of going from one enslavement to the next (under Egypt, Assyria, Babylon, Persia, Greece, and now Rome).

Lest the definition be perceived as theoretical, Jesus pointed out that it had been there in front of them from the beginning: "Just as the Son of Man did not come to be served, but to serve, and to give his life as a ransom for many" (v. 28). How could they miss it? Servanthood had been a running theme from the moment the disciples met Jesus. For three years he had ministered to them in both word and act. He welcomed the lowly and most vulnerable, continually redefining greatness (18:4).

Prophecies of old predicted that the coming Messiah, their leader,

---

33. R. T. France, *The Gospel of Matthew* (Grand Rapids: Eerdmans, 2007), 760.

34. For a fuller discussion of these terms, note my work *Missing Voices: Learning to Lead beyond Our Horizons* (London: Langham, 2019), 2–6.

would come as a suffering servant (Isa. 49:1–7; 52:13–53:12). Jesus could have made his leadership about showcasing his authority and asserting his power. He could have demanded that subjects serve his needs and wash his feet. He could have reminded everyone how great he was. Ironically, there were moments when this meek and mild leader expressed a forceful side, rebuking the wind, correcting his disciples, and telling the demons to go to hell. But in everything he did, he was ultimately in subjection to his Father, devoted to completing heaven's work and making the members of the Trinity known (John 17:4, 26).

Everywhere Jesus went, he did what servants do. He saved a family from embarrassment by providing wine (John 2:7–9), offered living water to a woman with thirst (4:10), raised a paralytic who could not stand on his own (5:8–9), fed a desperate crowd (6:11), gave sight to the blind (9:6–7), replaced grief with joy (11:43–44), and laid down his life for a world lost in sin (19:17–18). This is what leadership is.

But the disciples missed it, just as many leaders do today. The words of Jesus did not penetrate. It became apparent in the subsequent scene in the upper room that they still did not get it. Rather than see with eyes wide open, they were like some who habitually walk into screen doors. We all have the same propensity.

Jesus gathered them and once again defined leadership. Once more he turned their world order on its head (John 13:1–5). Against all protocol, he performed one of the most demeaning tasks of his day. He took a towel and a basin and washed the feet of his disciples, reversing all human assumptions of what it means to lead. The disciples were paralyzed. Ambition was still burning a hole in their stomachs.

To wash off the grime of the world, let alone touch someone's feet, was an act of profound subjugation.[35] The disciples found it necessary to rebuke Jesus (v. 8). As I note in *Under an Open Heaven*, CEOs do not refill the paper towel dispensers, up-and-coming kings do not unplug toilets, church leaders do not park cars, and worshipers with important roles do not assist

---

35. Andy Crouch, *Playing God: Redeeming the Gift of Power* (Downers Grove, IL: InterVarsity Press, 2013), 163.

a single mother who needs to pick up her children in the nursery.[36] And disciples don't wash feet. This is not what leadership means!

Actually, it is exactly what leadership means.

The upper room seemed to be a test of what Jesus taught earlier. Jesus was presenting them with the fundamental definition of a leader, but to use the words of N. T. Wright, "they had become used to the ordinary, shabby, second-rate sort."[37] They still didn't grasp reality (v. 12). John would get it later. With theological precision and clarity, in his gospel he explains Jesus's actions: "Jesus knew that the Father had put all things under his power, and that he had come from God and was returning to God; so he got up from the meal, took off his outer clothing, and wrapped a towel around his waist" (vv. 3–4). It was in light of Jesus's self-understanding, in his knowledge that he possessed the ultimate leadership status (power, authority, and divinity) that he rose to do the unthinkable.

Pause and reflect. Notice that there is no "nonetheless" in the language. No adversative phrase like "but he rose," as if to say that this is not typical of leaders. Rather Jesus served their most menial needs *because* of who he is. This is most significant to understanding leadership's meaning. In God's economy this is the logical movement. This is what leaders do. Especially those with great power and authority. This is what defines a leader.

After washing their feet, Jesus promised them they would be blessed if they got this (v. 17). But there would be no immediate blessing. As soon as the disciples finished the meal, they went at it again, bickering over who was the greatest (Luke 22:24).[38] Had they not just witnessed what it means to lead? Jesus again pointed out the world's definition of leadership as those who lord it over and exercise authority. And again he redefined leadership for those who follow him, underscoring what was counterintuitive: "You are not to be like that. Instead, the greatest among

---

36. John E. Johnson, *Under an Open Heaven: A New Way of Life Revealed in John's Gospel* (Grand Rapids: Kregel, 2017), 197.

37. N. T. Wright, *Simply Jesus: A New Vision of Who He Was, What He Did, and Why He Matters* (New York: HarperOne, 2011), 5.

38. There is no attempt to do historical reconstruction; the intent is simply to read the accounts in the order they appear.

you should be like the youngest, and the one who rules like the one who serves" (v. 26).

As with many of us, it was hard for them to get past a definition that had been hardwired into their egos from youth. Leadership was, "Serve me!" To the disciples' credit, they eventually moved on from their earlier assumptions. There was a radical break. After the cross, and following Pentecost, they would lead the church by serving, by pouring out their lives for others, and by dying in the process. They would learn what Augustine so eloquently wrote years later: "Where there's humility there is majesty; where there's weakness, there's might; where there is death, there's life."[39] If you want to get to the top, descend to the bottom. If you want to start a revolution, grab a towel and a basin. If you want to know what it means to lead, serve.

New Testament Leaders Underscore Jesus's Definition

As God's preeminent apostle and first Christian theologian, Paul chose servant language to explain his identity as well as define his leadership. It became his working introduction:

- "Paul, a servant . . ." (Rom. 1:1)
- "Paul and Timothy, servants . . ." (Phil. 1:1)
- "Paul, a servant of God . . ." (Titus 1:1)

These words represented a radical shift. There was a time when Paul's definition of a leader mirrored culture. Early on he was more interested in hobnobbing with the elite and separating himself from the *hoi polloi*. He was obsessed with getting to the top of his profession (Phil. 3:4–6). He prided himself on using the weight of religious authority to oppress others (Acts 26:10–11). But just as he did with the disciples, Christ stopped Paul in his tracks and transformed his life (9:3–6). Eventually, Paul came to grips with the necessity of the cross. It became a central focus of his theology. Consider these words: "I resolved to know nothing while I was

---

39. Quoted in Brooks, *The Second Mountain*, 260.

with you except Jesus Christ and him crucified" (1 Cor. 2:2). What was considered the most shameful death by the culture of his day reoriented Paul's life. He saw in Christ's death the ultimate act of servanthood. It turned his assumptions of leadership upside down. As McKnight writes, "Any kind of leadership that is soaked in *cruciformity* will become servant leadership."[40]

In due course, Paul composed a christological hymn. It stands forever as a theological statement of what, in essence, is leadership.[41] The lyrics declare that true leaders are willing to set their credentials aside. This is what Jesus did. Though coequal and coeternal with the Father and Spirit, Jesus did not come into this world to showcase his authority and make a display of his importance. Instead Jesus chose to empty himself, setting aside the full weight of his attributes. He emptied himself of his own prerogatives, gave up independence for dependence, laid aside his glory, and took on the form of a slave (Phil. 2:5–11).

Like his Savior, a transformed Paul approached everything in terms of service. He was a servant of the gospel (Eph. 3:7), a servant to his congregants (1 Cor. 3:5; Col. 1:25), a minister of the new covenant (2 Cor. 3:6), a servant of God (6:4), and a servant of Christ (11:23). He urged Timothy to step up and fearlessly lead, fulfilling his service (2 Tim. 1:7; 4:5; cf. Col. 4:17). He reminded the Ephesians that God has given to them leaders whose purpose is to equip the saints to do the work of service (Eph. 4:12).

Like Jesus, Paul determined to correct common misperceptions of how leadership is defined. Some, like those in Corinth, viewed their newfound community of faith in the same way they viewed the Roman imperial cult—as a place to gain influence and self-importance. Personality cults, personal rivalries, and personal comparisons dominated the ethos. They wanted Paul to be a leader like the world's leaders. They expected him to be a "super-apostle," operating like leaders at the head of the procession

---

40. Scot McKnight, *Pastor Paul: Nurturing a Culture of Christoformity in the Church* (Grand Rapids: Brazos, 2019), 25. McKnight refers to Michael J. Gorman's work *Cruciformity: Paul's Narrative Spirituality of the Cross* (Grand Rapids: Eerdmans, 2001) for his use of the term.

41. See Michale Ayers, "Toward a Theology of Leadership," *Journal of Biblical Perspectives in Leadership* 1, no. 1 (Fall 2006): 3.

(1 Cor. 4:8; 2 Cor. 11:5). They could not comprehend that Paul preferred to be regarded as a servant. This seemed an act of folly (1 Cor. 4:1, 10).

Moving to letters written by authors other than Paul, we find that they contended with the same temptations in their communities. John notes, "I wrote to the church, but Diotrephes, who loves to be first, will not welcome us" (3 John 9). How many Diotrephes types are still out there, treating the church as if it were a place to assert their rule and run their kingdom (v. 10)? How many would I face in my own church? Others, however, got it right. James introduced himself as a servant of God, as did Peter and Jude (James 1:1; 2 Peter 1:1; Jude 1). Peter admonished the early leaders of the church to be eager to serve, not lording it over those entrusted to their care (1 Peter 5:2–3). He came to realize that the proper authority of ministry is not an external, manipulative, alien power that distances itself from those under it but rather a legitimized and happily received influence that wishes only good for its recipient.[42]

A SERVANT DEFINITION GETS MIXED REVIEWS

This is true both within the church and outside the church. Some question the idea, viewing servant leadership as unrealistic. "It's a bad idea." "It's so impractical." This is how leadership consultant Mitch McCrimmon puts it. He argues that leaders as servants is one bandwagon that needs to be disrupted.[43] Why?

He, and others in his camp, argue that leaders must stand up, assert their authority, point to the future, and lead with boldness. They believe that it is difficult for leaders to do this with a posture of service. It is an unstable definition. It's fine to care for others and be patient with stragglers, but leadership isn't always about attending to the needs of others and pleasing them. There are moments when leaders must make it clear that followers

---

42. Thomas C. Oden, *Pastoral Theology: Essentials of Ministry* (New York: HarperOne, 1993), 53.
43. Mitch McCrimmon, "Why Servant Leadership Is a Bad Idea," *Management Issues*, August 16, 2010, https://www.management-issues.com/opinion/6015/why-servant-leadership-is-a-bad-idea.

need to get on the bus or get off. One cannot be like Moses, stuttering and stammering and interceding for others. No nice gestures at the expense of command and control. Gaining input is fine, but in the end the leader makes the decision. No waffling. No pusillanimity!

In their minds leaders who set out to serve confuse roles. Servant leader is an oxymoron. This is why, though it receives a certain amount of lip service, the definition is not widely embraced. Gardner, in *On Leadership*, notes that though the Bible "touches on the concept of leader as servant," the servant concept is not prominent in popular thinking.[44] The leadership industry wouldn't be a sixty-five-billion-dollar industry if servanthood was the marketing theme. Taglines like "Come Learn How to Lead as a Servant," "You Too Can Be a Slave," or "How to Put Others above You" will not work. Servile leaders, soft and passive, get run over.

Is there some misunderstanding of the biblical definition, or are these responses an effort to live in reality? Perhaps they are missing that Scripture never reduces servant leadership to pleasing others. Nor is there any suggestion that servant leaders are characterized as passive, lacking in courage or determination. Jesus's actions were anything but soft and nice. His was not a wild leadership suddenly domesticated by the cross. With the full heart of a servant, he confronted and corrected his followers (Matt. 17:17), spoke words that shook, leaving adversaries powerless (Luke 4:30), chased off demons (Mark 5:11–13), denounced hypocritical leadership in no uncertain terms (Matt. 23:13–36), and claimed lordship over everyone and everything (John 19:11).

The point made is this—to lead as a servant is not to diminish one's authority. Fleshed out, godly service can be the fullest expression of power. And one more thing, in response to comments like those of Gardner, the Bible does more than touch on the concept. Servant leadership is not some idea in a corner. As noted, it is Scripture's defining statement on what it means to be a leader.

On the positive side, some embrace the idea, viewing the servant model

---

44. John W. Gardner, *On Leadership* (New York: Free Press, 1993), 141–42.

of leadership as the key to success. Leaders who serve their followers, who place the good of others and the organization over their own self-interest, tend to generate a healthier, more effective workplace.

This was the finding of Robert Greenleaf, a retired telecom executive who wrote *Servant Leadership*. Though he attributed some of his thinking to his Quaker background, it was Hermann Hesse's novel *Journey to the East* that had the greatest influence on his thinking. Emerging in the 1970s, Greenleaf's concepts were described as unique, as groundbreaking.

One could fairly ask, had someone overlooked Jesus? More convicting is the question, didn't anyone see this definition lived out in the church?

Servant leadership suddenly became a new paradigm in corporate culture. Greenleaf was hailed as the founder of the modern servant leadership movement. His writings became part of the leadership lexicon, driven by people who were tired of ego-driven leaders and desperate for a better definition—leaders who were self-effacing and other-centered.[45] Recent studies affirm that servant leadership still works. Such leaders help followers reach their full potential.[46]

Optimistic as it sounds, this particular adoption of servant leadership practice misses its true meaning. Servant leadership can lead to beneficial results. People do respond in a positive way to those who come alongside and ask, "How can I help you soar?" But Christ's model was not simply about pragmatics. Serve as a leader because it works is not the principal motive. The servant language of Scripture transcends this.

By definition and design, servant leadership does not begin with us; it begins with service to God. Service has everything to do with our posture before God—not with what produces in the marketplace. This was Christ's motive. From the beginning it was always about his service to the Father. It wasn't what would bring pleasure to guests at a wedding event but what would fit within God's time frame (John 2:4). It did not matter if he alienated a religious establishment. Jesus came to serve the interests of

---

45. Kellerman, *The End of Leadership*, 181.

46. See Nathan Eva et al., "Servant Leadership: A Systematic Review and Call for Future Research," *Leadership Quarterly* 30, no. 1 (2019): 111–32, https://doi.org/10.1016/j.leaqua.2018.07.004.

the Father (5:19, 30). He did not minister so as to satisfy the customer. He served so as to satisfy the will of God (6:38). Christ served for one central purpose—to bring pleasure and glory to the Father.

Out of this vertical service, leadership moves horizontally. In obeyance to the divine moment, Jesus served the needs of a desperate groom (2:7–9). Out of serving the Father, Jesus asked the blind beggar, "What do you want me to do for you?" (Luke 18:41). Out of attending to the Father's will, Jesus washed the feet of his disciples (John 13:4–5). This is the pattern of servanthood, which becomes the essence of leadership.

Paul exhorted Timothy to present himself before God (2 Tim. 2:15). Only then could he do the work of service. The ultimate servant task is to place ourselves at God's disposal and leave the results to God. We are called to offer ourselves at the altar. This is our "intelligent service" (Rom. 12:1 YLT). More, it is our worship. Out of this—and only out of this—can we effectively lead. It requires:

- not looking out for our own interests but investing in the needs of others
- not ignoring the oppressed but standing up for them
- not holding others in debt but being in debt to others
- not inflicting pain but bearing one's pain
- not holding to one's rights but surrendering to the claims of others
- not working to gain power but aiming to release it.[47]

What all of this shows is that leadership, while having a servile component, is more about serving as the go-between.[48] Serving the purposes of God. Such service takes us to the depths of leadership's meaning. It is the point through which all other acts of leadership flow. *Diakonia* is the "essential layer of every theory, grade, or proper definition."[49] It was the

---

47. Max DePree speaks much to true servant leadership in his books, including *Called to Serve*, *Leadership Jazz*, and *Leadership Is an Art*.

48. McKnight, *Pastor Paul*, 25.

49. Oden, *Pastoral Theology*, 54.

theme of Jesus's most pointed discourse on leading and behind his most dramatic acts of leadership.

There is no better definition of a leader than one who serves the purposes of God. Those defined by this reflect the model of Jesus. They draw people to a purpose higher than themselves. Their acts of service transform the world in ways no amount of coercive leadership could ever do. Service to God is what dignifies leadership and invites an eternal reward (1 Pet. 5:4).

CONCLUSION

Those seven years in Holland taught me much about servanthood and leadership. Dying to self and washing feet. But there was still much to learn. When I began teaching leadership years later, I approached a lecture on leadership definition as part of the necessary preliminaries, an opening stage act before the real concert. Why give it much lecture time? The myriad of meanings offered by countless leadership scholars and models still left me with uncertainty. Who can say for sure what leadership is? Sometimes I wanted to exclaim with Kellerman, "I avoid like the plague definitions of leadership." So why try? Even scriptural models, as noted earlier in this chapter, led me to different assumptions. At best I could see common threads—followership, influence, and direction.

Thinking through a theology of leadership has changed this. It has forced me to give more space to defining leadership, to see it as an essential leadership question requiring a thoughtful theological answer. Everything begins here. Christ made it his mission to expose false definitions. By word and personal example, he defined leadership as *service*. This is what it means to lead, and it frames every other leadership question.

Just as the early apostles and early church leaders understood, embraced, modeled, and taught this definition, some voices still do. Shortly after Henri Nouwen left a prestigious academic post to minister to the mentally handicapped, he was invited to speak to leaders in Washington, DC. Not only was his mission to underscore the necessity of theology; his task was to define leadership. He chose the theme of servant leadership, and he challenged his audience to serve. And then he pointed them forward and said, "Here we touch the most important quality of Christian leadership in the future. It is not a leadership of power and control, but a leadership of powerlessness and humility in which the suffering servant of God, Jesus Christ, is made manifest."[50]

A question equally as challenging as definition is the question of need for leaders. Are leaders really necessary? Can we get on without them? Does God need leaders? Theology addresses these issues, the subject of our next chapter. But first a story, a working model of servant leadership.

✿ RUTH ✾

Ruth is a slave widow. She does not seem to be a likely candidate for servant leader. Does she even make the grade of one who leads—a person of influence and direction, one whom people follow? Ruth does not lead armies or nations or tribes. Unlike Deborah, a contemporary, she leads no one. Ruth doesn't even make the "Hall of Faith" in Hebrews 11. But here's a guess—if there were a Hall of Service, she might be near the top.

Ruth is a foreigner determined to serve her mother-in-law, Naomi. She takes the initiative to leave her familiar world in the interest of *khesed*, a Hebrew word meaning loving-kindness, loyal love.[51] She will break from her past and serve the same God as Naomi, taking refuge under his wings (Ruth 1:16; 2:12). Ruth is willing to do the menial and the mundane. She will work the fields of Boaz, accepting the scraps to provide for their needs. She is aware that she doesn't even make the grade of Boaz's maidservants (2:13). But this will change (3:9). Boaz will be in awe of Ruth's *khesed* (v. 10).

In time, Ruth marries Boaz and becomes a mother in the line of David

---

50. Henri J. M. Nouwen, *In the Name of Jesus: Reflections on Christian Leadership* (New York: Crossroad, 2000), 63.

51. See R. Laird Harris, Gleason L. Archer Jr., and Bruce K. Waltke, eds., *Theological Wordbook of the Old Testament*, 2 vols. (Chicago: Moody, 1980), 1:305–7.

and ultimately of Jesus (Matt. 1:5). As is fitting with her character, Ruth fades into the background of her own action. She will allow her son to be named by the women of the city, and they will choose Obed, a name derived from *'ebed*, which fittingly means "servant." Naomi will take the child and lay him on her lap while the women of the city declare, "Naomi has a son!" (Ruth 4:13–22). And somewhere in the background is a servant mother named Ruth who does not need the recognition. She will simply take it all in.

Ruth is an example of one who is comfortable letting others lead. She has no interest in seeking to push her way into the center. If she had any power, she would not seek to hoard it. If there were feet to be washed, she would grab a basin and remove the grime. She is, after all, a Moabite, a people described as God's basin for washing feet (Ps. 60:8). But lest anyone consider Ruth to be a nondescript alien who offers little to leadership studies, she served as a burst of light in a dark and bloody period.[52]

If you step back and note the setting, you will find she was the antithesis of a period of corrupt and failed leadership. At a time when there was no king and everyone did what was right in their own eyes (Judg. 21:25), Ruth led. Look closer, and you will discover that Ruth was never really in the shadows. She was known by "all the gate of my people" (Ruth 3:11 YLT). It's a way of saying that anyone who had anything to do with leading—fulfilling social, administrative, and business decisions—encountered Ruth (Deut. 21:19; Ruth 4:1). You couldn't miss her. She was a woman of *khayil*, which is no mean term. It declared that Ruth was a person of strength, power, might, and force. It would describe the fierceness of her future grandson, David (2 Sam. 17:10).

The word fits. As Waltke notes, this is part of an Old Testament narrative in which Ruth plays a leading role on a stage that is bigger than life. "She has the right stuff to be a mother in God's kingdom."[53] A willingness to glean the leftovers is critical to becoming a formidable leader.

---

52. Bruce K. Waltke, *An Old Testament Theology: An Exegetical, Canonical, and Thematic Approach* (Grand Rapids: Zondervan, 2007), 850.

53. Ibid., 865.

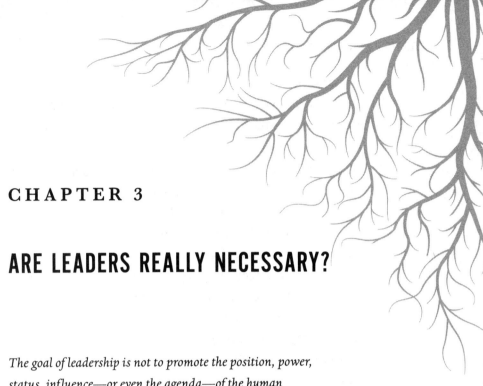

CHAPTER 3

ARE LEADERS REALLY NECESSARY?

The goal of leadership is not to promote the position, power, status, influence—or even the agenda—of the human leader. It is to accomplish God's purpose in the world.
—Justin Irving and Mark Strauss

The world was on the brink. A coalition of three military empires, under the autocratic leadership of Hitler, Mussolini, and Hirohito, had come together to remake the world in its own image. An unspeakable evil was descending on humanity. These empires almost succeeded, and they would have if not for one leader who emerged and turned the tide of history.

Listen to this conclusion about Franklin Roosevelt by historian Nigel Hamilton: "Had FDR, in the first year of America's involvement in World War II, not learned to wear the mantle of command so firmly, and to overrule his generals, it is quite possible Hitler would have achieved his aim when declaring war on the United States on December 11, 1941: winning the war in Europe." Hamilton adds, "It is a sobering reflection."[1]

---

1. Nigel Hamilton, *The Mantle of Command: FDR at War, 1941–1942* (Boston: Mariner, 2014), 442.

The unmistakable message of his book is this—the right leader is indispensable. Be it in Washington, on the athletic field, in the pulpit, within the corporate office, or in the theater of war, leaders make the difference. They shape history and determine destiny. Or do they?

Is this a mythical fantasy, something we want to believe? Just how essential are leaders? Do we really need them? Don't they create many of our headaches, even if some bring comic relief? How should we judge the concept of leadership? Are leadership hierarchies the solution—or the problem?

Many believe that leaders are fundamental, viewing them as the difference makers, the grand architects of history. Hamilton's story of FDR is one of many that support this. Behind every defining moment is a leader, one who provides a course and strengthens the resolve to press on. In his study on leadership, Bolsinger underscores that every living system requires someone to lead the necessary transformation. Leaders are essential for bringing people into the future, one they may be resisting. Look around. Great works, from cathedrals to spaceships to philharmonic orchestras, would be nonexistent if it were not for a leader who initiated, organized, enlisted, and tenaciously pressed hearts forward. If someone is not functioning as a leader, "the system will always default to the status quo."[2]

British historian Thomas Carlyle codified the long-standing idea that history's arc is bent by leaders. He claimed that history is no more or no less than—indeed is tantamount to—"the history of the Great Men who have worked here."[3] In one of his works, he made this summation: "All things that we see standing accomplished in the world are properly the outer material result, the practical realization and embodiment, of Thoughts that dwelt in the Great Men sent into the world: the soul of the whole world's history, it may justly be considered, were in the history of these."[4]

Other observers of history concur. John Keegan remarked that it was

---

2. Tod Bolsinger, *Canoeing the Mountains: Christian Leadership in Uncharted Territory* (Downers Grove, IL: InterVarsity Press, 2018), 21.

3. Quoted in Barbara Kellerman, *Leadership: Essential Selections on Power, Authority, and Influence* (New York: McGraw-Hill, 2010), 57.

4. Thomas Carlyle, *On Heroes, Hero-Worship, and the Heroic in History* (1840; repr., University of California Press, 1993), 3–4.

Lenin, Stalin, Hitler, Mao Zedong, Roosevelt, and Churchill who deter-mined the course of the twentieth century.[5] The effects still reverberate. Profiling Robert E. Lee, Martin Luther King Jr., Margaret Thatcher, and others, Stanley McChrystal, senior fellow at Yale's Institute for Global Affairs, concludes that leaders are critical to success.[6] They start compa-nies, invent things, lead nations, and hold court. They have the natural power to do what others cannot do, and what no amount of training will enable an ordinary person to do.

Behind their heroic ways is an extraordinary sureness. Leaders exude the kind of courage that compels others to follow. Roosevelt dominated both his colleagues and his subordinates "through his abiding confidence in himself and his own authority."[7] Those who worked with him referred to FDR as "the Boss." In his style of leading, no one challenged or contra-dicted him except General MacArthur, who, as Hamilton put it, "was God, and superior to everybody—as taught him by his mother!"[8] MacArthur saw himself as the central player in the grand narrative.

More than difference makers, leaders challenge the existing order and move people forward. Leaders point the way and create the momentum. They spurn the creeping inertia and sound the alarm. Leaders rouse slum-bering churches to action, warn nations of the perils of drift, alert cultures of the consequences of decadence and reinforce the convictions of those who follow. In the closing sentence of his book *Suicide of the West*, Goldberg warns, "Decline is a choice. Principles, like gods, die when no one believes in them anymore."[9] This is what leaders do—they inspire belief. They shake us out of our complacency and influence direction. They cast the vision, catalyze efforts, bring about results, sustain the action, and shape the values.[10]

---

5. Quoted in David Gergen, *Eyewitness to Power: The Essence of Leadership; Nixon to Clinton* (Boston: GK Hall, 2001), 11–12.

6. Stanley McChrystal, *Leaders: Myth and Reality* (New York: Portfolio/Penguin, 2018), xiii.

7. Hamilton, *The Mantle of Command*, 275.

8. Ibid., 276.

9. Jonah Goldberg, *Suicide of the West: How the Rebirth of Tribalism, Populism, Nationalism, and Identity Politics Is Destroying American Democracy* (New York: Crown Forum, 2018), 351.

10. Each of these are developed in my book *Missing Voices: Learning to Lead beyond Our Horizons* (London: Langham, 2019), 49–54.

Events suggest we would be stuck in the idle position without leaders. It's part of the reason so many lionize, romanticize, and aggrandize their role. Leaders meet this interior need to have an authoritative father figure to whom a follower can submit. Someone who will get people off the dime. As Gardner put it, "There is an element of wanting to be rescued, of wanting a parental figure who will set all things right."[11]

It's why the presidency remains "the center of our democracy," according to Gergen. The leader will always be "the single person who can engage the dreams and mobilize the energies of the country behind large, sustained drives."[12] We can criticize all we want, but someone has to organize and guide the wagon train forward. Many look to leaders as the ones who draw the lines and impose some form of stability and order, especially in perilous times.

Leaders also keep chaos from taking over; they maintain the well-being of an organization. Patrick Lencioni's books are devoted to developing healthy leaders and strong organizations. After making the case that the healthiest organizations have the competitive advantage, he writes this about leadership: "There is just no escaping the fact that the single biggest factor determining whether an organization is going to get healthier—or not—is the genuine commitment and active involvement of the person in charge."[13] Kingpins are the linchpins who bring about integrity and wholeness, keeping things together.

Leaders enable followers to overcome. When people are full of fear and losing confidence, great leaders restore trust. They lift our spirits. After studying nine great leaders of history, Andrew Roberts concludes that they all had a profound sense of self-belief. They were able to create sureness by making soldiers and civilians believe that they were "part of a purpose that [mattered] more than even their continued existence on the planet, and that the leader's spirit [was] infused into them."[14]

---

11. John W. Gardner, *On Leadership* (New York: Free Press, 1993), xv.

12. Gergen, *Eyewitness to Power*, 12.

13. Patrick M. Lencioni, *The Advantage: Why Organizational Health Trumps Everything Else in Business* (San Francisco: Jossey-Bass, 2012), 190.

14. Andrew Roberts, *Leadership in War: Essential Lessons from Those Who Made History* (New York: Penguin, 2019), 220.

The foregoing are just a few of the reasons to buy into leadership necessity (and leadership books!), but some are not so ready to invest. Reading these arguments, they might ask, "Aren't we overstating things?" "Haven't we elevated the role of leadership to mythic proportions?" "Do we make leaders a relentless focus out of our need for security?" "Is history the story of great men or the story of our propensity to make idols?" "Aren't leaders our basic problem?" "Aren't they like chairs in a hospital room—generally in the way?"

The questions are worth examining. Harvard professor Barbara Kellerman refers to this Great Man theory as "the knottiest of all leadership questions."[15] Do leaders matter, or can we live without them? Maybe it is time to take off the rose-colored glasses. Could it be assumptions are being made that ignore reality? Are we minimizing the role of followers? Won't leaders be ultimately judged by them?[16] Occasionally a Socrates, a Napoleon, a Lincoln, a Churchill, or a Gandhi arises. There are some "great men" who form a template for other leaders. But most leaders are not that consequential. A fair number are incompetent and hazardous to our health. And some are downright evil.

A growing number of leadership experts argue that it is time to dispel fictions and restate what is actual.[17] Leaders do not shape history. Leaders like to imagine they influence the times, but it is history that shapes them. A leader might think he has his hand on the tiller of history, but he is, at best, a star on the horizon.[18] In *The Myth of the Strong Leader*, Archie Brown exposes the idea, diligently promoted by leaders and their propagandists, that each of them are singularly wise, gifted, farseeing, and shapers of events.[19] This is, he writes, an illusion.

Leaders play some role, but they do not manipulate history. History will go where history goes. As Freud notes, "Events are less the result of

---

15. Kellerman, *Leadership*, 56.

16. Garry Wills, *Certain Trumpets: The Nature of Leadership* (New York: Simon & Shuster, 1994), 21.

17. McChrystal, *Leaders*, 7.

18. Ibid., 376.

19. Archie Brown, *The Myth of the Strong Leader: Political Leadership in the Modern Age* (New York: Basic, 2014), 359.

great men, more the hidden, general, and impersonal factors—the forcible influence of economic circumstances, changes in food supply, progress in the use of materials and tools, migrations caused by increase in population and change of climate."[20] To quote from Tolstoy, "A king is history's slave."[21] Leaders merely serve a predetermined course, and they often do it badly.

There are moments when leaders have not held things together; instead they have broken them. Leaders are the linchpins? Make this case to those living in current day Haiti or Lebanon or Afghanistan—or those who survived Chernobyl. Behind this toxic tragedy of epic proportion was incompetent and godless leadership. In his harrowing book *Midnight in Chernobyl*, Adam Higginbotham tells how people rose through the ranks and got to the top. It was based not on their performance but on their willingness to suppress their opinions, avoid conflict, and display unquestioning obedience before bullying superiors. Lies and deception were endemic to the system, trafficked in both directions. Falsified reports were passed up the chain of command, and at the top were leaders who had no real idea what was going on. All of which led to the worst nuclear disaster in history. Thanks to leadership failure at multiple levels, it may be thousands of years before the city is once again inhabitable.[22]

Going further back, when one surveys some of the "great men" in history, one finds that many were not so great. They were "more enamored of their own *image* of leadership than of the followers *or* the goal."[23] Some were merchants of death who took advantage of the power and position followers had given them and ruthlessly led. The world has long suffered under these narcissistic types, who are fueled by adoring sycophants and forced followers. Hitler, Franco, Gaddafi, Hussein, Kim—the list is long.

20. Sigmund Freud, *Moses and Monotheism*, trans. Katherine Jones (New York: Vintage, 1967), 136–40.

21. Leo Tolstoy, *War and Peace*, trans. Richard Pevear and Larissa Volokhonsky (New York: Knoph, 2007), 645–48.

22. Adam Higginbotham, *Midnight in Chernobyl: The Untold Story of the World's Greatest Nuclear Disaster* (New York: Simon & Schuster, 2019), 13–14.

23. Wills, *Certain Trumpets*, 268.

They were strongmen whose patronage networks "bound people to them in relationships of complicity and fear."[24]

It's time to face up to the facts. While some are dangerous, a significant number of leaders are simply bungling incompetents. This is especially true in the political realm. Barton Swaim, after writing speeches for an inept and immoral governor, asked this question at the end of his term: "Why do we trust men who have sought and attained high office by innumerable acts of vanity and self-will?"[25] Why do we follow leaders, given that so many have more energy than sagacity?

Are leaders indispensable? Leaders like to think they are the center of the universe, and they make the kinds of speeches that suggest we can't live without them. But many of us can. Eastern philosopher Lao Tsu verbalized what an increasing number believe—that leadership is not so critical. In the end, history is altogether independent of a leader's actions. Better a leader who is seen rather than heard. In the best scenario followers and leaders are equals who work together seamlessly. From *Tao Te Ching*, the most widely translated book next to the Bible, Lao Tsu wrote, "If he would lead them, he must follow behind."[26] In this way followers will not be harmed.

The point here is that the best leaders do not impress people with their necessity. They lead with "hands so light to the touch that they seem less real than imagined."[27] A leader's transformative power comes not from personal feats but from nonaction.

Journalist Yasmeen Serhan, quoting from another ancient Chinese philosophy—"A leader is best when people barely know he exists"—asks, "What if a leader doesn't exist at all?"[28] What if leadership has become passé? Unnecessary? Maybe we would be better off without leaders, espe-

24. See review of Ruth Ben-Ghiat's *Strongmen: Mussolini to the Present* in Tunku Varadarajan, "Lord of Misrule," *Wall Street Journal*, December 12–13, 2020, https://www.wsj.com/articles/strongmen-review-nostalgia-virility-and-power-11607727158.

25. Barton Swaim, *The Speechwriter: A Brief Education in Politics* (New York: Simon & Schuster, 2015), 197.

26. Lao Tsu, *Tao Te Ching*, trans. Gia-Fu Feng and Jane English (New York: Vintage, 1998), 66.

27. Kellerman, *Leadership*, 8.

28. Yasmeen Serhan, "The Common Element Uniting Worldwide Protests," *Atlantic*, November 19, 2019, https://www.theatlantic.com/international/archive/2019/11/leaderless-protests-around-world/602194.

cially given the widespread leadership failures. People are beginning to question assumptions. In politics, legislators are asking why the executive branch of government should have so much power. And polls suggest that less and less constituents have confidence in these same representatives. If there is any certainty, it is this—today's audacious hope is tomorrow's material for SNL, and the next day's forgotten name.

In the corporate world, office space that was once designed to decree hierarchy is being converted to floor plans that break down the walls. A number quote from the likes of Ori Brafman and Rod Beckstrom, who have written a popular book challenging the notion of leadership layers.[29] The absence of structure, leadership, and formal organization, once considered a weakness, has become a major asset. Command and control have shifted to cooperate and collaborate. The mantra is, flatten or be flattened.

The same question is being asked in the sports world. "Why do we need captains?" It has prompted some teams to remove designations. They have openly soured on the idea of a leader. Writes Sam Walker, "Captains have become unfashionable—like pleated slacks, Rollerblades, and gluten."[30] Teammates ask, "Are they really necessary?"

In the religious realm, the Protestant Reformation began this leveling long ago. "Do we need the papacy?" In some congregations today, people are asking, "Do we need pastors?" "Do we need preaching?" There was a day when preachers came to the pulpit with a word from God. Pastors adhered to a traditional homiletic, one in which they followed in the tradition of Greco-Roman oration. They set forth their authoritative arguments, and parishioners dutifully took notes. Today, in a growing number of churches, there is a new homiletic, one in which preachers are no longer singular voices standing in the pulpit. They have moved out among the congregants to converse, facilitate discussion, and collaborate in the quest to find truth together.

---

29. Ori Brafman and Rod A. Beckstrom, *The Starfish and the Spider: The Unstoppable Power of Leaderless Organizations* (New York: Portfolio, 2006).

30. Sam Walker, *The Captain Class: A New Theory of Leadership* (New York: Random House, 2017), 265.

Sure, these all sound like a fever dream of an anarchist-Marxist collective at a bourgeois liberal arts college. That's how Brian Klaas puts it in his book *Corruptible*.[31] But could it be that if one gazes back far enough into history, the world was free of hierarchy. Klaas goes on to argue that the three-hundred-thousand-year history of our species was a nonhierarchical, flat society. Hierarchy only became the norm in more recent history.[32]

Maybe we can learn from the past and head toward it. Without the rigidity of a singular voice, be it a preacher, political leader, CEO, or captain, people seem to be finding a newfound liberty. Leaders are becoming less relevant to the day-to-day work. Educators who teach leadership are acknowledging this trend toward a post-leader age. Followers are on the rise and leaders are in decline.[33] At the same time, anarchist philosophers and libertarian thinkers are also on the increase, asking, "Why should we do another person's will? It's time to get on without leaders, for the underlying problem of culture is the very existence or concept of leadership itself."

We see this in the current leaderless protest movements that are occurring in various parts of the world. Have you noticed that an increasing number have no definable person leading the charge? Almost every night, the news in my city of Portland reports on the endless demonstrations. Hundreds gather to throw rocks, burn buildings, or barricade streets. People are tired of the perceived corruption, abuse, hypocrisy, racism, and incompetence of governing authorities. What is striking is the absence of a recognizable, charismatic individual who is leading the charge. In the spirit of our age, people are asking, "Who needs to have such a person?" Social media will do. People are networked and in regular communication with one another. Information power is diminishing leaders and leveling the playing field.[34]

---

31. Brian Klaas, *Corruptible: Who Gets Power and How It Changes Us* (New York: Scribner, 2021), 17.
32. Ibid., 23.
33. Note Kellerman's informative overview in her chapter "Historical Trajectory," in *The End of Leadership* (New York: Harper Business, 2012), 3–24.
34. Ibid., 46.

Even those who are leaders in their fields (a.k.a. the experts) are being challenged. There was a day when we looked to them to learn from, be influenced by, and follow their knowledge. But things have changed. We are convinced we have the same access to the same information. In *The Death of Expertise*, Tom Nichols sees the emergence of a flattened culture in which every person's opinion about everything must be accepted as equal to everyone else's. But this, as he notes, can be scary: "Never have so many people had so much access to so much knowledge and yet have been so resistant to learning anything."[35]

Where does all of this leave us? How should we frame leadership importance? These two positions are hotly contested and can leave us in a bit of a dilemma. Are leaders essential? Yes. Wait, no. Well, maybe.

By the sheer volume of books written about leadership, not to mention the billions invested in the leadership industry, leadership would appear for many to be essential. Yet there seems to be a growing pushback to the role of leaders. Some of the most disparaging remarks in the media are reserved for those at the top. And this has become a daily occurrence. Followers and leaders appear to have a love-hate relationship. We can't live with leaders, and we can't live without them. N. T. Wright observes, "Some of us heave a sigh of relief: *Someone's in charge! Chaos will be averted!* Others of us, meanwhile, groan: *This is tyranny! We don't want anybody reigning over us! We want to be free!*"[36] Part of it is that leaders are as capable of leading us to the abyss as to the sunlit uplands.[37]

Essential? Nonessential? Maybe the words mysterious and menacing are more appropriate. This is how Wills describes both leadership and followership.[38]

What we need is a centering voice, one that rises above pragmatics and puts the importance of leadership in perspective. This is where theology comes in.

---

35. Nichols, *The Death of Expertise*, 2.

36. N. T. Wright, *After You Believe: Why Christian Character Matters* (New York: HarperOne, 2010), 73, italics in the original.

37. Roberts, *Leadership in War*, xii.

38. Wills, *Certain Trumpets*, 21.

GOD'S VIEW ON THE NEED FOR LEADERS

How does God view all this noise? What does he say to a culture that works itself into a frenzy deciding the next leader? What are his words for those who prefer the absence of any authority, who would just as soon be free of any leadership?

LEADERS ARE NOT SO ESSENTIAL TO GOD

As much as leaders might be impressed with the thought that they are necessary, even critical to the Divine and his purposes, theology teaches that they are not. This might surprise and offend some. Prime Minister Winston Churchill of England was convinced of his necessity to the universe. On the eve of his seventy-fifth birthday, he was asked if he was ready to die. His hubristic response was permanently engraved on his burial stone: "I am ready to meet my Maker. Whether my Maker is prepared for the great ordeal of meeting me is another matter."

What most "great" leaders overlook is that God met them long before they met themselves. God's word to Jeremiah applies to everyone who wears the mantle of leadership: "Before I formed you in the womb I knew you, before you were born I set you apart" (1:5). God knew Churchill's words before he ever made an utterance in Malta or spoke to his nation. He ordained every day and determined every step of Churchill's life and wrote them in a book copyrighted in eternity past (Ps. 139:4, 16).

Nothing in Scripture suggests that any leader in any realm has—or could ever—impress God. No one is essential to God's purposes. There are no achievements that could ever amaze him. When we stand before God, any notions of self-importance turn to vapor. Ask Nebuchadnezzar, whose words, "By my mighty power and for the glory of my majesty" (Dan. 4:30) were met with a voice from heaven declaring, "Your royal authority has been taken from you" (4:31; cf. Acts 12:23).

God is self-sufficient. He is from himself, independent and unconditioned.

There is no incompleteness needing completeness. God would not be at a loss if leaders—or anyone—did not exist. God is not bound by any necessity except to be who he is. "Need," wrote Tozer, "is a creature-word and cannot be spoken of the Creator."[39] It's time to resist the familiar flow of our thoughts. God does not need air, food, shelter, or the latest technology. He does not need our money nor depend on our availability. He is not counting on us to protect his interests or defend his name. He is not the man upstairs who needs our help making his way up and down the steps. God is beyond the created order and beyond the Beyond.[40] He is not reliant on anyone to carry out his will, since all things have their beginning and ending in him.

Theologians call this aspect of God's being *aseity*. Like all God's attributes, this one exceeds the capabilities of our imagination and is difficult to explain. Here are some attempts.

- God is self-sufficient; his being and existence are not contingent on anything in the universe.[41]
- God is radically independent of all creaturely power and being.[42]
- God does not need us or the rest of creation for anything.[43]
- God depends on no cause external to God.[44]

The psalmist wrote words that redirect the attention: "Not to us" (Ps. 115:1). It's all to God, the one in heaven who does whatever he delights (v. 3). The world is God's, and everything in it (24:1; 50:10–12). He has no want. He suffers no privation. This was Paul's first "Theology Proper" lesson to the intellectuals at Athens: "The God who made the world . . . is not served by human hands, as if he needed anything. Rather, he himself

---

39. A. W. Tozer, *The Knowledge of the Holy* (New York: HarperCollins, 1961), 39.

40. Mark Galli, *Karl Barth: An Introductory Biography for Evangelicals* (Grand Rapids: Eerdmans, 2017), 46.

41. Michael F. Bird, *Evangelical Theology: A Biblical and Systematic Introduction* (Grand Rapids: Zondervan, 2013), 128.

42. Donald G. Bloesch, *God the Almighty: Power, Wisdom, Holiness, Love* (Downers Grove, IL: InterVarsity Press, 1995), 88.

43. Wayne Grudem, *Systematic Theology: An Introduction to Biblical Doctrine* (Grand Rapids: Zondervan, 2009), 160.

44. Thomas C. Oden, *Classic Christianity: A Systematic Theology* (New York: HarperOne, 2009), 40.

gives everyone life and breath and everything else" (Acts 17:24–25). The question by Eliphaz, "Can a man be of benefit to God?" (Job 22:2) assumes a negative answer. It is God who is of benefit to man.

God shapes the events. Sooner or later leaders come to realize they do not have their hands on the tiller of history. They do not turn the wheel (Pss. 33:14–20; 40:5; 44:1–6). Leithart makes the point with humble clarity: "We can no more bring the world under our complete control than we can guide the wind into a paddock for the night. We can no more give permanent form to the world than we can sculpt the evening breeze into solid shapes."[45] Nothing of our leadership is enduring. Our projects have the permanence of cloud castles on a windy day.[46] It is God who makes and establishes. It is God who wakes kings in the night to do his shaping (Est. 6:1).

Leaders like to see themselves as those who affect the affairs of life. But look at the record of the kings in the historical section of the Old Testament and the phrases "as the LORD had said" (1 Kings 14:18), "according to the word of the LORD" (15:29), and "in accordance with the word of the LORD" (2 Kings 9:26; 14:25). Each make this point: the leaders of Israel lived out a script not of their making. They rose and then receded into the background. God's word through his seers determined the rise and fall of dynasties and kingdoms.[47]

Still, some imagine that God is part of the cloud of witnesses watching their race (Heb. 12:1). But God is no spectator bound by events he cannot control. He's not a stagehand serving the stars onstage. To those who say, "By the strength of my hand I have done this, and by my wisdom" (Isa. 10:13), God responds, "Does the ax raise itself above the person who swings it, or the saw boast against the one who uses it?" (v. 15). To those who would quarrel and challenge their Maker, God asks, "Does the clay say to the potter, 'What are you making?'" (45:9).

A leader may think he has the power to bend the course of history, only to find that history rushes past him. One's reign is but a moment; one's

---

45. Peter J. Leithart, *Solomon among the Postmoderns* (Grand Rapids: Brazos, 2008), 68.
46. Ibid.
47. Peter J. Leithart, *1 & 2 Kings* (Grand Rapids: Brazos, 2006), 18.

accomplishments are soon in ruins. We have a hard time absorbing this. The prophet asks, "Do you not know? Have you not heard? . . . He [God] brings princes to naught and reduces the rulers of this world to nothing [*tohu*, "void," "waste," "nothingness"]. No sooner are they planted, no sooner are they sown, no sooner do they take root in the ground, than he blows on them and they wither, and a whirlwind sweeps them away like chaff" (40:21, 23–24).

Mortality is the great leveler. No matter rich or poor, human or animal, powerful or weak (Eccl. 3:19–21). Great leaders who were great deciders and great builders eventually sleep the sleep of death. "The lowborn are but a breath, the highborn are but a lie" (Ps. 62:9). The ordinary come and go; those who think, talk, and act as if they will always be in power are deluded. Together their weight is not even a vapor. That we shed a million flakes of skin every hour is a reminder that "silently and remorselessly we turn to dust."[48]

To this knottiest of all leadership questions—Does the leader make history, or does history make the leader?—theology gives an unambiguous reply: A leader does not make history, nor does history make a leader. Both are made by God.

Again and again we find that God alone is indispensable. The opening words of Genesis declare who is necessary. Before the acts of creation, God "hovered" over the darkness, suggesting his power over the formless void. He alone set everything in motion (1:1). He took nothing and made it something, turned formlessness into form, and changed emptiness into fullness. He set the proper cadence of command, execution, and assessment. He commanded ("And God said" [v. 3]), he executed ("and there was light" [v. 3]), and he assessed ("God saw all that he had made, and it was very good" [v. 31]). And not only that but it is God—not leaders—who holds things together (Col. 1:17).

In the memorial services I have conducted as a pastor, I often come back to the centering words of Psalm 39. It was written by a world leader, one who in a circumstance of life was exposed to "the fatal insufficiency

---

48. Bill Bryson, *The Body: A Guide for Occupants* (Prescott, AZ: Anchor, 2019), 11.

of all that is earthbound."[49] This is a reality of life. Death has a way of confronting our sense of indispensability, as does this psalm. Here we are reminded that the span of our years is as handbreadths, as nothing before God (v. 5). Leaders might wonder how the world will make it without them, but from the standpoint of the psalmist, we are but a "mere phantom" (v. 6), a shadow whose presence is fleeting. We heap up our achievements and leave behind our earnings for God knows who. And these will soon disappear, as quickly as the memory of our existence. Parishioners can only pause, assess, and in some cases redirect.

God's purposes will be accomplished. God "works out everything in conformity with the purpose of his will" (Eph. 1:11). He ordains and uses whomever and whatever he decrees for his purposes, ones that "stand firm forever" (Ps. 33:11). To the mightiest superpower and super leader of the day, God declared, "Surely, as I have planned, so it will be. . . . The LORD Almighty has purposed, and who can thwart him?" (Isa. 14:24, 27).

Any of us who lead, who even for a moment have considered the thought that God relies on us to accomplish his mission, may find ourselves in the same storm as Job. It was there that God ordered Job to brace himself for God's withering questions. In this moment God brought Job's demanding spirit and assumption that God owed him anything back to earth (Job 38:1–41:34). It is God who leads, and what he wills he achieves. He alone fixes the limits for the seas (38:10), gives orders to the morning (v. 12), knows the way to the abode of light (v. 19), and speaks with a voice that thunders (40:9).

Everywhere one looks in Scripture, God underscores the point. To leaders who assume their essentiality, God makes it certain that his rule is above theirs (Dan. 2:21). He alone is the Most High (Ps. 83:18). He is the king who rules the world, the warrior who destroys the armies, and the judge who administers justice. He is the ruling Lord; everything else derives from him, leans upon him, and is understood with reference to

---

49. Derek Kidner, *Psalms 1–72* (Downers Grove, IL: InterVarsity Press, 1973), 156.

him.[50] He directs the course of man (Prov. 21:1). He determines mankind's outcomes (v. 31). Even the world's most powerful, most pagan rulers serve God's rulership (Isa. 44:28; 45:13; Jer. 27:6–7). Kings put into action what God puts in their hearts (Ezra 1:1; 7:27).

When leaders assume they are the center, God reminds them they are the circumference (John 19:11). When they become impressed with their towering heights, God brings them back to earth like lofty trees reduced to stumps (Ezek. 31:10–11; 32:1–16). When they seek to reject the authority of God, he laughs (Ps. 2:2–5). When they go their own way, God brings about circumstances to remind them, "I am the LORD" (Ezek. 29:6; 32:15). In God alone is a leader's trust (Prov. 3:5–6). When leaders trust in their own rule, their endeavors will end up a barren waste (Jer. 17:5–6).

Whew! This is a lot of theology to make a simple point: leaders are unnecessary to God. Still, we need every one of these words, for we often become obsessed with who is leading. We polarize and end relationships over who we think should lead. At the same time, leaders forget and get out of their lanes. A sense of self-importance is deeply embedded in all of us. The deeper our venture into Scripture, however, the more "radically decentered" we become. At the core of our being we find not ourselves. We find another, and that other is God.[51] Any assumptions of our necessity are stripped away.

LEADERS PLAY A SIGNIFICANT ROLE

It would be a misjudgment, however, to conclude that leaders are irrelevant, and that humanity can live without them. Having established God's aseity, Scripture underscores, both in statements and stories, that leaders are an integral part of God's design and purpose.

God has chosen to create for his purposes leaders who serve under his

---

50. Ludwig Kohler, *Old Testament Theology* (Philadelphia: Westminster, 1957), 30. Note Gary Smith's article "The Concept of God/the Gods as King in the Ancient Near East and the Bible," *Trinity Journal* 3 n.s. (1982): 18–38.

51. Leithart, *Solomon among the Postmoderns*, 131.

authority. Though self-sufficient, God governs by gracious self-giving.[52] We are God's vice-regents, representing the Sovereign. To us has been given the authorization to subdue, oversee, and take care of his creation (Gen. 1:28; 2:15). Taken together, the verbs suggest not exploitative use of the earth but a gentle yet firm care and enhancement of the earth and its creatures.[53]

God could have designed things differently. He could have kept leadership all for himself. The potter could have molded clay vessels to be passive bystanders, mere chattels having no authority, no power to assert themselves, and no concept of what it means to lead. We could have been made to be mindless followers, like livestock moving from one pasture to another.

Instead God has chosen to share leadership. These words in *After You Believe* make the point: "Precisely because God is the God of generous, creative, overflowing love, his way of running things is to share power, to work through his image bearer, to invite their glad and free collaboration in his project."[54] From the beginning, God gave the earth to man (Ps. 115:16), a statement that we are stewards entrusted with responsibilities. God designed creation to flourish when guided by capable leadership.

Because of this, God has gifted certain ones to lead (Rom. 12:6–8). Trace their stories in Scripture, and one finds that leaders are markers in the turning points of the narrative. At each turn God raises leaders—Abraham, Joseph, Moses, Deborah, David, Solomon, the prophets. This is how Stephen and Paul framed their stories (Acts 7:2–50; 13:16–41). When Jesus left this earth, he delegated leadership to those he called to lead (John 21:15–17; 20:21). Entering heaven to take his throne, he did not downgrade us and reduce us to pawns or ciphers.[55]

---

52. Walter Brueggemann, *Genesis: Interpretation; A Bible Commentary for Teachings and Preaching* (Louisville: Westminster John Knox, 1986), 33.

53. Walter Brueggemann, *Theology of the Old Testament: Testimony, Dispute, Advocacy* (Minneapolis: Fortress, 2005), 460.

54. Wright, *After You Believe*, 76.

55. N. T. Wright, *Simply Jesus: A New Vision of Who He Was, What He Did, and Why He Matters* (New York: HarperOne, 2011), 213.

That God has delegated his rule should astound us. Job was overwhelmed that God would make so much of man and give him so much attention (Job 7:17). The psalmist found it amazing that God is ever mindful of who he has created. It's beyond comprehension that God has placed men and women to be rulers over all his works (Ps. 8:4–6).

In the hands of God, leaders play a critical role in *setting the direction*. Leaders who "show the way forward" is an unmistakable theme in Scripture. Without a leader, people are usually harassed and helpless, scattered "like sheep without a shepherd" (Matt. 9:36). When Saul was slain, the nation was confused and hopeless (1 Sam. 31:7). People abandoned what ground they had taken. Leaders are summoned by God to point the way. They infuse a sense of purpose and meaning into people's lives. As other leadership theorists have noted, effectual leadership takes followers, with their advice and consent, to a new and better place.[56] Leaders like Moses and Joshua illustrate this. Conversely, when Israel did not heed them, life was a series of dead ends (Deut. 1:42–46).

Leaders are also used by God to *bring order out of chaos*. From the beginning humanity was placed in the garden to be a creative and stabilizing force (Gen. 1:28). Ever since humanity's fall, the advent of sin, and the disruption of order, leaders have been summoned to put things back together. Fallen humanity tends to rebel against order, which manifests itself in awful ways, including racism, defaced beauty, deception, and corruption. Leaders serve as shields against such disorder. The godly ones call out idolatry and turn people back to true worship (Ex. 32:19–20).

Bringing about order and harmony is the reason God raises up leaders in the church. God has given gifted leaders to *prepare God's people* (Eph. 4:12). Behind the word *katartizō* is the task of mending, repairing, restoring back to a fit and ordered state (Gal. 6:1).[57] In a repaired condition,

---

56. Kellerman, in *Leadership*, references Mary Parker Follett and James MacGregor Burns to describe what they see as leadership at its best (p. 104).

57. Reinier Schippers, "right, worthy," in *The New International Dictionary of New Testament Theology* (Grand Rapids: Zondervan, 1978), 3:350.

congregants are equipped to do the work of ministry and arrive at God's intended outcomes (Eph. 4:13).

Consider the evidence of history. Where chaos reigns, there is usually an absence of leadership. Leaders *sound the warning* and make clear the consequences of sin (Ezek. 3:17–21). Sometimes they serve as intermediaries to protect people from themselves. In other moments they beg for God to forgive people's failures (Ps. 106:23). Moses often found it necessary to make such intercession (Num. 11:2; 14:19). It is one of the basic functions of spiritual leadership.[58]

Because leaders are God's instruments to bring law and order, they sometimes serve as God's "agents of wrath" (Rom. 13:4) to bring punishment on those who cross the line (Prov. 20:8, 26). When leaders uphold God's justice and exercise their gifts, the land enjoys a certain stability (29:4). This is why a king's mother pleads that her son stay sober and keep his wits so that he might judge rightly (31:1–9). It's why we are admonished to submit to and honor those who lead (1 Tim. 2:1–2; 1 Peter 2:13–14). Leaders are called to protect the rights and well-being of those they lead, giving voice to the needs of the downtrodden and distributing wealth and resources fairly. They are summoned to steady an unsteadied age, and when they do, the Lord is moved to bring rest (2 Chron. 15:15).

Without the strong presence of the right leader to tend the garden, it's natural for the wilderness to take over. Once Moses withdrew his presence, Israel descended into revelry and unrestraint (Ex. 32:1). In the time of the judges—in which warlords fought for turf—confusion, division, idolatry, and dysfunction took hold. Kept in front of the reader are the words, "In those days Israel had no king; everyone did as they saw fit" (Judg. 17:6; 21:25).

Here is the warning for us: when God chooses to judge a land, one of the severest sentences is the removal of leadership. This was the warning of Isaiah: "The Lord . . . is about to take [away] . . . the hero and the warrior, the judge and the prophet, the diviner and the elder, the captain of fifty and the

---

58. Ruth Haley Barton, *Strengthening the Soul of Your Leadership: Seeking God in the Crucible of Ministry* (Downers Grove, IL: InterVarsity Press, 2008), 143.

man of rank. . . . [The LORD says,] 'I will make mere youths their officials.' . . . People will oppress each other. . . . Jerusalem [will stagger]" (Isa. 3:1–5, 8). When times are leaderless, bedlam reigns and people will become desperate for anyone with any semblance of authority. Isaiah forewarned Israel of this: "A man will seize one of his brothers in his father's house, and say, 'You have a cloak, you be our leader; take charge of this heap of ruins!'" (v. 6).

There's more. Leaders give direction, bring order, prepare people, sound the warning, as well as *lead the fight*. Every day is a battle. We face conflict on multiple fronts, be they physical or emotional or spiritual. Entrenched forces of evil plot and strategize. Confrontation saddles many of our moments. One commentary sums it up this way: "The Bible teaches an enmity that goes to the bone."[59] It is part of the metanarrative. Eliminate enemies from the biblical story, and you eliminate most of the biblical story.[60] The battle that began in Genesis will not end until death and Hades are thrown into the lake of fire (Rev. 20:14).

Someone has to rise and protect and lead followers to war against instigators of turmoil and destruction, against those who make life wretched and impossible.[61] Many of the Old Testament leaders were called to the task of deliverance. Moses stood at the place of battle and, lifting his arms in intercession, determined the outcome. Leaders are anointed to deliver (1 Sam. 9:16). Someone must stand in the gap (Ezek. 22:30). It's the same in the New Testament. Those who lead the church are summoned to be overseers fighting the good fight (1 Tim. 6:12). They serve as prophetic voices who sound the alarm (Acts 2:17).

Finally, God uses leaders to fill the space and *bring presence*. An integral purpose of leadership is to be with those that one leads. It comes back to servanthood. There are occasions when followers need, more than anything else, a leader's "withness," a presence that goes beyond emails and Instagram and text messages. This is what authenticates leadership.

When God summoned leaders in Scripture, his promised presence

---

59. Leithart, *1 & 2 Kings*, 151.
60. Ibid., 146.
61. Brueggemann, *Theology of the Old Testament*, 272.

changed everything. Sending Moses to Pharaoh, God declared, "I will be with you" (Ex. 3:12). Prior to leading Israel into the land, God said to Joshua, "As I was with Moses, so I will be with you" (Josh. 1:5). Similar words were imparted to Gideon, Saul, David, Solomon, Asa, and Jeremiah. These stories serve not only as an assurance of power but a model for leadership.

The incarnation of Jesus is God's definitive example. He came to be with us, for we are relational, physical beings. When Jesus left this earth, his departing promise to the disciples was, "Surely I am with you always, to the very end of the age" (Matt. 28:20). Richard Bauckham's book *Who Is God?* captures the significance: "To discover that God is 'with' us is probably the most important discovery anyone can make, for, once made, it colors all of life's experiences."[62] We realize we are not going it alone.

In the same way, when leaders are present, they provide the needed confidence. Those who choose to lead from a distance lose credibility, as well as create insecurity for those who follow. Sadly, more and more leaders aspire to build large operations, as if to distance themselves from their essential task to be present to those they lead. And this is often when leaders, particularly pastors, get in trouble. Failure of presence and sin often go together.

Ruth Graham made this point in a *New York Times* article following the recent moral failure of a celebrated pastor. Listen carefully to her observation of what led to his unfortunate choices: "No pastor of a big church can have personal relationships with every parishioner. But Mr. Lentz was unusually remote, according to current and former congregants. He seemed to disappear for months at a time, appearing onstage at church only intermittently."[63]

Like so many megachurch pastors, this religious leader rarely mixed with churchgoers. There was no witness in his leading. This likely went back to his failure to be with God. Leaders like him ignore Scripture's clear word that God's desire is to be with us, just as we are to be with one another.

---

62. Richard Bauckham, *Who Is God? Key Moments of Biblical Revelation* (Grand Rapids: Baker, 2020), 10.

63. Ruth Graham, "The Rise and Fall of Carl Lentz, the Celebrity Pastor of Hillsong Church," *New York Times*, December 5, 2020, https://www.nytimes.com/2020/12/05/us/carl-lentz-hillsong -pastor.html.

One cannot use the excuse of a preference for privacy, an introverted personality, or a killer schedule to justify separation and absence. Separation diminishes leadership and misses the purpose for which one is called.

CONCLUSION

This chapter began by outlining reasons commonly given for and against leadership. Both sides have fair points to consider. Leaders do make a difference, though our tendency has been to elevate their influence to mythic proportions. Leaders can be consequential or inconsequential, a cause for celebration as well as grief.

In our age, the voices on both sides have grown more virulent. We see dominant leaders who are bent on asserting their importance, while followers choose to follow no matter what. We are also seeing a growing resistance. Many are fed up with leadership failure, be it moral or a matter of incompetence. Not enough attention has been given to the important part followers play. Too often leaders have relegated those they lead to a passive role—simply instruments for their endeavors.

Theology, I believe, brings needed perspective. God's words put us in our needed place, shattering the pride of those steeped in the illusion of self-belief and self-confidence. As much as we would like to think God needs us, he does not need anyone or anything.

At the same time, Scripture underscores that leaders are an essential part of God's design. Thinking back on my life, it was a leader who:

- persuaded me of the truth of the gospel
- planted a seed that grew my life in a new direction
- taught me to take a stand for my convictions
- showed me the power of vision

Leaders do matter. They give direction, bring order, and provide presence. This is the message from Genesis 1 to Revelation 22. When leaders are faithful to God's will for their lives, people as a whole rejoice and give thanks. Such leaders lift us out of our petty preoccupations, carry us above the conflicts that tear a society apart, and unite us in the pursuit of objectives worthy of our best efforts.[64]

Defining leadership and making a case for the importance of leaders are logical starting points. But how does one become a leader? This too needs a theological answer, which brings us to the next chapter. But first a brief story addressing leadership's necessity.

☙ DAVID ❧

If anyone demonstrated leadership's importance, it was David. Anointed by God to lead Israel through a turbulent time, David was a warrior who took on Goliath, conquered the Philistines, brought Jerusalem under capable rule, and recovered the ark. What would God do without David?

David went on to establish his reign and build his mansion, but as he looked out from his palatial setting, he saw a disturbing sight. He could not get it out of his mind. Outside there was a homeless person living in a temporary shelter, and his name was Yahweh. The incongruity ruined David (2 Sam. 7:1–2). Something had to be done.

The heavens waited breathlessly for someone to act. Wasn't it David who recovered the ark of the covenant from Kiriath Jearim, where it had been marooned for twenty years (1 Sam 7:2)? David knew it was up to him. He had made the vow, "I will not enter my house or go to my bed, I will allow no sleep to my eyes or slumber to my eyelids, till I find a place for the Lord, a dwelling for the Mighty One of Jacob" (Ps. 132:3–5).

Everything pointed to the fact that David was God's man for God's hour.[65] David knew it, the people knew it, and more importantly, David's pastor knew it. Nathan could see that David's mission was vital to the security of

---

64. James MacGregor Burns, *Leadership* (New York: Open Road Media, 2012), 452.
65. Eugene H. Peterson, *Leap Over a Wall: Earthy Spirituality for Everyday Christians* (New York: HarperCollins, 1997), 155–68.

God's presence in Israel. Building a temple would provide a needed haven. (Perhaps it would help to localize and tame some of God's wilderness wildness.) But before David could build any walls, he hit a wall. It seemed everyone was consulted but God. God would need to step in and bring needed clarity. And God did.

For all of us, there are moments when God must push the pause button and make it clear that those he summons are not necessary to him. In David's case it began with the question, "Are you the one to build?" (2 Sam. 7:5). Men of war lead God's armies, but building temples belongs to others. It's easy to assume we know God's will. We speak for God. We know his mind. He needs us to fulfill multiple roles!

Like so many of us, David got it wrong. But God was not finished with his conversation. Sitting David down, he asked, "Did I ever request a temple?" It might have struck David in this moment that God never requested a permanent residence. The curtained, canopied tabernacle was God's design in the first place (v. 7). One can hear God asking, "Are you trying to domesticate me? Buy me off as your patron god? Have you not considered that even heaven, the highest heaven, cannot contain me, much less a temple?"

We can get caught up with our plans, our purposes, having become so impressed with our importance. If we are not careful, we can assume we are necessary to getting things done. In the case of David, God had to deal with David's sense of self-importance, reminding him that leaders are not so essential. Only God is. If we have any role, it is because of God (v. 8). If there have been any triumphs, they came because of him (v. 9). Any sense of security? It is because of him (v. 10). Any space, any rest we have experienced, it is all because of him (v. 11).

In one brief moment God turned everything on its head. He reversed the subject of the verbs, using the first-person pronoun twenty-three times (vv. 8–16). It is God, not David, who will build a house (v. 11). Like every leader—every leader—it is David who needs God. We may win the battle in the field, but one of our greatest threats will always be the creeping sense of self-importance ever whispering, "You are indispensable to God and others."

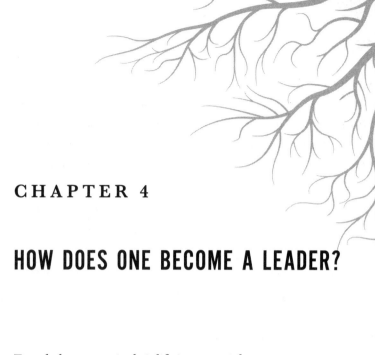

CHAPTER 4

HOW DOES ONE BECOME A LEADER?

To each there comes in their lifetime a special moment
when they are figuratively tapped on the shoulder and
offered the chance to do a very special thing, unique to
them and fitted to their talents.

—Winston Churchill

Do you ever ask yourself, "How did that person become a leader? Did he have the right connections? What was involved? Is it because she had what it takes?" We might ask these of ourselves: "How can I become a leader? How did I come to leadership? Was it a matter of fate or having the right gifts or earning the appropriate credential or being in the right family?" Secular theory has developed several common assumptions about how leaders are made.

Some believe that leadership begins with an ambitious spirit. William "Boss" Tweed seemed destined to lead. After all, he lusted to lead. He chased after power from an early age, rising from alderman to county commissioner to state senator. Eventually, Tweed was the political boss of New York. By the second half of the 1800s, he had grown to symbolize New York City politics.

If you were to ask people how he rose to become grand sachem of Tammany Hall and party leader, they might point to his toughness, his ability to organize, and his mastery of the system. He was the guru of backroom deals. He knew how to leverage authority, manipulate people, and milk the system. In the process he enriched himself and his cronies.[1]

I've met people like this. They tell you that if you want to rise to power and lead others, you have to have this kind of determination and drive. You must strive for influence, pursue power and wealth, establish the right networks, and hobnob with the prominent. You have to take things into your own hands and maneuver through the complexities with those same hands on the levers. Leading is all about positioning yourself to be in the right place at the right time.

Churchill did this. Early on he plotted out how he would become a leader. He was determined to get to the top. He believed it was his destiny, and he had the ambition to match. In a speech to the House of Commons, he admitted, "I am certainly not one of those who need to be prodded. In fact, if anything, I am a prod."[2] He was willing to pay the price. If it meant becoming a hero, he would leave his comforts, travel for weeks by ship, and engage in the Boer War. He rode his horse so as to show himself brave and be noticed by the troops. He confided to his younger brother, "There is no ambition I cherish so keenly as to gain a reputation for personal courage."[3] He was certain it was by his exploits that he would get to the top.

Others would say that while ambition has its place, there is no substitute for the gift of leading. One must show some talent, some genetic evidence for leading. Some researchers claim to have discovered a "leadership gene," a bit of genetic code identified as rs4950, underscoring that some are born to lead.[4] Hence, their leadership comes naturally, even effortlessly. All the drive and determination in the world cannot substitute for this. As

---

1. Stanley McChrystal, *Leaders: Myth and Reality* (New York: Portfolio/Penguin, 2018), 248–65.

2. Candace Millard, *Hero of the Empire: The Boer War, a Daring Rescue, and the Making of Winston Churchill* (New York: Anchor, 2016), 12.

3. Ibid., 7.

4. Klaas, *Corruptible*, 46.

with a capable musician or a proficient athlete, the inbred ability is either there or it is not.

What explains the impact of Steve Jobs and Michael Jordan, these "hypermagnetic global icons"? There was this innate, competitive drive that enabled them to push their organizations to unprecedented success. It was in their nature to "scare the hell out of people." That's how Sam Walker described them in an article for the *Wall Street Journal*.[5] As with other impressive movers and shakers, leadership was part of their DNA. Jordan had intuitive vision, exhibiting outstanding leadership traits. Jobs could see products and applications of which no one dared—or were able—to dream. He had the charisma that convinced others he could do almost anything. As a result, he revolutionized six industries.

David Gergen, after surveying numerous world leaders, came to a similar assessment: "It certainly appears that many of the best of the past century—Churchill, the Roosevelts, Gandhi, Mandela, Golda Meir, Martin Luther King Jr.—had leadership in their bones."[6] They had a natural ability to foresee a crisis and inspire people to action.

This follows a trait theory of leadership. There are certain innate qualities that define leaders. These traits include intelligence, confidence, charisma, determination, sociability, and integrity.[7] If one is not conscious of one's leadership gift, circumstances will eventually draw out one's awareness. Some gifts emerge out of emergencies and in some cases are generally so powerful and revolutionary that they pose a challenge to the existing order.[8]

In his early days, few saw Harry Truman as a leader. Most dismissed this future American president as weak and ineffectual, a kid with no athletic or leadership skills. But this homebody was sent to fight in WWI, and

5. Sam Walker, "Michael Jordan Didn't Manage People, He Lit Them on Fire," *Wall Street Journal*, May 16, 2020, https://www.wsj.com/articles/michael-jordan-didnt-manage-people-he-lit-them-on-fire-11589601602.

6. David Gergen, *Eyewitness to Power: The Essence of Leadership; Nixon to Clinton* (Boston: GK Hall, 2001), 13.

7. Peter G. Northouse, *Introduction to Leadership: Concepts and Practice* (Thousand Oaks: SAGE, 2015), 21–29.

8. Max Weber, *The Theory of Social and Economic Organization*, ed. Talcott Parsons (New York: Free Press, 1947), 328–29; 358–63.

the war became his crucible. His natural ability to lead—there from the beginning—emerged, and he returned from Europe a different man.[9] Yet the same man. With the mantle of leadership passed to Truman, no one could have predicted that the first four months would be the most challenging of any American presidency. Never had fate "shoehorned so much history" and shaped the world, writes Baime.[10] It would require someone like Truman, someone who had leadership built into him.

Not everyone agrees that gifting is essential to guiding others. Most books on leadership argue that leading comes by learning. Some, like Peter Drucker, acknowledge that there may be "born leaders," but there surely are too few of them to depend on.[11] The gap must be filled by leaders who, though not gifted, are trained.

Leadership, according to this position, is not some elite club for those with the right genes. The idea that leaders are born is, in the words of Gardner, "sheer nonsense."[12] "The most pernicious myth about leadership" is how Kouzes and Posner describe the misguided notion that leadership belongs to those who are innately endowed.[13] Leadership can happen anywhere and at any time. Warren Bennis, in his influential book *On Becoming a Leader*, says that leaders are "made, not born, and made more by themselves than by any external means."[14] Want to be a leader? Invent yourself!

This opinion is consistent with some of the earliest writers on leadership. Ancient sages, like Confucius, considered education to be the critical factor for those who would wish to command.[15] The skills necessary

---

9. Warren G. Bennis and Robert J. Thomas, *Geeks and Geezers: How Era, Values, and Defining Moments Shape Leaders* (Boston: Harvard Business Review Press, 2002), xxiii-xxiv.

10. A. J. Baime, *The Accidental President: Harry S. Truman and the Four Months That Changed the World* (New York: Mariner, 2017), loc. 89 of 8945, Kindle.

11. Peter Drucker, "Not Enough Generals Were Killed," in *The Leader of the Future*, ed. Francis Hesselbein, Marshall Goldsmith, and Richard Beckard (San Francisco: Jossey-Bass, 1996), xi.

12. John W. Gardner, *On Leadership* (New York: Free Press, 1993), xix.

13. James M. Kouzes and Barry Z. Posner, *The Leadership Challenge* (San Francisco: Jossey-Bass, 2007), 15.

14. Bennis, *On Becoming a Leader*, 5.

15. See Barbara Kellerman, *Leadership: Essential Selections on Power, Authority, and Influence* (New York: McGraw-Hill, 2010), 15.

for leading come as one develops leadership intelligence. Studying the principles of leadership includes learning how to lead teams and direct organizations to be missional, visionary, strategic, and tactical. By mastering such concepts, one is enabled to motivate people to take action, handle conflict, and recognize when to transition.

Leadership educators like Barbara Kellerman of Harvard believe we can learn leadership from adolescence all the way into adulthood.[16] It requires time and attention, searching for substantive books written by respected voices. One can talk about methods, but one must read the great leadership literature, acquiring a fixed body of knowledge.[17] As one studies the research of leadership theorists, one must then put it to the test.

Choosing leadership books will require a fair amount of sifting. There's a lot of chaff on the bookshelves. Look at the contents, read the reviews, but do this with a critical eye. Study leadership in its multiple contexts. These include military (Mattis's *Call Sign Chaos* and McChrystal's *Leaders*), political (Burns's *Leadership*, Gardner's *On Leadership*, and Gergen's *Eyewitness to Power*), and corporate (DePree's *Leadership Jazz* and Lencioni's *The Advantage*). One should also read great biographies of leaders—Roosevelt (*The Mantle of Command*), Churchill (*Hero of the Empire*), Bonhoeffer (*Bonhoeffer: Pastor, Martyr, Prophet, Spy*).

Not all learning is found in books. Leadership comes from observing others in action. This, writes Michael Useem, is one of the most effective ways of learning to become a leader. Analyze what others have done when their own leadership is on the line.[18] Learning also comes from on-the-job training. We can read and study and attend seminars, but much of leading is developed in the task itself. Conducting meetings, setting a vision, working with a team, confronting criticism, standing alone, building relationships, holding people accountable. Nothing prepares like the actual doing, in which we will succeed and fail—and become a leader in the process.

---

16. Ibid., xix.
17. Ibid., xiii.
18. Michael Useem, *The Leadership Moment* (New York: Three Rivers, 1998), 3.

Taken as a whole, the argument of these writers is that leadership is less intrinsic to a person's composition and more about learned behavior. Nurture is more important than nature. This means that the skill to lead is accessible to anyone who wants to be a leader. It will, however, require discipline, as well as discernment. Leadership cannot be acquired in a weekend; it is not a set of correspondence courses over two days or two semesters. There is no microwave theory of leadership. Instead, to become a leader, one must devote one's life to learning theory and practice, acquiring and critically reading the best resources available.

In this matter of how one becomes a leader, others would point out that a number of leaders are the product of their birthright. It has little to do with drive and everything to with descent, nothing to do with blood and everything to do with bloodlines, less to do with learning and everything to do with lineage. A father passes the mantle of command to a son. A king bestows the crown to a queen. The directorship of a corporation is handed off to a family member.

We see this on the world stage, though it is becoming less common. There are only some forty or more hereditary monarchs still in existence. Kim Jong-il of Korea passes on to Kim Jong-un what was passed on to him—the right to be head of state. Elizabeth II receives the crown and will pass it on one day. Such leaders have a sense of historic destiny, of something passed on to them from past centuries. Napoleon, founder of modern France, was convinced his leadership was an inheritance passed on from Julius Caesar and Alexander the Great.[19] It explains why many of his leadership techniques were replicas of theirs.

Leadership by heritage explains why most leaders are male. Much of the history of leadership has been the story of men passing leadership on to their sons. This, according to McChrystal, helps to explain why so much of the Great Man theory of leadership is "patently patriarchal."[20]

---

19. Andrew Roberts, *Leadership in War: Essential Lessons from Those Who Made History* (New York: Penguin, 2019), 1.

20. McChrystal, *Leaders*, 374–75.

Finally, some would say leadership acquisition is less about any of the foregoing and more a matter of chance. Destiny determines life. Test pilot Chuck Yeager, when asked to explain his extraordinary achievements and level of influence, replied, "I was just a lucky kid who caught the right ride." Such people believe that there are external, inexorable forces at work, an inevitable set of circumstances that result in leadership. John F. Kennedy, in explaining his heroic status, which propelled him to the presidency, stated, "They sank my boat." The reality, and the myth of PT-109, changed everything for him.

Situations arise, and those who rise to the occasion usually end up as the leaders.[21] David Brooks makes a similar point, noting that we don't create our lives. Rather we are "thrown by fate, by history, by chance, by evolution, or by God into a specific place with specific problems and needs."[22] What is necessary is to keep one's eyes wide open. As Mattis puts it, "To each there comes in their lifetime a special moment when they are figuratively tapped on the shoulder and offered the choice to do a very special thing, unique to them and fitted to their talents."[23]

As you pause to reflect on the foregoing views to leadership acquisition, what is your story? Do you trace your rise to leadership to ambition? For as long as you can remember, has there been a fire in your belly, a directed focus, a determination to move people forward? Has this ability to lead been there all along, a defined part of your being that comes without much effort? Maybe you have never been quite sure if leadership defines you, but you have devoted a fair amount of time to studying the subject. Unnatural as it sometimes feels, you can capably lead. Or perhaps leadership was passed on to you whether you wanted it or not. Maybe it is unhappily yours. Perhaps it is simply your destiny.

Regardless of our perceptions of how leadership comes about, God's Word gives us the greatest clarity. What do his words reveal?

---

21. Leonard Sweet, *Summoned to Lead* (Grand Rapids: Zondervan, 2004), 12.

22. David Brooks, *The Road to Character* (New York: Penguin, 2015), 21.

23. James Mattis, *Call Sign Chaos: Learning to Lead* (New York: Random House, 2019), 54.

GOD'S DESCRIPTION OF LEADERSHIP ACQUISITION

On the subject of becoming a leader, leadership books and the biblical texts appear to overlap. We look at a number of the biblical accounts, and we see some of the same categories. But look closer. What God has to say transcends our assumptions. Beyond our personal desires, someone, something else, is at work. We are not alone in this. What appears to be a biological trait goes beyond one's DNA. Something of the Spirit has been actively involved. Learning leadership goes beyond hardbacks and life circumstances to God-ordained movement and divine lessons. Fate may seem to be in play, but it receives no press in Scripture. There is no such thing as chance, destiny, or luck in God's kingdom.

To all of this debate, theology declares that God determines the course.

Ambition? In a number of biblical stories, people chased after leadership—or at least accused others of doing so. Resentful followers challenged Moses, asking, "Why then do you set [yourself] above the Lord's assembly?" (Num. 16:3). They accused him of wanting to "lord it over" them (v. 13). As far as they were concerned, his quest to lead was the result of an ambitious streak, one likely influenced by his upbringing in Pharaoh's court.

During the Old Testament monarchy, a number of go-getter types (Jeroboam, Baasha, Jezebel, Athaliah) maneuvered to get their names on the door. Adonijah, who the writer points out was never corrected by his father, "put himself forward" in hopes of succeeding David (1 Kings 1:5–6). He did what the ambitious do—get endorsements, secure alliances, receive divine blessing, host dinners for the influential, kiss babies, and make cabinet promises (vv. 7–9). Adonijah had everything going for him but access.

For various pagan kings, the pinnacle of leadership was to become as gods. Rulers like Nebuchadnezzar and Darius wanted complete control and fealty. They challenged anyone who did not bow down before them (Dan. 3:1–15; 6:6–9). We see similar behaviors played out today in multiple realms. Obeisance or off with your head!

This is not to say that all ambition is wrong. Those without drive and desire are often adrift and complacent. In the parable of the talents, God has little good to say about those who play it safe (Matt. 25:26–27). We're encouraged to seek God's blessing, expand our horizons, and look for opportunities to influence. God fulfilled Jabez's audacious request for greater impact and blessed him (1 Chron. 4:9–10). In Ecclesiastes the sage exhorted the wise to take certain risks and cast their bread upon the waters (Eccl. 11:1). Some see these words as a metaphor for maritime trade and expansion. Qohelet was urging his intended readers to go for it.[24] It is folly to keep your ship in the harbor. Wisdom implores us to get out in the whitewater. Only fools make up excuses and stay within the secure (Prov. 26:13).

In similar manner, 1 Timothy 3:1–7 lays out rigorous qualifications for church leadership, beginning with aspiration. At its root the term in the original describes a stretching out of one's heart. If there isn't some level of eagerness to lead, some passion to give direction to leaderless parishioners—some *ambition* to be part of a leadership team—one is disqualified from the start.

In sum, Scripture tells us ambition does play a role in leadership acquisition. The question of acquiring leadership comes down to whether it emerges from holy ambition or is driven by the wholly ambitious, whether it is impelled by a desire for personal gain or motivated by service to God and others, the very definition of leadership. Ambition that God honors is generated by the Spirit of God for the glory of God.

What about *gifting*? What does God reveal? Leadership in Scripture is recognized as a *charisma*, a gifting "according to the grace given to each of us" (Rom. 12:6). The word speaks to something more than natural talent. In a definite moment, one is acted upon by God. Whether at physical or spiritual birth or in certain crises moments, leadership is a divine endowment that becomes a part of one's identity.

Paul uses two words to describe the gift of leading, and both are interchangeable. The first is *proistēmi* (v. 8). In classical literature the term referred to military or state leadership. In the context of a letter to people in Rome, Paul exhorted those with this leadership gift to exercise it with

---

24. See Craig G. Bartholomew, *Ecclesiastes* (Grand Rapids: Baker, 2009), 336.

a sense of urgency. Leaders are to be anything but complacent and half-hearted in their governing. They are gifted for a mission, and those who follow are exhorted to pay close attention (1 Thess. 5:12).

In 1 Corinthians, Paul speaks again to gifts, noting that the Spirit "distributes them to each one, just as he determines" (12:11). One's acquisition of leadership is God's prerogative, not ours. Instead of *proistēmi, kybernēsis* is used (v. 28). Some attempt to make a distinction in these terms, one referring to leadership and one to management, but there is no justification for such a difference . *Kybernēsis* was used of sailors in the Mediterranean, particularly of the helmsmen (*kybernētēs*).[25] It is comparable to the expression "ship of state," having a relationship with the Hebrew *takhbulot*, another nautical term. Those with the gift are like steering ropes of a ship, ensuring that it is well-steered.[26]

In the selection of leaders, it is reasonable—prudent actually—to assess someone's skills for leading. What evidence indicates that leadership is part of a person's being, a person's giftedness and strength? It is a disservice to press one to be someone they are not.

Acquiring leadership is also about *learning.* Those summoned to lead must understand the complexities of leadership and what is involved to be effective. No one in the scriptural accounts gets a pass. Would-be leaders were sent to leadership school. There were no Harvards, no Wharton Schools of Business, nor were there any Amazon lists of leadership bestsellers. Instead there were wildernesses and caves and struggles with enemies. The prophets served as some of the leaders' best professors, God's iron sharpening iron (Prov. 27:17; 2 Chron. 20:37). And there was Jesus, whose leadership course began with the words, "Follow me." Jesus provided the ultimate role model in leadership development as he trained twelve ordinary men to lead the effort to fundamentally change the whole world.

Those who are wise are aware that God is always teaching. His lessons often underscore what one reads in books, but they go further. God may

---

25. Larry Coenen, "bishop," in *The New International Dictionary of New Testament Theology* (Grand Rapids: Zondervan, 1978), 1:193.

26. Bruce K. Waltke, *The Book of Proverbs: Chapters 1–15* (Grand Rapids: Eerdmans, 2004), 96.

use a relational challenge to refine one's sensitivities. He will close doors to try our patience, as well as open doors to test our faith. Some of our greatest leadership lessons come in failure. A leader who looks to God to get through a leadership breakdown finds it is often one's best training ground. Have you discovered this?

In God's design, leadership is also about *inheritance*. In one sense all of us who lead have received our mandate from those who have gone before us. For some, leadership comes as a physical inheritance. Many in Scripture acquired leadership by birthright, something God sanctioned. Behind Jacob's call to lead was Isaac passing the mantle of leadership (Gen. 27:29). Samuel appointed his sons as judges (1 Sam. 8:1), and David transferred the throne with these words to Bathsheba, "Solomon your son shall be king after me" (1 Kings 1:30). From priests to kings to prophets, leadership acquisition in the Old Testament was often a matter of being born in the right tribe, in the right family, and in the right moment. Many of the genealogical lists bear this out.

What can we conclude? To this point, a review of theology and leadership acquisition gives more than a spiritual coating to common assumptions. Behind one's ambition, God may be doing something profound, something in the heart that may shake the earth. Beyond leadership talent, leading is a supernatural gift for a supernatural work. We can learn some things about leading, but if we are willing to enter God's classroom, we will gain insights that go beyond the most notable leadership texts. We find in all of this that the words of God cannot be domesticated to fit into our ideologies and categories. It is nothing less than a strange, emancipatory voice among us, freeing us to move beyond the seen to the unseen.[27] How one becomes a leader is nothing less than a holy work.

Destiny? The role of chance in becoming a leader is where theology and common notions part company. Acquiring leadership is not a matter of fate. It might appear to be about one's destiny. At least that's what Uhtred, the hero in the popular series *The Last Kingdom*, says about life. In every

---

27. Bradford Winters, "A Conversation with Walter Brueggemann," *Image* 55, https://image journal.org/article/conversation-walter-brueggemann/.

episode, he rides off into the sunset declaring, "Destiny is all." Theology takes us to a more intentional universe. Leadership isn't a matter of some external, inexorable force that controls all events and determines one's leading. Leadership acquisition is far more personal.

LEADERSHIP IS A SUMMONS

In terms of becoming a leader, this is theology's most important lesson. This takes us to the root of the matter. All my assumptions of how I became a leader begin here. Divine calling is a dominant theme, one that moves from the beginning of Scripture to its end. Hence, it involves some space to develop.

A summons to lead fits within a larger summons. God stretches out his hand and orders the whole universe—the heavens, the sun, the moon, and the stars—and they stand in position together (Isa. 48:13). God summons all creation to himself. This includes every leader, no matter the context or size of one's realm. God's is a call so decisive that everything we are, everything we do, and everything we have is invested with a special devotion and dynamism lived out as a response.[28]

Humanity is created and ordained to maintain and enforce God's claim to dominion over the earth (Gen. 1:26–28). Leaders do not derive their legitimacy from the consent of the governed, nor do they draw their power from their own determination (or some impersonal force). They receive their authority to lead from the sanction of God. King Nebuchadnezzar, ruler of the largest empire the world had seen, was sobered by the realization that a leader's power is relative in relation to God's power. God alone is "sovereign over the kingdoms of men and gives them to anyone he wishes" (Dan.4:17). Paul's command to "present yourself to God" (2 Tim. 2:15; cf. Rom. 12:1) is the natural response of one who has been summoned.

---

28. Os Guinness, *The Call: Finding and Fulfilling God's Purpose for Your Life* (Nashville: Nelson, 2003), 4.

This should be the first responsibility of a leader's day, followed with a request that echoes Isaiah's: "Here am I. Send me!" (Isa. 6:8).

Over and over Scripture affirms that leadership is a summons determined in eternity past. In the end, this is how one becomes a leader. Long before anyone becomes aware he or she has been summoned to lead, God has been at work crafting us for his purposes. Ruth Haley Barton imagines God saying to Moses, "Now that you know who you are, I am calling you to *do* something out of the essence of your being."[29] Our calling is inextricably interwoven with God's predetermined work.

Prior to Samuel's summons, God was at work in Samuel, establishing his stature and increasing his favor with God and men (1 Sam. 2:26). David was placed in a pasture to learn how to lead sheep before God summoned him to lead a nation (2 Sam. 7:8). God revealed to Isaiah that the voice he would use to cut a nation's heart, the polishing that would be essential to display divine splendor, and the gifting to lead and guide the nation were all initiated in the womb (Isa. 49:1–5). The prophet Jeremiah, who was about to be summoned to shatter and form worlds by his speech, was made aware that God had been shaping his voice from the very moment of conception (Jer. 1:4–5). Looking back after his encounter on the road to Damascus, Paul came to the realization he had been set apart from birth and called to lead the church (Gal. 1:15).

From the beginning, and in secret, God weaves the skills necessary for one to command (Ps. 139:15–16). Election into God's leadership purposes is based not on proven ability or skillful scheming but on God's meticulous work.[30] This vocation comes not from some external voice calling us to be something we are not but from an internal voice of the heart calling us to be the leaders we are made to be.[31]

Leadership is a summons that comes in multiple ways. There is no set script when God calls leaders. The language shifts to accommodate

---

29. Ruth Haley Barton, *Strengthening the Soul of Your Leadership: Seeking God in the Crucible of Ministry* (Downers Grove, IL: InterVarsity Press, 2008), 73.

30. Eugene H. Peterson, *Leap Over a Wall: Earthy Spirituality for Everyday Christians* (New York: HarperCollins, 1997), 18.

31. Barton, *Strengthening the Soul of Your Leadership*, 77.

the manifold ways God summons. Look and you will discover a variety of verbs. These include "establishes," "calls," "raises," "appoints," "sends," "places," and "ordains." In some cases a divine summons comes in the form of a dialogue ("Whom shall I send?" [Isa. 6:8]). In other cases it comes in a dream (Gen. 37:5–7). In other situations God simply speaks: "I will take you, and you will rule" (1 Kings 11:37). *In every encounter God is always the subject.*

Scripture reveals that a divine summons has nothing to do with popularity or promise of potential. God's call often comes seemingly out of nowhere to those one would least expect. Big always starts with little. Consider the many examples. When God decided to save a world, he spoke to an unknown named Noah, summoning him to set a plan in place (Gen. 6:13). Moses was another nobody, long forgotten by those in power, but he was summoned by God to lead God's people. God showed up in a burning bush and called Moses during his daily routine of leading sheep and eking out a living (Ex. 3:2–10; 1 Sam. 12:6).

The command to take off his shoes tells us that when God summons a leader, it is a sacred act carried out on holy ground (Josh. 5:15). It is an exhortation to pause and take note. It is a call to service, the essence of leading, conforming to ancient Near Eastern culture, where those who served took off their shoes.[32]

Every leadership story appears to be a summons. This is why it is such a vast theme. When God decided to bring Israel into the land and give it to his people, he summoned Joshua and commanded him to arise and get ready "because you will lead" (Josh. 1:6). When God determined to deliver his people from the enemies surrounding them, he sent the angel of the Lord to Gideon with the question, "Am I not sending you?" (Judg. 6:14). In some cases the summons was less overt though just as certain. In the life of Samson, the Spirit of the Lord stirred something inside (13:25).

For Saul, who belonged to the least of the tribes, God's summons came in the form of an anointing (1 Sam. 10:1). The same was true of David (1 Sam. 16:12–13; 2 Sam. 5:2, 12; 6:21). The psalmist describes God's

---

32. R. Alan Cole, *Exodus: An Introduction and Commentary* (Downers Grove, IL: InterVarsity Press, 1984), 65.

summoning of David with dramatic effect: "Then the Lord awoke as from sleep, as a warrior awakes from the stupor of wine. . . . He chose David his servant and took him from the sheep pens" (Ps. 78:65, 70).

Anointing, like the command to remove one's shoes, underscores that acquiring leadership is a sacred responsibility. It is the moment when God chooses to permeate a leader with divine activity and promise. One is called to no longer live for lesser things but live for God and his purposes. Would that every leader had an epitaph less Churchillian (see chap. 3) and more Davidic: "When David had served God's purpose in his own generation, he fell asleep" (Acts 13:36).

In certain moments a summons is discovered in the depths of one's soul. News of Jerusalem's wretched condition moved Nehemiah to grief. God spoke through Nehemiah's tears, giving a summons that was confirmed after months in prayer (Neh. 1:4–11). This is the testimony of a number of leaders—something is "ruined" inside. One can no longer tolerate the status quo. An unsettling spirit takes hold and will not let go until one lays hold of God's call.

God spoke disquieting words to Esther through her cousin Mordecai, suggesting that her position in the court had less to do with her beauty and more to do with a divine call to lead (Est. 4:14). For the prophets the call from heaven came in a heavenly vision (Isa. 6:1–13), a word from God (Jer. 1:5), and an order to stand up and go (Ezek. 2:1–3). For the disciples it was a visit by the Messiah to their workplace (Matt. 4:18–20). For Paul it was a blinding light and a visit from Ananias (Acts 9:1–6; 22:10).

Every leader has a story of how they were summoned to leadership, whether they realize it or not. Look deep enough, and you will find a divine call to rise and lead. What is your story?

We discover that a divine summons to lead takes precedence over our plans. Leaders have their leadership designs. They should. But in the end God determines their steps (Prov. 16:1–3, 9). Sometimes leaders learn this the hard way, something we saw when David took the presumptuous lead to build the temple (2 Sam. 7). Nebuchadnezzar needed to lose his mind and become like the animals of the field to grasp that God does as he pleases (Dan. 4:34–36).

Sometimes a divine summons seems to make no sense. It might even be met with defiance and disobedience. We don't always embrace God's orders. Fleeing to Tarshish was a statement from Jonah that there was no way he would go to a terrorist state and preach repentance (Jonah 1:1–3). Who of us have not had a moment when we initially pushed back from God's calling to lead?

I have had my share of moments when wills converged, when, like Jacob, I have wrestled. We learn that God's summons is seldom custom designed to fit our tastes and preferences—but is divinely fit for us. Those leaders who desire authenticity will find themselves driven to evaluate their choices. They will be forced to discover where egotistic impulses might be pulling them away from a higher order, a greater calling and purpose.[33] Ultimately, God's will will be done.

On occasion a summons is extended to those who have their own gods and live out a certain evil. Holy or unholy, leaders are the "vehicle of his revelation or a channel of his power."[34] God summoned a sorcerer named Balaam (Numbers 22–24). He called pagan kings like Nebuchadnezzar to carry out his will, even bestowing on him the title of "my servant" (Jer. 25:9; 27:6; 43:10).

In Isaiah 44, after declaring his sovereignty over all creation, God referred to Cyrus the Great as "my shepherd [who] will accomplish all that I please" (v. 28). Here was a Persian king of whom God said, "I summon you by name and bestow on you a title of honor, though you do not acknowledge me" (45:4). Sometimes God's purposes are realized even when our efforts are consciously motivated to obstruct them.[35]

In every situation, leaders govern within the bounds of divine mandate (Isa. 10:5–6; 37:26–27; Amos 9:7). Caesar Augustus issues his decree and orders his census. Whether he realizes it or not, he has been summoned

---

33. Justin A. Irving and Mark L. Strauss, *Leadership in Christian Perspective: Biblical Foundations and Contemporary Practices for Servant Leaders* (Grand Rapids: Baker, 2019), 43.

34. See the introduction to commentary, Arthur E. Cundall and Leon Morris, *Judges & Ruth* (Downers Grove, IL: InterVarsity Press, 1968), 15–48.

35. Donald G. Bloesch, *God the Almighty: Power, Wisdom, Holiness, Love* (Downers Grove, IL: InterVarsity Press, 1995), 119.

to send Joseph and Mary to Bethlehem to fulfill Old Testament prophecy (Luke 2:1–7; Mic. 5:2). God is the main—not the supporting—actor. We have bit parts in his play.[36] How God summons leaders and accomplishes his purposes, in conjunction with their effort and striving, is a mystery.[37] His thoughts are not our thoughts (Isa. 55:8–9). Becoming a leader and leading are on God's terms. We see this in the biblical stories. We see it in ours.

Leadership acquisition is more than a summons to serve God; it is a *partnership* with him. Leaders are summoned to join with God in carrying out his will. This is leadership's ultimate design—fitting into his timing and leading into his future. God declares words that echo ones delivered to Eli: "I will raise up for myself a faithful priest, who will do according to what is in my heart and mind" (1 Sam. 2:35). No matter where you lead (a business, a nation, an athletic team, a university, a church) or what title you carry, the ultimate intention is a joint venture of human and divine.

Scripture illustrates in numerous places: "You led your people like a flock by the hand of Moses and Aaron" (Ps. 77:20). "I will make you like my signet ring, for I have chosen you" (Hag. 2:23). "Unless the Lord had given me help, I would soon have dwelt in the silence of death" (Ps. 94:17). It was this way from the beginning. We were called to be an extension of God's leadership, doing this work of leading together (Gen. 1:28).

The Lord sent for Jerub-Baal, Barak, Jephthah, and Samuel, but it was God who delivered Israel from the hands of their enemies (1 Sam. 12:11). Through her divinely inspired song, Hannah could see a day when God would summon and give strength to the king of his choosing to lead through him (2:10). God goes out with the armies, and the armies follow his lead. It's a joint operation.

In the context of the church, God summons leaders to partner with him in the formation of the body of Christ. Paul uses the phrase "fellow workers" to describe his co-ministry with God (1 Cor. 3:9 ESV). God invites us to join with him in praying, feeding the hungry, and shepherding his

---

36. Kevin J. Vanhoozer, "Letter to an Aspiring Theologian," *First Things*, August 2018, 31.
37. Bloesch, *God the Almighty*, 116.

people (John 6:5–13; Acts 20:28; 1 Peter 5:1–3). It is a collaborative effort, as it was with Father and Son (John 20:21).

Summoning leaders to action means that God has chosen to work through human instrumentality. Finite leaders join the infinite being, the One who is the source and ground of all finite beings.[38] He invites us to join the One who is radically independent of all creaturely power, the One who is self-sufficient, self-sustaining, and self-existent. As Bloesch notes, "He exists by his own power, but he seeks to fulfill his plan and purpose in cooperation with his people whom he empowers by his Spirit."[39]

Keith Johnson adds, "We have not been united to Christ to live as mere spectators to his work; we have been united to him to live as his partners."[40] He summons leaders to carry out his purposes in a covenant partnership, "drawing out possibilities within them for the creation of a promising future."[41] As coleaders, we move together in the same direction, on the basis of divine superintendence and Spirit empowering.

Listen to Paul's own testimony: "I worked harder than all of them—yet not I, but the grace of God" (1 Cor. 15:10). It's important to get this right. At its heart theology is more than missional—it is co-missional.[42] The operative word is "with" (Gen. 28:15; 39:2; 1 Sam. 16:18; Ps. 23:4; Matt. 28:20). We who lead serve his purposes "by intention or by accident."[43] The responsibility of a summons is to keep one's face turned in God's direction to advance God's kingdom.

Together, leaders who get in line with God's purposes bring restoration to a broken world (Matt. 28:18–20; Col. 1:28–29). We work alongside God as his stewards, building his house—not masters on our own, building

---

38. Ibid., 34.

39. Ibid., 88.

40. Keith L. Johnson, *Theology as Discipleship* (Downers Grove, IL: InterVarsity Press, 2015), loc. 878, Kindle.

41. Ibid., 115.

42. John R. Franke, *The Character of Theology: An Introduction to Its Nature, Task, and Purpose* (Grand Rapids: Baker, 2005), 166.

43. Rick Langer, "Toward a Biblical Theology of Leadership," in *Organizational Leadership: Foundations & Practices for Christians*, ed. John S. Burns, John R. Shoup, and Donald C. Simmons Jr. (Downers Grove, IL: InterVarsity Press, 2014), 68.

our empires.[44] It may not be efficient as the world measures efficiency. It may seem to take an inordinate amount of time and resources. Leading together can add to a long, arduous journey, calling for faith at every turn.

Leadership is a bidding that has its risks. Acquiring leadership to carry out a divine summons amounts to a fatal call.[45] Deadly in every case, because to respond to a summons begins with dying to ourselves and our plans. Ignoring or running from God's summons can lead to the greater danger of missing God's purpose for our leadership and facing a certain futility. Jonah discovered this. In the end God always find us. As a Puritan pastor once wrote, "He has messengers enough to overtake us."[46]

CONCLUSION

Theology expands our thinking—even our imagination—on leadership acquisition. We might debate gifting versus learning, destiny versus choice, but in the end it is about something larger. There is a divine summons at work. Leaders are not called into existence by the circumstances. It can appear this way, but something else is going on. Something far more profound. Events, it turns out, are not products of purely immanent factors and causes.[47] Context is not assigning us. God is.

A theological historiography reveals that leadership is a matter of divine providence, divine intervention, and divine permission. Calling and appointment come from God; everything else—ambition, gifting, training, inheritance—is secondary.[48] The people of Israel are corrected for assuming they can set up kings without God's consent (Hos. 8:4). God

44. Miroslav Volf and Matthew Croasmun, *For the Life of the World: Theology That Makes a Difference* (Grand Rapids: Brazos, 2019), 141.

45. Barton, *Strengthening the Soul of Your Leadership*, 84.

46. Richard Baxter, *The Reformed Pastor: A Pattern for Personal Growth and Ministry* (Portland: Multnomah, 1982), 130–31.

47. Peter J. Leithart, *1 & 2 Kings* (Grand Rapids: Brazos, 2006), 34.

48. Langer, "Toward a Biblical Theology of Leadership," in *Organizational Leadership*, 75.

does the making, as David acknowledges: "You have made me the head of nations" (Ps. 18:43). *There is no such thing as a self-made leader.*

Whatever authority leaders acquire and whatever intentions they have are derived from God. "No one from the east or the west or from the desert can exalt themselves. It is God," writes the psalmist (Ps. 75:6–7). In him we live and move and have our being (Acts 17:27–28). There is no worldly rank that is anything but provisional.[49] Leaders are sovereignly conscripted. We find a narrative that is less about men and women pursuing leadership and more about God pursuing and using those who would be leaders. In the end leadership is a sacred summons to fulfill the will of God. That's it.

I can attest to this. One night my spiritual godfather entered an ice cream shop where I was working. He had taken an unusual interest in my life, convinced I had leadership potential. Squeezing through a myriad of customers, he whispered over the counter, "You need to give your life to ministry. Join us and change the world." But I had my plans. I was headed for the Air Force Academy.

Over the course of a year of preparation to obtain an appointment, I had no rest. Like a seed lodged into my soul, God's call began to grow, pushing out other plans and ambitions. It was a most restless year. This man's invitation had ruined me—in a good way. Eventually, I accepted his challenge.

Looking back, I realize that coming to leadership was less about me and my desires and more about a divine summons. It was God's idea. While I realize that coming to leadership requires ambition, gifting, and learning, it is in the end a bidding from God. And who knows how and when it will come.

We are all in a story, one God is writing (though providence would say it has already been written). The leadership stories of Scripture invite us to live into them, but we must also find our own. There is a script that has been given to us within this narrative, a role that when we find it we find ourselves.[50]

---

49. Derek Kidner, *Psalms 73–150* (Downers Grove, IL: InterVarsity Press, 1975), 272.
50. James K. A. Smith, *On the Road with Saint Augustine: A Real-World Spirituality for Restless Hearts* (Grand Rapids: Brazos, 2019), 163.

Seeing our leadership as a call to partner with God in his story is a sobering task, one to be taken on with a theological seriousness. Once acquired, one must stay with it. There will be certain assurances, certain demands, certain costs, and certain surprises. We have been called to enter into a covenant, into "an intense mutuality with Yahweh."[51] At the end of our leadership, we might realize that we have embodied and enacted God's will, not our own. And this is so much better.

God has sought and continues to look for one who will respond to his summons, enter his story, and stand in the gap and lead (Ezek. 22:30). In ways predictable and unpredictable, he moves to and fro, summoning those he chooses as leaders. And then, when God finds people willing to serve his purposes, they are "used to the limit."[52] But what's required? Does character matter? This is where we go next. But first a curious story of the acquisition of leadership.

SAUL

In the story of Saul (1 Sam. 9–31), the storyteller begins with the words "There was a Benjamite, a man of standing." It sets up an expectation. God is about to do something, and in typical fashion, he will act in ways we do not anticipate.

Looking at the life of Saul, I can't help but ask, "How in God's name (and I mean this literally) did Saul become a leader?" Few leaders have been so flawed, so disparaged as him. The ending verse of the previous chapter gives us a clue as to where this is going. God speaks to the judge of Israel and says, "Listen to them [the Israelites] and give them a king" (8:22). Samuel is tasked to find a leader, but it is not all on him. Behind this is a

---

51. Walter Brueggemann, *Theology of the Old Testament: Testimony, Dispute, Advocacy* (Minneapolis: Fortress, 2005), 453.

52. J. Oswald Sanders, *Spiritual Leadership: Principles of Excellence for Every Believer* (Chicago: Moody, 1967), 17.

summoning God. The narrator takes us behind the scenes to discover how one becomes a leader.

Leadership is going through a sea change in Israel. The people are weary of warlords. Monarchs are the wave of the future. Samuel must shift with the current and make the transition. Immediately the story goes in an unanticipated direction. It makes no sense that the future of Israel should come from the smallest tribe, one that has been decimated by internal rivalries and fratricidal wars. Benjamin is the "little tribe" in which brothers kill brothers. But out of this no-name place is a family with some influence and a son who is head and shoulders above everyone else. He has a commanding presence that makes him unique (9:2; 10:24).

Like some of us, Saul is not initially looking to become a leader. He is introduced as a man looking for lost donkeys. The God of the universe is in search of a king, and Saul can't even find missing livestock. Like many of us, Saul doesn't come with an impressive resume. Where is there any ambition, let alone gifting? He appears to be a man devoid of spiritual sensitivity, unaware that in the neighborhood is Israel's most famous and honored spiritual leader since Moses—Samuel. As time goes by, deep fissures in Saul's character will be exposed, the kind that will disqualify him from leading. But in this moment God has his eyes on Saul. He is leading Samuel to the leader of his choice: "This is the man I spoke to you about; he will govern my people" (9:17). As Brueggemann underscores, "The choice of Saul is rooted precisely in the intention of God."[53] This goes for every leader.

Up to the city, up to the high place, up to the head of the table. Saul is on the ascent. A special portion has been set aside for the man who would be king. In this intimate moment Samuel sets Saul apart and confers divine authority on him (10:1). This is huge. As Barton notes, "When God calls, it is a very big deal."[54] Saul is called to keep God's people within their boundaries. He has God's stamp of ownership. He is God's choice, which conveys a special status even David must respect when he has the chance to kill Saul.

As with any summons, it will require confirmation. Two men will come to

---

53. Walter Brueggemann, *First and Second Samuel* (Louisville: John Knox, 1990), 73.
54. Barton, *Strengthening the Soul of Your Leadership*, 74.

Saul and verify that the donkeys are found, just as Samuel said. Three men will give a meal of consecration. A procession of prophets will greet Saul, and the Spirit will anoint this emerging leader by rushing upon him. Saul will be this prophetic, priestly king (v. 6). There will be this explosive surge of strength, and Saul will become another man. Saul will become who he was intended to be from the beginning (Gen. 1:28). It will be evident God's presence has intersected Saul's person and will now be *with* Saul. God's signature act is to be with the leaders he calls.

Some (like Isaiah) seek God's calling before it comes. Others (like Moses) argue with God when God appears. Still others (like Jonah) bolt and run. A fair number anesthetize their vocational conscience with familiar routines so as to avoid it. This is Saul.[55] Saul seems in a daze. Ambivalent. He has no idea how Samuel came up with such a preposterous idea (1 Sam. 9:21). Samuel will spend the evening talking to Saul. Conversation is not the language used. Only Samuel's words are recorded, and it appears that Saul was speechless. Asked by his family about his time with Samuel, Saul keeps it to himself. At his inauguration he hides out among the baggage (10:22). After the festivities Saul returns to the familiar routines of the fields to continue life as before. Eventually, Saul will do what the circumstances require, but only for a season.

This is often what happens. God shows up, but we are uncertain. Do I want this? Is this my strength? He summons us to lead, but as with Saul, it may take a crisis to get us in step. Nonetheless, God will seize our moment and do what must be done. He will—he must—change us into a different person. Into the person we were called to be from the beginning—a prophetic, royal priest who must command.

---

55. I couldn't resist this option, borrowed from Eugene H. Peterson, *Under the Unpredictable Plant: An Exploration in Vocational Holiness* (Leominster, UK: Gracewing, 1992), 11.

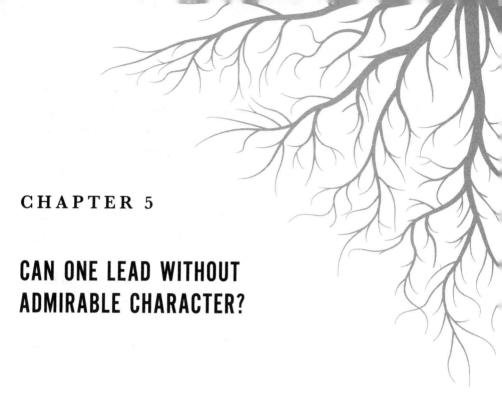

CHAPTER 5

CAN ONE LEAD WITHOUT ADMIRABLE CHARACTER?

If you have integrity, nothing else matters. If you don't
have integrity, nothing else matters.
—ALAN SIMPSON, INTRODUCING GERALD FORD AT HARVARD

In 2013 an old, substandard ship called the *Rhosus* sailed into the Black Sea port of Batumi to pick up its cargo. The 2,750-ton shipment, a chemical compound used for building bombs, never reached its destination. It ended up stored in Warehouse 12 of a Beirut port. For seven years Lebanese officials, lawyers, judges, and a Russian shipper bickered over what to do with the volatile materials.

It all became mired in bureaucracy, one in which a criminal oligarchy had created a spoils system that excluded all but their own. A government filled with empty suits had been tolerated and abetted by a population that has known no other kind of leadership. No one stepped up to give direction and avert a disaster. Meanwhile the stockpile of explosive materials sat, unsecured.

On August 4, 2020, the inevitable happened. At approximately six o'clock that evening, a nearby fire lit the fuse, triggering a blast reminiscent of a nuclear bomb. Bodies, trees, and cars were tossed through the air, leaving two hundred people dead, more than five thousand injured, a port district destroyed, more than a quarter million people homeless, and billions of dollars in damage. A nation's worst nightmare became reality.

As time has progressed, no president or prime minister or head of army or port authority or judge has taken responsibility. No one. Credible leadership is nowhere to be found. As of this writing, the government cannot run its currency, supply the necessary power, cure its sick, or protect its people.[1] Events will have passed by the time of publication, but it is likely things will be the same.

Sadly, Lebanon is not unique. We shake our heads at the sheer incompetence. But it runs much deeper. Under such feckless leadership is a failure of character. A radical corruption is at work in the interior of the soul, and it appears to be spreading.

In his introduction to *Character Counts*, Os Guinness asks the question, "Where has all the character gone?"[2] The world stage is littered with leaders void of virtues that lead to moral excellence. One does not have to travel to Beirut. I see it in my own city. My own country. In the church. Moral failures coddled and enabled by sycophants. Superficiality has replaced authenticity, and celebrity has replaced substance. There is no shortage of leaders, but it is getting harder to find a leader with interior substance. Too many are cutting their conscience to fit this year's fashions.[3] How did we get into this mess? Is it a failure of preparation? Could it be we have never fully addressed the question of whether character matters?

Professors like Jeffrey Pfeffer of Stanford acknowledge and lament the

---

1. This is how Robert Fisk, who lived in Beirut as a long-term journalist, described his city shortly before his death. Robert Fisk, "11 August 2020: How Do You Save a Truly Corrupt Country Like Lebanon?" *Independent*, November 10, 2020, https://www.independent.co .uk/news/long_reads/robert-fisk-lebanon-beirut-explosion-corruption-government-resign -hezbollah-assad-sisi-b1642016.html.

2. Os Guinness, *Character Counts: Leadership Qualities in Washington, Wilberforce, Lincoln, and Solzhenitsyn* (Grand Rapids: Baker, 1999), 14.

3. Warren G. Bennis, *On Becoming a Leader* (New York: Addison-Wesley, 1989), 41.

trend. Speaking to prominent and educated business leaders in Belgium, Pfeffer remarked, "I find it depressing that after decades of books, lectures, leadership-development programs, and all the other components of the large leadership industry, virtually every shred of evidence shows most workplaces filled with distrustful, disengaged, dissatisfied, despairing employees."[4] But it's not just a failure on the part of the leadership industry. Other university professors, such as Barbara Kellerman of Harvard, recognize a growing gap between the teaching of leadership in the academy and the practice of leadership in the field.[5] Until character is addressed, all the theories of effectual planning and decision making and the like won't matter. But this will not be easy.

The very subject raises a number of questions. What do we even mean by character? This is the first question. Joseph Epstein recently reviewed Marjorie Garber's book *Character: The History of a Cultural Obsession*. He was struck by the length of the book and asked, "Can an examination of the single word 'character' sustain a book of 383 pages and another 40-odd pages of endnotes?"[6] It turns out that it can. The meaning of *character* continues to morph. Could it be that *character* has become so fluid and so arbitrary that it has become a "bland, sanctimonious, and empty word"?[7]

Maybe, but if we are going to speak to leadership and character, we have to define our terms. It might help to go back to the original meaning of the word. *Character* spoke to that which was engraved or imprinted on something. *Character* described the inner form, what Guinness refers to as the "essential stuff" that makes anyone or anything what it is.[8] Character hence is something different than personality or charisma, the persona we see on the outside. Character goes to the heart.

---

4. Jeffrey Pfeffer, *Leadership BS: Fixing Workplaces and Careers One Truth at a Time* (New York: Harper Business, 2015), 193.

5. A gap Harvard professor Barbara Kellerman notes in her *End of Leadership* (New York: Harper Business, 2012), loc. 58 of 4487, Kindle.

6. Joseph Epstein, "Where the Self Meets the World," review of *Character: The History of a Cultural Obsession* by Marjorie Garber, *Wall Street Journal*, July 18–19, 2020, https://www.wsj.com/articles/character-review-where-the-self-meets-the-world-11594998822.

7. Ibid.

8. Guinness, *Character Counts*, 12.

Character, by this definition, is who a leader is in the dark when no one else can see, *when one is most oneself.* Character is what is left when all the trappings of leadership—the titles, the impressive dress, the entourage, the crowds, the crafted speeches—are stripped away. Consider Adolf Hitler. Andrew Roberts devoted a chapter both to his outward charisma and to his more hidden character. Though he was presented as a charismatic near deity, underneath Hitler was, in Roberts's assessment, "a banal, soulless little weirdo," "a terrible know-it-all, bore, and conspiracy theorist," and "a pathetic excuse for a human being."[9] This was his essential stuff.

Or take Robert E. Lee, the Confederate general whose monuments are beginning to come down. He has been revered in institutions like West Point for his dignity, rectitude, and composure on the battlefield. At the same time, Lee is remembered off the battlefield for his insecurity, petulance, impatience, contempt, racism, and violent temper. Some would even include treason.[10]

But maybe this definition is too limiting. Wouldn't it be more accurate to say that character is not just a part but the sum of who a leader is, *both* in public and in private? Isn't character the aggregate of a person's thoughts and acts? Add up one's attitudes, ideas, motives, words, and actions, and over time they form a picture. This is how Dallas Willard describes it: "Our character is that internal, overall structure of the self that is revealed by our long-run patterns of behavior and from which our actions more or less automatically arise."[11] N. T. Wright puts it more graphically, describing character as "the pattern of thinking and acting which runs right through someone so that wherever you cut into them (as it were), you see the same person through and through."[12]

---

9. Andrew Roberts, *Leadership in War: Essential Lessons from Those Who Made History* (New York: Penguin, 2019), 68–69, 90.

10. Mackubin Thomas Owens, "The Enigma of Robert E. Lee," *National Review,* October 4, 2021, https://www.nationalreview.com/magazine/2021/10/04/the-enigma-of-robert-e-lee/#slide-1.

11. Dallas Willard, *Renovation of the Heart: Putting On the Character of Christ* (Colorado Springs: NavPress, 2002), 142.

12. N. T. Wright, *After You Believe: Why Christian Character Matters* (New York: HarperOne, 2010), 27.

Can One Lead without Admirable Character?

Character gets to authenticity, to who a leader is, inside and out. And this can be good or bad. Stalin was the same monster through and through. He was "an ambitious, cynical, cunning, murderous, vengeful, narcissistic, imperious, self-centered paranoiac."[13] What he was onstage was what he was offstage. On the other hand, Abraham Lincoln exhibited a moral excellence that was consistent with his heart. He was a leader with the kind of sound mind and character we want to remember. For these, we create monuments.

Given that character describes the sum total of a leader, good or bad, the term is neutral. We need an adjective to qualify the word, differentiating a leader with good character (i.e., *moral excellence*, a soundness of heart that chooses to do what is right) from a person whose character is flawed (i.e., *moral failure*, a perversion of heart that chooses to do what is wrong).

As we working through meanings, the subject of character raises a second question—Does moral excellence in a leader matter? It's one thing to come together on a definition. It's another to insist that principled character be a priority in the leaders we choose. Our age is more and more enamored with performative leadership. This was discussed back in chapter 1. Part of the breakdown can be traced to leadership curriculums that give more attention to the pragmatic how ("How to Assert Your Leadership," "How to Inspire People to Follow") and less attention to the who ("Who I Am as a Leader," "The Importance of Self-Leadership").

In a number of fields, results are what ultimately matter. Accomplishments are what we choose to remember. Stanley McChrystal, after profiling thirteen diverse leaders, concluded, "Our profiles are a reminder that those who emerge as successful leaders are not necessarily those with the best values."[14] Their careers might have been marked as a straight line of ascent, all onward and upward, but their personal lives were marred by "bumps and potholes along the way."

T. S. Eliot was a literary giant, but his wife would show up at his

---

13. Roberts, *Leadership in War*, 95.
14. Stanley McChrystal, *Leaders: Myth and Reality* (New York: Portfolio/Penguin, 2018), 395.

lectures with a sign that read, "I Am The Wife He Abandoned."[15] The gap between the persona of Walt Disney and his private character was described as "a chasm."[16] The same could be said of Leonard Bernstein. He was a genius onstage but a failure in his personal life.[17] We tend to let achievements eclipse these.

Is moral character that essential to being a world leader? Alexander the Great created one of the world's largest empires by the age of thirty. His armies would follow him to the ends of the earth. But character? He had multiple wives, lived out a number of sexual distortions, and died after a two-day drinking binge.[18]

Over the course of our own history, we have had our share of flawed leaders. Recent presidents like Lyndon Johnson, Richard Nixon, Bill Clinton, and Donald Trump have been regarded by many as accomplished political leaders. Even though they lacked a moral compass, and self-knowledge seems to have escaped them, followers rationalized and minimized their moral failures because of their achievements. Lies, sexual debauchery, and authoritarian leadership were overlooked as long as unemployment was low, the stock market maintained its value, and the right person sat on the court bench.[19]

It's the same in the corporate world. Board members demand results. If you want to be a high-profile leader, you will need a dominating nature and an aggressive will. Even Pfeffer acknowledges that getting things done often requires behavior that some people might find repugnant.[20] Leaders must deal with certain realities if they are going to succeed. One of them is that outcomes—not principled leadership—are what matters.

Steve Jobs of Apple was one of *the* remarkable business leaders of his

---

15. Joseph Epstein, "The Perfect Critic," Review of *The Complete Prose of T. S. Eliot* by Ronald Schuchard et. al., *Wall Street Journal*, November 27–28, 2021, https://www.wsj.com/articles/the-collected-prose-of-t-s-eliot-review-tradition-keeper-of-the-flame-joseph-epstein-11637943045.

16. McChristal, *Leaders*, 51.

17. Ibid., 142.

18. Thomas R. Martin, *Ancient Greece: From Prehistoric to Hellenistic Times* (New Haven: Yale University Press, 2013), 197.

19. Ramesh Ponnuru, "Character Effects," *National Review*, November 7, 2019, https://www.nationalreview.com/magazine/2019/11/25/character-effects.

20. Pfeffer, *Leadership BS*, 207.

time. He set a standard for innovative leadership. Excellent character was another matter. Colleagues referred to the "hero/shithead" dichotomy—those under his leadership were one or the other, sometimes on the same day.[21] Though he was often rude and abusive to those he led, people looked past his nasty edge. For most, product development was more important than heart development.

Not everyone dismisses moral character. A number would argue that principled leadership is essential to impacting people's lives, values, and relationships. Sam Walker has spent eleven years researching the accomplishments of more than twelve hundred sports teams across the world. His mission has been to determine the one thing that elite teams have in common. His conclusion: "The most crucial ingredient in a team that achieves and sustains historic greatness is the character of the player who leads it."[22] More often than not, a captain with integrity is the difference between winning and losing.

Leaders who have been most revered are those who have exhibited moral excellence. Influencers like Wilberforce, Lincoln, Mandela, Tubman, and King are remembered for their deeds as well as their solid character. Moral strength generated their accomplishments. Duty to family and devotion to God compelled Harriet Tubman to give herself to dismantling slavery. As a result, people followed. In their book *Moral Leadership*, Gushee and Holtz say, "There is something in the human spirit that simply cannot help but gravitate to people who have led lives of great moral purpose."[23] These are the leaders who do not demand blind fanaticism. They create commitment and enthusiasm.

The reality is that when you minimize the need for excellence in character, you will likely be left with an environment that is toxic, dysfunctional, and dictatorial, where the morale is low and the turnover is

---

21. Walter Isaacson, *Steve Jobs* (New York: Simon & Schuster, 2011), 561.

22. Sam Walker, *The Captain Class: A New Theory of Leadership* (New York: Random House, 2017), xvii.

23. David P. Gushee and Colin Holtz, *Moral Leadership for a Divided Age: Fourteen People Who Dared to Change Our World* (Grand Rapids: Brazos, 2018), 3.

high. Over time, trust will be replaced with mistrust, the enthusiastic will give way to the dispirited, and order will turn to chaos.

A study of character raises a third question—What do we use to judge character? We have noted that character is not so easy to define, and the importance of ethical character for effective leadership is up for debate. The reference point for moral excellence is also shifting. Given our culture's growing secularity, more and more are turning to their own criteria. What constitutes a virtuous leader? Many are moving from traditional assumptions and shared ideals. Moralism and its rules are becoming a matter of opinion. In some cases we have redefined moral excellence to be as inane as "Be true to yourself."

Still, most agree that a larger honesty is essential. In their exhaustive research, Kouzes and Posner found that the most important trait of a leader isn't one's negotiating skills or force of personality; it is integrity.[24] As a whole, people value truthfulness rather than deception, loyalty rather than betrayal, self-effacement rather than self-promotion, compassion rather than oppression, decency rather than indecency, and cooperation rather than exploitation. Followers want a leader who can express the values that hold a society together. They look for a leader with the moral fiber that lifts followers out of their petty preoccupations, carries them above the conflicts that tear a society apart, and unites them in pursuits worthy of their best efforts.[25] Who wants a leader who believes he is the most important person in the room?

Though we may disagree on where to set the guideposts, most want leaders of some moral rectitude. Leadership professors like Peter Northouse point out that leadership comes with an enormous ethical responsibility.[26] The problem is that we are becoming pretty confused when it comes to the lines. Moral convictions are becoming increasingly subjective. What

---

24. James M. Kouzes and Barry Z. Posner, *Credibility: How Leaders Gain and Lose It, Why People Demand It* (San Francisco: Jossey-Bass, 2003), 12.

25. John Gardner, quoted in James MacGregor Burns, *Leadership* (New York: Open Road Media, 2012), 451.

26. Peter G. Northouse, *Introduction to Leadership: Concepts and Practice* (Thousand Oaks: SAGE, 2015), 261.

happens when there is no truth but only versions? How can we judge character if there is no moral center and only sides?

More than ever universities are challenged to find a moral basis that leadership studies can agree on, a standard of moral excellence that defines moral character. Without a criterion that transcends us, we are letting the one who has the greater power decide. It's critical that both leaders and followers get beyond themselves to find their bearings, but is this possible?

Let's face it, some of our existing notions about leadership and character need the work of a wrecking crew. Given the number of empty suits that sit at executive desks, stand in pulpits, and lead industry, it's obvious there is a crisis of character. Our only hope is to get beyond ourselves, our confusions, and many of our false assumptions. Here again we need to slow down to catch up with God. We need to see with greater precision and embrace what God has to say about character.

GOD'S WORD ON THE CHARACTER OF A LEADER

There is no ambiguity in Scripture when it comes to the importance of proper character. It is not a subtheme to leadership success and stability. Charisma, exceptional energy, and audacious initiatives are impressive attributes, but they cannot make up for moral deficiencies. A leader unconcerned with moral deficits is no more useful to God than is silver full of dross to a silversmith (Prov. 25:4).

The consequences of minimizing the importance of principled character will catch up with every leader and their followers. This is the warning of Scripture. Without the right heart, leaders will go into dark places, cave to their base impulses, and abuse those they have been called to serve. Whatever is within will eventually come out (Matt. 15:16–20).

Most leadership failures in Scripture had little to do with personality conflicts, unexceptional performance, or failed expectations. They had everything to do with unprincipled hearts. Character is the part-gyroscope, part-brake that provides the leader's strongest source of bearings and restraint.[27] Without a clear set of moral principles in place, leaders like Saul, Manasseh, Caiaphas, and Herod were leadership disasters. Once promising, they became empty souls, as significant as "foam on the surface of the water" (Job 24:18). Here, then suddenly gone, and even more quickly forgotten (v. 24).

Without the right character, self-serving leaders not only destroy themselves but end up dismantling the world.[28] The social order comes apart. A large bureaucracy becomes necessary to fill the void and manage the corruption and disorder. This is the point of Proverbs 28:2: "When a country is rebellious, it has many rulers, but a ruler with discernment and knowledge maintains order." If things do not change, a corrupt leadership will interfere with both God's blessing and God's presence (2 Kings 17:18).

Theology gives the reference points for leadership character. Scripture is not vague or ambivalent here. God does not leave it up to us to draw the lines. Left to our own designs, our own feelings, and society's vague notions, boundaries and borders lack precision.

Western culture in particular has looked to ancient philosophers like Plato and Socrates and Aristotle for guidance in drawing the lines. Traditionally, four virtues have been recognized as classic (or cardinal): wisdom (*sophia*), prudence (*sōphrosynē*), justice (*dikaiosynē*), and courage (*andreia*).[29] Historically, we have measured character by one's mastery of these human ideals, as well as other morals that hinge on these. The problem is that they begin and end with us as the model.

Theology confirms what life reveals, that pursuing human ideals will not bring us to the outcomes of true character. As Bloesch puts it, "Natural virtues (such as justice, courage, temperance, and wisdom) are praiseworthy in their own right, but they are deficient in producing a righteous life."[30] Wright imagines the apostle Paul being asked for his opinion about

---

27. Guinness, *Character Counts*, 20.

28. Walter Brueggemann, *1 & 2 Kings*, Smyth & Helwys Bible Commentary (Macon: Smyth Helwys, 2018), 3.

29. Wright, *After You Believe*, 34.

30. Donald G. Bloesch, *The Paradox of Holiness: Faith in Search of Obedience* (Peabody, MA: Hendrickson, 2016), loc. 284 of 4654, Kindle.

these Greek ideals: "It is fine up to a point and as far as it goes, but it can't give what it promises. It's like a signpost pointing in more or less the right direction (though it will need some adjustment), but without a road that actually goes there."[31]

Ultimately, any definition of true character must find its reference point in God and his character. This is theology's lesson. A person aspiring to be a leader with gravitas, having the full weight of character, must begin with Paul's exhortation: "Follow God's example" (Eph. 5:1). This is what roots true character. It's in God's being we find ideals that lead to what a Hellenistic ideal—or any other cultural model—cannot.

With God as the source, Scripture gives a number of virtue lists. Peter urged his readers to make every effort to supply moral excellence in their faith, and then gave a list of ideals (2 Peter 1:5–7). They begin with and then go beyond our earthbound virtues, enabling us to participate in the divine nature. The Beatitudes of Jesus serve as another list of moral qualities (Matt. 5:1–11), describing the character of those devoted to God's kingdom.

In various epistles, Paul laid out a set of virtues for every leader. To the Galatians he gave a list that evidences the filling of the Spirit (Gal. 5:22–23), to the Colossians he defined the moral qualities leaders are to wear (Col. 3:12–14), and to the Corinthians he pointed to faith, hope, and love as the cardinal graces (1 Cor. 13:13). James, as another apostolic voice, used the wisdom from above as the broad category under which he specified a set of godly character qualities a leader should pursue, ones that stand in contrast to the earthly and unspiritual (James 3:17–18).

This is not about pick and choose. It is important for leaders to go after all these virtues, for each is kept in place by the other.[32] They all require the development of "habits of the daytime heart in a world still full of darkness."[33] Different lists might suggest different prioritizations, but they are to be embraced as a whole. Nonetheless, five are especially critical to principled leadership.

---

31. Wright, *After You Believe*, 36.
32. Wright, *After You Believe*, 195.
33. Ibid., 137.

Love

Following the exhortation to be imitators of God, Paul commands, "And walk in the way of love" (Eph. 5:2). For Paul, love was the cardinal virtue, the defining grace, because love is what God most requires of himself. It characterizes his very nature (1 John 4:8).[34] Love is both a virtue to pursue and a gift to be received, and it begins with loving God (Matt. 22:37).

Love did not make Aristotle's list of cardinal virtues, but it crowns God's list. Divine love, embraced in the life of a leader, becomes something unconditional and covenantal.[35] It is not an overstatement to say that love should be the dominant character quality of a leader. A survey of God's Word affirms this. Love is the character attribute that unites all the other virtues (Col. 3:14). As McKnight puts it, "Love, then, is not one of the virtues; love is the one and only virtue that creates space for all of the other virtues."[36] It is the crowning gift of the Spirit, the first of God's graces (Gal. 5:22; 1 Cor. 13:13; cf. 2 Peter 1:5–7).

In the end, measuring one's character by love is setting the bar as high as it will go.[37] Jesus referred to love as "the first and greatest commandment" (Matt. 22:38). The Torah is reduced to this, just as character is. Love for God cannot be second to the love of self, power, money, achievement, career, or anything else. Leaders who love eschew abuse. They lift spirits, extend kindness, give generously, and show respect. They care more for a person's needs than a person's performance.

Justice

A leader of principle is a leader who is not only loving but just. Love and justice, kindness and truth, compassion and righteousness are tied together and are behind every divine act (Isa. 30:18). Like love, justice runs deep in God's being (Ps. 36:6). It must run deep in the heart of a leader. Just as

---

34. Ben Witherington III, *Who God Is: Meditations on the Character of Our God* (Bellingham: Lexham, 2020), 5.

35. Scot McKnight, *Kingdom Conspiracy: Returning to the Radical Mission of the Local Church* (Grand Rapids: Brazos, 2014), 169.

36. Ibid., 168.

37. Wright, *After You Believe*, 184.

justice is the foundation of God's throne, it must symbolize the power of a leader (89:14). Speaking of this justice, Culver notes that it is "doubtless the most important idea for correct understanding of government—whether of man by man or of the whole creation by God."[38]

The world has always been desperate for leaders who are fair-minded. Stories of victimhood and injustice drive many of our headlines. In Scripture many of the pleas directed toward a leader related to injustice (1 Kings 3:16–27; 2 Kings 8:3). Leaders who make justice a leitmotif of their leading bring evenhandedness to an uneven world. They do not show partiality or take bribes. They cannot be bought, and they do not minimize what is right. Rightness can never be secondary or subservient to expediency, achievement, or personal satisfaction.

True leaders and true faith model justice. God is not impressed with leaders who go through the motions, who plead to him for justice but live unjust lives (Isa. 58:2). Isaiah flips our assumptions of what constitutes religiosity—fasting and Sabbath keeping—and every other ritual. Those with the heart of God devote themselves to loosening the chains of injustice, freeing the oppressed, providing food for the poor, and clothing the naked (vv. 6–7). These are the leaders the world longs to follow.

Humility

Humility is a virtue that joins other godly ones like patience, purity, gentleness, and kindness. These qualities are associated more with divine ideals than with human ones. They point to moral excellence as God defines it.

Humility is a priority for those of principle. It has been described as the framework in which all virtues live.[39] This is a stunning statement, given it is left off of other virtue lists. Without humility, without an understanding of our proper place in the order of creation, we cannot cultivate the other virtues like love and justice.[40] We fall prey to arrogance, a vice that

---

38. Robert D. Culver, "shapat," *Theological Wordbook of the Old Testament* (Chicago: Moody, 1980), 2:948.

39. Willard, *Renovation of the Heart*, 209.

40. Karen Swallow Prior, *On Reading Well* (Grand Rapids: Brazos, 2018), 208.

is behind almost every leadership failure. Too many imagine they are like gods, ignoring the fact they are transient and dispensable. All eventually drop like flies on the windowsill.

If God is to elevate a leader, it begins with one's willingness to descend (Matt. 23:12). Here, one is unconcerned with getting one's way, promoting one's name, advertising one's accomplishments, and seeking for some recognition. Leaders who are modest do not need the applause of the crowd. They are okay with being in the shadows. They know this is a rare trait, for most leaders like to be seen. They view self-effacement as an indication of weakness. Crowds tend to gravitate to leaders who are brash, popular, forceful, and heroic. People will tolerate their braggadocious behavior as long as they get things done. But it is a failure, both of character and of leadership. Humility brings us back to the very definition of leadership, which is one of servanthood.

Integrity

Leaders who have integrity realize that this, in the main, is what matters. Without it nothing else, be it achievements or status, counts in the end. Acts of justice, love, and courage—absent of integrity—are superficial at best. Humility without integrity corrodes into false humility.

Integrity comes from a Hebrew root *tmm*, from which come words describing something that is whole, sound, and solid. Leaders of true character are complete, straightforward, and dependable. The antonym is a root describing something incomplete, unsound, and twisted. These are leaders who lack credibility. They bend the truth and change memories. They have a propensity to exaggerate or understate the facts. They make promises but fail to follow through.

In his book on leadership, Bobby Clinton refers to integrity as the heart of moral character.[41] It is the substance and the core because integrity gets back to the heart of God. God is the God of truth (John 3:33). It is impossible for him to lie (Heb. 6:18). Whatever God promises, he fulfills (Num. 23:19).

---

41. J. Robert Clinton, *The Making of a Leader: Recognizing the Lessons and Stages of Leadership Development* (Colorado Springs: NavPress, 2012), 58.

Whatever God says about himself is trustworthy. Whatever he does is congruent with who he is.[42]

Leaders of integrity take their cues from God. They seek to imitate his uprightness, but it requires constant vigilance. It takes but a bit of folly to destroy integrity. One small indiscretion, one flippant remark, one indecent touch can ruin one's reputation, destroy one's character, and call into question one's leadership (Eccl. 10:1).

Diligence

Though not found in the virtue lists of Scripture, diligence (thoroughness, attentiveness, carefulness) is a core value in the broader narrative. Leaders of moral excellence will not tolerate a leadership that is haphazard and neglectful.

Just as diligence is a mark of an ordered and wise life, slothfulness reveals something disordered and foolish in the soul. Proverbs is all about wise character, and some of its severest warnings are directed toward the sluggard (24:30; 26:14–16). Missing is a sense of care, which is the literal description of akēdia, a Greek word used twice in the Septuagint and often used interchangeably with laziness. Quoting from Sayers, Leithart adds that akēdia is the evidence of deep sin. It is "the accomplice of the other sins and their worst punishment. It is the sin which believes in nothing, cares for nothing, seeks to know nothing, interferes with nothing, enjoys nothing, loves nothing, hates nothing, finds purpose in nothing, lives for nothing, and only remains alive because there is nothing it would die for."[43] This is the antithesis of a virtuous leader.

Leaders who ignore these five traits—who are unloving, unjust, crooked, arrogant, and unconcerned—are hollow leaders. They contribute to the moral rot of a nation. No matter their achievements, they are unworthy of a following. Whatever they may have once done well will not be remembered (Ezek. 3:20). On the other hand, leaders who manifest the character of love, justice, integrity, humility, and diligence serve the

---

42. Thomas C. Oden, *Classic Christianity: A Systematic Theology* (New York: HarperOne, 2009), 69.
43. Peter J. Leithart, *1 & 2 Kings* (Grand Rapids: Brazos, 2006), 114.

divine purpose for which they were summoned. These are the leaders who transform the world. They are the ones followers will go to the depths for. They are the leaders who are loved.

How does one acquire moral excellence? Scripture is unambiguous. We cannot develop leadership character on our own. It does not reside within. No matter how deep one penetrates the soul, one will find no true north. Instead, if one is honest—brutally honest—one discovers a desperate condition the deeper one goes. David Brooks, in his *Road to Character*, uses the phrase "crooked timber," borrowing a line from Immanuel Kant.[44] We are all fundamentally flawed, having a "weird fascination with sin."[45]

No matter our achievements, the soul runs amiss, and true character escapes our grasp. To put it bluntly, we are all under sin, dead in our transgressions and sins, living off incoherent dreams and illusions (Rom. 3:10–11; Eph. 2:1; Col. 2:13).[46] This is not easy to acknowledge. Dallas Willard, who taught philosophy at USC, writes, "Our social and psychological sciences stand helpless before the terrible things done by human beings, but the warpedness and *wrungness* of the human will is something we cannot admit into 'serious' conversation."[47] Some prefer to believe that—at the core of our being—we are okay, but this is to bypass reality.

In telling the biblical story, God is not hesitant to deconstruct Scripture's major characters, exposing their uncultivated inner lives and their defective leadership.[48] Crooked timber is everywhere; there are no straight arrows. Noah got drunk and exposed himself (Gen. 9:20–22). Abraham caved to domestic pressure and sired a child through an Egyptian maidservant (16:3–4). Moses let his anger get the best of him and lost the privilege to enter the promised land (Num. 20:11–12). Eli

---

44. David Brooks, *The Road to Character* (New York: Penguin, 2015), 10.

45. Ibid., 13.

46. Ibid., 200.

47. Willard, *Renovation of the Heart*, 46. David Brooks, in an op-ed piece, discussing the moral failure of our current age, adds, "Human beings exist at moral dimensions both too lofty and more savage than the contemporary mind normally considers." "This Is Where the Fever Breaks," *New York Times*, January 7, 2021, https://www.nytimes.com/2021/01/07/opinion/capitol-riot-republicans.html.

48. Paul Copan, *Is God a Moral Monster? Making Sense of the Old Testament God* (Grand Rapids: Baker, 2011), 67.

refused to restrain his children, and his sons made themselves contemptible (1 Sam. 3:12–14). Saul was a mix of piety and impulsivity, like a vase with a crack (15:10–11).

This "weird fascination with sin" that began with Adam continued through the account of Israel's kings. David became preoccupied with power and acquisition, allowing passion to get the best of him (2 Sam. 11:1–5). The rest of the story of these rulers is one cycle of rise and fall after another. Even those who were models of faithfulness, like Asa, Jehoshaphat, Hezekiah, and Uzziah, all fell in the end.

The rapid-fire style of the writer in Kings moves from one story of moral failure to another. After a while the narrative becomes what Leithart calls "monotonous and boring."[49] But then, sin is, in the end, tiresome and deadening. The New Testament is another collection of malevolent kings, corrupt priests, and greedy saints. Even the disciples come off as impulsive and prone to faithlessness. Paul was an apostle with gravitas, but there were moments when he seemed to lose his patience and disrupt relationships (Acts 15:37–39). We find ourselves with Job, declaring, "Man is born to trouble as surely as sparks fly upward" (Job 5:7). Something is terribly wrong.

Character failure, both within and outside the Bible, is endemic. "There is no one who does good, not even one" (Ps. 14:3). More, it is intrinsic: "All our righteous acts are like filthy rags" (Isa. 64:6). At work in the hearts of all humanity is sin, a depravity that goes back to the roots of our existence. Back to when a darkness worked to seduce and deceive humankind. Evil intruded into space and time. Yielding to it, humanity is shot through with sin. Genesis 3:1–7 describes a free movement of our first parents that contradicted the disposition to affectionately follow God and carry out his rule.[50]

This explains why character is impossible to build on our own. It accounts for why so many workplaces are dysfunctional—why current books on leadership include titles like *Leadership BS* and *The End of Leadership*. Sin has a blinding effect, causing leaders and would-be leaders to

---

49. Leithart, *1 & 2 Kings*, 110–13.
50. See Marguerite Shuster, *The Fall and Sin: What We Have Become as Sinners* (Grand Rapids: Eerdmans, 2003), 30–36.

stumble in the dark, exhibiting impulsive, dishonest, and arrogant behaviors. Until we come to an admission of our true nature and our helplessness to bring about interior change, we will not be so inclined to seek a solution. Our character will remain flawed and our leadership inept.

Some believe further education and certain regimens will help to address our character deficiencies. More and more people are demanding that educators do a better job of training, and while this is encouraging, it falls short. Unprincipled leadership isn't an issue of ignorance; it's more an issue of denial. Most refuse to accept—or admit—that a more radical evil is at work, one that added courses cannot correct (though we try). As Willard puts it, "We are like farmers who diligently plant crops but cannot admit the existence of weeds and insects and can only think to pour on more fertilizer."[51]

When we're in the presence of God's majesty, our moral corruption is obvious, having no human remedy. The damage is beyond us, our learnings, and our intentions to correct and rebuild. It's more than a distortion of character; it is alienation from God.

No matter our efforts, we need the saving work of Jesus. Only God can do the repair, and he has. God, out of his infinite love for us, has sent his Son to pay the price for our failures and change our character. Everything we do is framed within this act of grace.[52]

We have been invited into a union with him, in which the old heart, with its habits and patterns, died on the cross with him (Rom. 6:6). When he rose and ascended, we rose to new life (Eph. 2:6). This is why the gospel is such good news for everyone, particularly those who lead and aspire to a life of excellent character. It addresses our human condition "appropriately, pertinently, and effectively as nothing else has, does, or can—and in generation after generation, culture after culture, and life after life."[53] Because of Jesus's redemptive work, we are forgiven (Heb. 10:22), reconciled with God

---

51. Willard, *Renovation of the Heart,* 46.
52. Wright, *After You Believe,* 258.
53. Os Guinness, *Prophetic Untimeliness: A Challenge to the Idol of Relevance* (Grand Rapids: Baker, 2005), 13.

(2 Cor. 5:19), set free (Rom. 6:6), and given a new life (1 Cor. 6:11). We can lead knowing we are no longer bound to our past.

Only in receiving Jesus's saving work can a leader become a leader of principle. Otherwise leaders will continue the same bad habits and hang on to the same disordered feelings. They will lead in ways no one will care to remember. Once spiritually healed, we will still need the ongoing work of the Spirit. Even with God's initial saving work, there is no guarantee a leader will become a leader of moral excellence. Though one has been given the authority and power to overcome deep internal flaws, one must commit to ongoing spiritual disciplines.

This journey is lifelong. The biblical virtues will be irrelevant words on a page until they become daily routines. It begins with a thousand small choices, ones requiring effort and concentration, and then on the one-thousand-first time becomes automatic.[54] Character development involves self-denial and rigorous training (1 Cor. 9:24–27; 1 Tim. 4:7). It demands keeping company with the right people (Prov. 13:20). Once you begin to allow others to leech your integrity, they will drain you dry.

One must engage in the constant practice of presenting oneself to God for his purposes (Rom. 12:1). It means times of solitude, meditating and reflecting on God's Word—slowing down to catch up with God. Peterson uses the language of "eaten, chewed, and gnawed" to describe the discipline of reading and meditating.[55] God's revelation will not transform a soul until it enters the soul's bloodstream.

Developing love requires learning God's love and praying for those we might be disinclined to love. Justice will require a deep understanding of divine righteousness and the courage to carry it out. Integrity will require a daily regimen of self-examination, standing before God, acknowledging every weakness, and moving to confession and repentance. Humility will come as we daily acknowledge our insufficiency (John 15:5). Diligence will demand the discipline of ridding oneself of any signs of lethargy, beginning with laziness at the center of the soul.

---

54. Wright, *After You Believe*, chap. 1.
55. Eugene H. Peterson, *Eat This Book* (Grand Rapids: Eerdmans, 2005), 11.

All of this relies on the indwelling power of the Spirit. We will have to keep in step with him if we hope to change (Gal. 5:25). We will need community. Virtues like kindness and compassion and patience cannot be developed in isolation. We will need to live out the one anothers (welcoming, forgiving, encouraging, bearing, spurring, and submitting to one another). The end, the *telos*, is "attaining to the whole measure of the fullness of Christ" (Eph. 4:13).

CONCLUSION

Moral excellence matters, especially when it comes to leadership. Followers may turn a blind eye to a leader's indiscretions, so long as their needs are met, but God does not ignore how one lives. Leaders without gravitas and moral rectitude may have their season, but they eventually become paragons of mediocrity. Without true character, one's life has the propensity to give way to the darkness, to occasional behaviors that are destructive.

Theology also corrects any assumption that moral character can be achieved on one's own. We might exhibit some outward virtues by our own efforts, but apart from Christ the heart remains ruined. Its corruption due to sin has a way of coming to the surface, be it in fits of anger, misguided wants, or self-centered and immature acts. Without a radical change in the interior, leaders lose their bearings, lack the restraints to govern their most intrinsic desires, and lead with little depth.

Coming to Christ and discovering the power of the gospel begins the transformational process. Leadership books might promise alternatives, but there is no other way to real change. Once on the journey of faith, we are on a potter's wheel, where God is forming, shaping, creating in his leaders a growing capacity to show forth his character (Isa. 64:8). Our character will not be perfected this side of eternity. We will have to work out our salvation daily (Phil. 2:12), but in the process there is great promise we will powerfully lead.

The stories of biblical leaders are, in the main, accounts of regression that call for reflection. Unfortunately, contemporary examples of moral failure suggest we are not taking heed. The power of the old life persists, with the capability to take leaders down. But we can—and must—resist. We must also insist that the leaders we choose to follow not neglect the essential habits of character formation. There can be no compromise, no excuse making, no waffling—no overlooking deficiencies as long as the leader performs. A failure of character will lead to more harbor explosions.

A life of character is the first step in becoming a credible leader. There is more, and we will see this in the next two chapters. But first another working model, a leader with moral excellence.

ༀ MOSES ༀ

David Baron wrote a book entitled *Moses on Management: 50 Leadership Lessons from the Greatest Manager of All Time*. It prompted one reviewer to write, "How could someone who took forty years to make an eleven-day journey possibly be the greatest manager of all times?"

It's a fair question. Were Moses here, he might agree. "A management book? Really? If it weren't for Jethro, my leadership would have been synonymous with chaos!" But here's where there is less debate—Moses was a leader of substance, a man of character. It's not that Scripture presents Moses (or any leader except for Jesus) as some polished ideal. His faith had its share of rough edges. Early on, his leadership was raw and unrefined.[56] Challenged to lead, he dithered. Pressed to his limits, he was inclined to doubt. At one point God came close to killing Moses (Ex. 4:24), and at another Moses reproached God with language tantamount to "to hell with it!" There were moments when he just came to the end of himself (Num. 11:15). But these are margins outside the main body of his life.

Over time Moses's character deepened. He became a man of faith. He stepped out when all he could see was desert and all he could follow was a

---

56. Ruth Haley Barton, *Strengthening the Soul of Your Leadership: Seeking God in the Crucible of Ministry* (Downers Grove, IL: InterVarsity Press, 2008), 39.

cloud. He led three million people toward the promised land, with nothing but the promise of God. He rebuked sin, and with great moral fierceness he laid down the law of God. By faith Moses believed the giants would be swallowed up because the Lord was with them (14:9). He pressed on, even though his hopes were delayed forty years. No wonder the book of Hebrews prefaces Moses's life with the words "By faith" (11:24).

Perhaps the most definitive statement of Moses's character is found in Numbers 12:3: "Now Moses was a very humble man, more humble than anyone else on the face of the earth." It's an astounding statement. It seems over the top. If tradition is right, Moses wrote Numbers, and this is Moses describing himself. But this was no proud boast. It was simply a record of who he was, a declaration that he was utterly dependent on God, and it was backed up in countless ways.[57]

We see it the moment Moses was summoned. Moses recognized his limitations. He was raised in a royal court, but he never forgot that he was rescued from the bulrushes as an infant. He identified with the oppressed and was chased out of town. As for leadership, Moses was, by his own admission, "singularly ill-equipped."[58] He never lost his amazement that God would appear to him and call him into service. Moses grew into leadership and accepted early on that leadership meant serving God's purposes. This became his unshakable mission.

From the mundane (dispensing the rules for keeping the camp clean) to the more significant (ten commandments that reveal God's character), Moses humbled himself before God and served his interests. When the Spirit chose to rest on others besides Moses, he was not threatened. Rather Moses wished all God's people were prophets (11:29). When criticized—and he was mercilessly disparaged—he used his energy to carry the people into the presence of God.[59] In most cases he left his defense to the Lord. When God told Moses it was time to go to the mountain, ending Moses's dream to be

---

57. Leonard J. Coppes, "'ana," *Theological Wordbook of the Old Testament* (Chicago: Moody, 1980), 2:682.

58. Eugene H. Peterson, *Christ Plays in Ten Thousand Places: A Conversation in Spiritual Theology* (Grand Rapids: Eerdmans, 2005), 151.

59. Ibid., 142.

in the promised land (27:12), Moses accepted God's will for what it was. It was far more important than his.

Character does not come automatically, and it didn't for Moses. Moses owed a great deal to the desert. If Egypt was his university, the wilderness was graduate school. It was here in solitude and exile that Moses was tested, reduced to the last extreme of helpless nothingness. Here he died to his own strength, forsaking his own plans and surrendering to God's purposes. In the barren he was shaped to be a man of God. In time Moses discovered who he was—and who he was not.

The humility of Moses should not be confused with shyness or softness. Behind a modest heart was steel-like courage. Moses was willing to stand at the fateful intersection between God's people and God, a place that is not for the faint of heart. It required entering God's presence, which has its own risks. Approaching the holy mountain held its own terror (Heb. 12:18–21). But Moses could approach it because his walk was blameless. He met the requirements of those invited to God's holy hill (Ps. 15:1–2).

We know that Moses spent a lot of time with God, allowing God to refine his character. We know because the phrase "the LORD said to Moses" is the most repeated phrase in the book of Numbers. No one had more exposure to God than Moses. In God's presence, Moses prayed for wisdom and pleaded for God's mercy. More than once his intercessions averted God's wrath on the nation (Num. 14:11–16).

By the end, every aspect of Moses's leadership character was God-defined and God-refined, as well as God-saturated. Little wonder his life ends with these words from God: "Since then, no prophet has risen in Israel like Moses, whom the LORD knew face to face. . . . No one has ever shown the mighty power or performed the awesome deeds that Moses did in the sight of all Israel" (Deut. 34:10, 12). One cannot help but pray, "Please, God, raise another Moses, a leader of character for our day!"

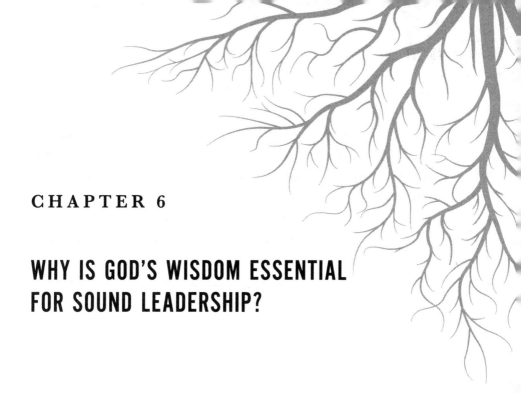

CHAPTER 6

WHY IS GOD'S WISDOM ESSENTIAL FOR SOUND LEADERSHIP?

To reject wisdom as a way of life, or Christ as the
embodiment of wisdom, is not like leaving the dessert
untouched after a good meal; rather, it is like refusing
the very nourishment without which human beings
cannot truly flourish.
—MIROSLAV VOLF

Plenty of leaders have lived on whims and illusions. George De Long was a naval officer who led the ill-fated USS *Jeannette* expedition in the late 1800s. He lived during a time when people were obsessed with exploring the North Pole. In the minds of many, this was the purest of wildernesses, having its own lonely grandeur. There were thick, misty atmospheres and blood-red halos to experience.

But it was more. Explorers like De Long had a fantastical notion that a warm Pacific current extended to the polar cap. One simply had to work through the outer crust to discover a Caribbean-like world teeming with marine life. Under this dome was Shangri-la, where one might even find God's elect.[1]

As it turned out, De Long's voyage was a fool's errand. The ice pack crushed his ship, De Long died of starvation, and many of his crew perished. The arctic is no paradise where life approaches perfection. One will not find Santa Claus and his elves making their toys. It is a barren landscape where numerous adventurers have frozen to death.

The world has always had its share of leaders, some fools, whose eyes "wander to the ends of the earth" after idealistic but unrealistic goals (Prov. 17:24). Rare are those who are sagacious. We might prefer more familiar words like wise, prudent, and understanding. These are leaders who see the world as it really is, and they have a knack for fitting themselves into it.

In his chapter "Sin and Folly," Plantinga describes the wise as those who "tear along the perforated line."[2] They conform to the design of the Designer. They give attention to how life goes—its times and seasons, its patterns and dynamics, its laws, and its rhythms.[3] In contrast to the De Longs of the world, wise leaders live with the sober realization that things are not always as they seem. As the proverb puts it, "There is a way that appears to be right, but in the end it leads to death" (14:12).

Wisdom is a leadership imperative. Few, if any, leaders would disagree. Who wants to be known as someone dim-witted, a hapless leader whose follies lead to one disastrous consequence after another? Most can see that operating with some common sense is necessary, especially in these loud, binary times. What good is an education if you haven't developed some mastery of life?

But how does one become wise? Where is wisdom to be found? What are our cultural assumptions?

Some leaders turn to Himalayan guides, ancient Greek philosophers,

---

1. Hampton Sides, *In the Kingdom of Ice: The Grand and Terrible Polar Voyage of the USS* Jeannette (New York: Anchor, 2014), loc. 891 of 1077, Kindle.

2. Cornelius Plantinga Jr., *Not the Way It's Supposed to Be: A Breviary of Sin* (Grand Rapids: Eerdmans, 1995), 115.

3. Cornelius Plantinga Jr., *Reading for Preaching: The Preacher in Conversation with Storytellers, Biographers, Poets, and Journalists* (Grand Rapids: Eerdmans, 2013), 70.

or self-help books. Most draw wisdom out of life experiences. In his *Lead with Wisdom*, Mark Strom writes, "Wisdom is not to be found in a database; it grows out of the experience of living the life of the human herd and absorbing the lessons which that experience inevitably teaches us about who we are."[4] The wise leader is the one who observes certain patterns:

- Shut mouths catch no flies.
- A large chair does not make a king.
- Too many cooks spoil the broth.
- If you take big paces, you leave large spaces.

The good news is that one doesn't have to live seventy-plus years to acquire some understanding. According to Robert Fulghum, some of the most helpful wisdom is learned in kindergarten: Play fair. Share. Don't take things that aren't yours. Don't hit people. Put things back where you found them. Clean up your own mess.

Ironically, kids who heed these rules end up acting more grown-up than many grown-ups.

Some contemporary writers, like Jordan Peterson, offer their own set of operating rules, practical wisdom, for an untutored generation.[5] Other contemporary writers like Edith Hall and Eric Weiner point us back to early philosophers and their love of wisdom (*Aristotle's Way: How Ancient Wisdom Can Change Your Life* and *The Socrates Express*). In his *Practical Wisdom*, psychologist Barry Schwartz cautions, however, that there is no recipe, formula, or set of techniques for acquiring wisdom.[6] Wisdom is disarmingly human: always within reach yet somehow elusive.[7] A fair amount can be learned through reading various philosophers, but it is not some mysterious gift owned by a handful of sages—white-haired wizards.

---

4. Mark Strom, *Lead with Wisdom: How Wisdom Transforms Good Leaders into Great Leaders* (Milton: Wiley, 2013), loc. 481 of 7127, Kindle.

5. Jordan Peterson, *12 Rules for Life: An Antidote to Chaos* (Toronto: Random House, 2018).

6. Barry Schwartz, *Practical Wisdom* (New York: Riverhead, 2010), 8.

7. Strom, *Lead with Wisdom*, loc. 465 of 7127, Kindle.

More than anything else, wisdom is gained through one's own experience, empathy, and intellect.

Turn to Old Testament scholars of wisdom, like Gerhard von Rad, and you will find they too put a premium on life experience as a main source of wisdom. The first sentence of his *Wisdom in Israel* reads, "No one would be able to live even for a single day without incurring appreciable harm if he could not be guided by wide practical experience."[8] Encounters with life teach a leader to understand events, foresee reactions, and apply the appropriate resources.

Yet, despite all of the wisdom resources available and all of the years of accumulated experiences, much of society is in a wisdom deficit. Lance Morrow's recent article, "You Are Living in the Golden Age of Stupidity" is an indictment of our age. We have lost our bearings at the highest levels. He writes, "Stupidity is entitled to no moral standing whatever, and yet it sits in a place of honor at the tables of the mighty; it blows in their ears and whispers promises."[9] Morrow adds, "It's a short ride from stupidity to madness. Soon people aren't quite people anymore; they are cartoons and categories . . . They engage in what amounts to an Oedipal rebellion against reality itself."[10]

Survey the landscape, and it is clear that many leaders are not tearing along the perforated line. The chaos, which is inherent in life (but made worse by a growing relativism), is leading to a shortage of good judgment.[11] This is particularly evident in political, corporate, and ministry worlds. Leaders are banging their shins and scraping their elbows on a regular basis.[12] Too many are making idiotic decisions, overpromising, and screwing up. They chase after fantasies and turn into flakes. Lacking self-awareness, an increasing number are like roosters taking credit for the

---

8. Gerhard von Rad, *Wisdom in Israel* (Nashville: Abingdon, 1972), 3

9. Lance Morrow, "You Are Living in the Golden Age of Stupidity," *Wall Street Journal*, August 29, 2021, https://www.wsj.com/articles/idiocy-stupidity-afghanistan-covid-vaccine-maga-trump -civility-privacy-common-sense-11630271666.

10. Ibid.

11. In the introduction to Peterson's *12 Rules for Life*, Norman Doidge speaks to the foolishness of our age (xvi–xvii).

12. Plantinga, *Not the Way It's Supposed to Be*, 119.

sun's rising. After watching yet another leadership failure, one national columnist could not but describe a major political leader's descent as falling from guiding father figure to authoritarian nincompoop.[13]

What explains this? Part of it might be the human tendency to observe life experiences but refuse to learn from them. Lots of leaders suffer a collective amnesia. They have this rich repertoire of patterns enabling them to recognize new situations and new problems as familiar, but they forget.[14] Like fools, they have to learn the same lessons again and again.

It could also be the particular wisdom many have chosen to embrace. Much of our practical wisdom tends to flow from self-love and run into self-interest.[15] It goes only so far, like cold remedies that address the symptoms rather than the cause. In our cleverness we tell ourselves we are the answer to all our problems. We heed the voice, "You just need to invest in you, believe in you, trust in you, and prioritize you." The result of such mindless advice is a leadership that cannot discern the lines between virtue and vice, wisdom and folly. When this happens, leaders eventually devolve and end up a shell of who they were. This is what folly does. It hollows out a leader.

We have to find a better way to wisdom. We have to find a better wisdom, one that goes beyond the sort that allows God only a crowning touch to what has already been settled by humanity. Ours is becoming a leaderless and decadent society, in which the wisdom we once revered has disappeared. We are left with "a territory of darkness, a posthuman landscape" that is "stuck, tired, distracted, repetitive, irritable, bored, boring, or just 'comfortably numb.'"[16] Standard answers will not solve the growing chaos. It's not enough to create a set of rules and abide by them. Rules, unleavened by judgment, can be obtuse and even dangerous.[17]

---

13. Peggy Noonan, "Andrew Coumo Plots His Survival," *Wall Street Journal*, March 18, 2021, https://www.wsj.com/articles/andrew-cuomo-plots-his-survival-11616108915.

14. Elkhonon Goldberg, *The Wisdom Paradox: How Your Mind Can Grow Stronger as Your Brain Grows Older* (New York: Gotham, 2005), 89.

15. Stephen Charnock, *The Existence and Attributes of God* (Grand Rapids: Baker, 1979), 601.

16. Daniel E. Burns, "Our Post-Pandemic Decadence," review of *The Decadent Society: America Before and After the Pandemic,* by Ross Douthat, *National Review*, July 12, 2021, https://www.nationalreview.com/magazine/2021/07/12/our-post-pandemic-decadence/.

17. Barry Schwartz, *Practical Wisdom* (New York: Riverhead, 2010), 118.

GOD'S NECESSARY WISDOM FOR LEADERSHIP

There is a better wisdom for leading. Incomparably better. Proverbs refers to God's wisdom as supreme, one worthy of pursuing no matter the cost (4:7). It alone enables a leader to be faithful to reality and effective in exercising judgment.

Preparing the church's future leaders, Jesus made it clear that featherbrains need not apply. The world is too dangerous. His warning still stands: "I am sending you out like sheep among wolves" (Matt. 10:16). The words are unnerving. Sheep are not known for taking down wolves. The metaphor suggests utter helplessness, setting up this command: "Therefore be as shrewd as snakes and as innocent as doves."

Such wisdom, he is telling us, has its own power. The Old Testament wisdom books affirm this. "Wisdom," writes Qohelet, "is better than weapons of war" (Eccl. 9:18). By divine wisdom war is waged (Prov. 24:6). Snakes and doves trump wolves. So to navigate through this life, those who intend "to save a city" (see Eccl. 9:15) must have a certain savvy. They will need to be shrewd, snakelike sheep. In a world out of step with God's intentions, where leading can be a perilous assignment, God exhorts leaders to be both astute and blameless. Carry yourself with a dovelike innocence but be smart. In some cases be cunning, just as God is. He shows himself pure to the pure and shrewd to the crooked (Ps. 18:26). God can match the faithless in the capacity to throw a curve ball or bend a free kick.[18]

Reading the account of God and Ahab in 1 Kings 22:19–22, Leithart concludes, "Yahweh is the ultimate trickster that outfoxes all human attempts to escape him. Yahweh is not only cunning. He is transcendently, infinitely cunning."[19] He requires something of this in those he summons to lead (Josh. 8:1–29; 1 Sam. 16:14).

In the parable of the shrewd manager, Jesus urged his followers to be like a calculating businessman, cleverer than those of the world (Luke 16:8). God expects those he calls into leadership to be shrewd when it comes to

---

18. John Goldingay, *Psalms: Volume 1: Psalms 1–41* (Grand Rapids: Baker, 2006), 270.
19. Peter Leithart, *1 & 2 Kings* (Grand Rapids: Brazos, 2006), 164.

strategic thinking, long-term planning, and implementing goals. Leaders have to be astute when dealing with adversaries. Too often, however, Christians are seen as naive, simplistic, and gullible. Some believers get the "innocent as doves" part down but hesitate to act with shrewdness.

It is not that God commends dishonesty or ungodly aggressiveness. Gentleness and humility are necessary to leading, but these are not the same as being naive and indiscriminate. One can be kind and at the same time be sharp-witted. The admonition of Matthew 10:16 tells us that there are times when the two complement one another.

The call to possess this wisdom pervades the pages of Scripture. All theology is wisdom, and once this is recognized, the whole Bible becomes wisdom—"searching, finding, articulating, living."[20] God's intent is to cast a vision of what constitutes a wise and ordered life. To miss this is to miss one of Scripture's most significant themes. In his *Jesus the Great Philosopher*, Pennington goes so far as to conclude, "The point of the whole Bible is to give wisdom that leads to life in his kingdom."[21] Here is what one discovers:

God's Wisdom Is beyond Us

Like other wisdom writers, Old and New Testament sages paid attention to life and how it works. It was their profession to explore and hunt for divine wisdom. Their findings, put in poetic verses, stand as mini dissertations. Sages like Solomon and Agur distilled years of experience into two or three lines, giving the leader, as McKane puts it, "a comprehensive competence which enables man to steer the whole of his life surely."[22] Read Proverbs, and you will gain practical advice on everything from entering into contracts to waking people up (6:1–5; 27:14).

Unlike the wisdom of this world, however, one finds that the wisdom of God is not inspired by philosophical theory. It is more than a set of

---

20. Scot McKnight, *Five Things Biblical Scholars Wish Theologians Knew* (Downers Grove, IL: InterVarsity Press, 2021), 10.

21. Jonathan T. Pennington, *Jesus the Great Philosopher: Rediscovering the Wisdom Needed for the Good Life* (Grand Rapids: Brazos, 2020), 51.

22. William McKane, *Proverbs: A New Approach* (Philadelphia: Westminster, 1970), 20.

theoretical contemplates or practical rules for success.[23] Some may view God's wisdom as "a long list of platitudinous advice."[24] But look further, and you will find that it is not a species of human wisdom. The wisdom of Scripture transcends this world.

Given this, the wisdom of God is not easy to systematize or categorize. It has a depth that cannot be plumbed (Rom. 11:33). It is beyond narration, too high for a fool. When the foolish attempt to employ God's proverbs for their purposes, they can do great damage (Prov. 26:7–9). Juxtaposing one's buffoonish behavior with divine proverbs is like putting firearms in the hand of a child.[25]

When Tozer wrote his theology of God, one senses he took language and stretched it as high as vocabulary could go. This is most obvious in his chapter on divine wisdom. He wrote, "When Christian theology declares that God is wise, it means vastly more than it says or can say, for it tries to make a comparatively weak word bear an incomprehensible plenitude of meaning that threatens to tear it apart and crush it under the sheer weight of the idea."[26] No wonder an attempt to do a theological analysis of divine wisdom can feel so overwhelming.

Proverbs, one of divine wisdom's principal voices, opens by telling us that divine wisdom has a vastness that cannot be captured in one word. There is a piling on of terms in 1:2–4, what Von Rad refers to as a "stereometric way of thinking"[27] and Kidner describes as a "rainbow of constituent colors."[28] Internalizing the wisdom represented by these words, a leader will manifest multiple dimensions of sagacity: discipline, under-standing, prudence, knowledge, discretion, discernment. All are critical to leadership success.

---

23. Michael Horton, *The Christian Faith: A Systematic Theology for Pilgrims on the Way* (Grand Rapids: Zondervan, 2011), 104.

24. William H. Willimon, *Pastor: The Theology and Practice of Ordained Ministry* (Nashville: Abingdon, 2016), 255–56.

25. Bruce K. Waltke, *The Book of Proverbs: Chapters 15–31* (Grand Rapids: Eerdmans, 2015), 353.

26. A. W. Tozer, *The Knowledge of the Holy* (New York: HarperCollins, 1961), 65.

27. Von Rad, *Wisdom in Israel*, 13.

28. Derek Kidner, *Proverbs: An Introduction and Commentary* (Downers Grove, IL: InterVarsity Press, 1984), 36.

Why Is God's Wisdom Essential for Sound Leadership?

Part of what distinguishes this otherworldly wisdom is that God designed these capacities to operate in the moral realm of righteousness, justice, and equity (v. 3). The wisdom of God is about shrewdness as well as ethics, cleverness as well as character. It is living with God on his terms.

Compare this with any other concept of wisdom, and you will find it shines brighter because there is no distracting plurality of gods and demons, no influence of magic, and no cultic licensing of immorality to muffle the voice of conscience.[29] There are false wisdoms that market their wares, but they mislead and destroy (9:13–18; Isa. 47:10). They have all the staying power of sandcastles at high tide. In God's wisdom, there are no impurities that compromise its message, no proverbs that are eventually washed out to sea. This is why leaders from around the world were drawn to the wisdom of Solomon (1 Kings 4:29–34). They could see that it was in a class all its own. Leaders like the queen of Sheba became converts, "won by Solomon's sapiential evangelism."[30]

When God's Son entered the world, he came as a sage speaking in similar sapiential language (parables, riddles, proverbs). But this was more than speech patterns that could be compared to the material in Proverbs, Ecclesiastes, Wisdom of Solomon, and Sirach. This was wisdom in the flesh.[31] One wiser than Solomon had stepped onstage (Matt. 12:42). The words and acts of Jesus personified wisdom (1 Cor. 1:30), for in him are hidden all the treasures of wisdom (Col. 2:2–3).

Leaders who give themselves to emulating Jesus and the wisdom of God will find that it makes the wisdom of the world's experts seem rather anemic.[32] Even foolish! This is God's assessment, conveyed through the apostle Paul (1 Cor. 1:20; Col. 2:9–10). The wisdom of God does not come to nothing, like so much of the world's wisdom (1 Cor. 2:6). No other wisdom can compete with his (Prov. 21:30).

---

29. Ibid., 21.

30. Leithart, *1 & 2 Kings*, 78.

31. Ben Witherington III, *Biblical Theology: The Convergence of the Canon* (New York: Cambridge University Press, 2019), 77.

32. Tremper Longman III, *The Fear of the Lord Is Wisdom: A Theological Introduction to Wisdom in Israel* (Grand Rapids: Baker, 2017), 263.

God's Wisdom Enables Effective Leadership

Divine wisdom is written for all, but it is aimed at present and future decision-makers. The setting of Proverbs and Ecclesiastes was the royal court, what Michael Fox refers to as "the decisive locus of Wisdom creativity."[33] Wisdom was conveyed through God's king and copied by those who served at his command (Prov. 25:1). Hence, while God's wisdom is critical for everyone, it is especially applicable to those who lead.

What happens when leaders decide to make God's revealed wisdom a life pursuit, a daily discipline? What characterizes their lives and leadership?

Wise Leaders Are In Step with Reality

If leaders meditate on the myriad of proverbs, allegories, mini-narratives, and riddles found in the Wisdom Books, they will question ventures that promise a pot of gold. They will come to grips with their limitations and reject illusions of grandeur. The Lord is the maker of all, rich and poor, powerful and powerless, and this reality has a flattening effect (Prov. 22:2). Unless God aids our reason, we lack understanding (30:2). Wisdom has a way of bringing us down from our self-constructed perch and away from our grandiose schemes.

The school of wisdom intends to help leaders reckon with an all-embracing order and an inscrutable power for life. No human ingenuity can discover these on its own.[34] There is an inescapable cause and effect: whatever one sows, one will inevitably reap. Sow righteousness and receive a reward; sow trouble, and your life will be filled with grief (11:18; 12:21). If leaders are too sluggish to consider emerging opportunities, there will be no future (10:4). Dishonest gains will not lead to long-term profits (v. 2). If you build an empire at the sacrifice of relationships, you will live a lonely existence (Eccl. 4:7–8). This is how it goes with life.

The reality-based leader will spot other patterns. Life has an ebb and flow. There will be gains and losses, high points and low points, booms

---

33. Michael V. Fox, *Proverbs 1–9* (New Haven: Yale University Press, 2000), 10.

34. Walter Brueggemann, *Genesis: Interpretation; A Bible Commentary for Teachings and Preaching* (Louisville: Westminster John Knox, 1986), 317.

and busts, bull markets and bear markets, high approval ratings and low approval ratings. We won't always hit home runs. A season of congregational growth is often followed by a season of loss. Leadership will sometimes seem like a zero-sum game (3:1–8). Like the sage, a leader ponders, "What is the gain?" (cf. v. 9). Those of us who lead will sometimes wonder if our leading has made any difference. Wisdom urges us to anticipate such moments and hold on to what ultimately counts.

The wisdom of God teaches that there is more to life than meets the eye. God has planted eternity in the heart (v. 11), an act Roland Murphy describes as "divine sabotage."[35] Leaders who live in the real world know there is something, someone, beyond the here and now. God has placed us in this middle zone, where we live between time and time without end, between impermanence and permanence, incompletion and completion, finiteness and infiniteness, brevity and eternity. Efforts to understand the past and probe the future are subverted by "heavenly-imposed limitations."[36] The wise come to grips and cope with this. Wisdom calls it trust (Prov. 3:9–10).

The prudent realize that while life and one's leadership should be approached with a certain urgency, one should also help one's followers to relax and seize the moments God serves up (Eccl. 5:18–20). Wisdom tells us that whatever we think we control is an illusion. We lead for only so long. Every leader has a shelf life. Today's affirmation of a leader is tomorrow's rejection; time and familiarity take their toll (4:13–16). Reality says to hold loosely to your position and seize fervently the time you have left.

Leaders who live in reality are also aware of the effects of praise. Applause comes with being onstage. It can be an encouragement; it can also be one of a leader's greatest tests (Prov. 27:21). A leader can turn approval into self-congratulation. Being at the center can lead to self-absorption. The constant admiration can lead one to make outrageous promises. It can deceive one into hanging on too long. All of these have their price.

---

35. Roland Murphy, *Ecclesiastes*, WBC (Dallas: Word, 2015), 256, 39.
36. Dan Loy, "The Divine Sabotage: An Exegetical and Theological Study of Ecclesiastes 3," *Conspectus* 5, no. 1, (March 2008): 116.

Realists realize that pride is behind many of our misbehaviors. It's the mother hen under which all other sins hatch. Adulation is addictive. Unchecked, the ego inflates to undue proportions. Arrogance overlooks realities and prompts an affair with self. This is the surest way to lose God's favor and forfeit the honor he wants to give a leader (16:5). Egoism is the precursor to shame, embarrassment, conflict, and collapse (v. 18). If there is to be any praise, wisdom says, let it come from others (27:2). The wisest of leaders know they aren't as essential as they imagine. It is God who directs the heart and secures the victory (21:1). It's easy for people to assume it's all about the leader, but everything ultimately comes from God (29:26).

Wise Leaders Collaborate on the Essentials

Nothing in divine wisdom glorifies stand-alone leadership, the kind that prefers isolation and independent decision making. Still, leaders tend to have this heroic notion that imagines themselves as rugged self-starters, self-reliant players.[37] But operating with this kind of separation, according to the wisdom of Proverbs, is to play the fool (18:1).

Shrewd leaders acknowledge that it is impossible to lead by their own wisdom. It is folly to bypass wise counsel—even if one is certain he has things figured out. Proverbs instructs, "Surely you need guidance to wage war, and victory is won through many advisers" (24:6). Unlike the fool, who finds no pleasure in understanding, the wise build teams and seek out guidance before deciding (18:2, 15). Many of a leader's strategic moves are complex and many-sided. It is necessary to search things out, looking at possibilities from multiple angles. It is what keeps a leader sharp (27:17). It also defines a leader's glory. There is something remarkable about being an inquisitive leader, one who digs for truth and seeks after knowledge (25:2).

Failure to capitalize on the wisdom of others is folly, but it is utter madness to go it alone without God. The wise leader makes it a daily practice to lay one's whole life and plans before God. The wise know that while

---

37. See my chapter on teams in *Missing Voices: Learning to Lead beyond Our Horizons* (London: Langham, 2019), 157–85.

they have their dreams, it is foolish to set out on their own. It is mindless to attempt anything apart from God. Ultimately, it is God who sets things in motion (16:1, 9). God sees out into the future as well as deep into the heart. He knows our motives (v. 2). At the end of the day, only the fool goes with one's gut. The wise look beyond themselves and their feelings and ask, "Does this reflect divine wisdom?" If so, they step out in faith and trust God (3:5–6; 16:3). If not, they wait, knowing that God specializes in placing himself where paths meet and decisions must be made (8:2). Leaders who lean on themselves invariably take the wrong fork.

God imparts his wisdom through Scripture, through circumstances, through other people and even through nature (Ps. 19:1–4). When we lose our way, wisdom tells us to go to the ant (Prov. 6:6). When we lose our stride and our courage, God may direct us to consider the lion and learn what it means to lead an army (30:30–31). When we keep making the same mistakes, God may point us to a dog and its revolting tendency to return to its vomit (26:11). When we are big on promising but slow in delivering, God may speak to us through the clouds that pass by without providing the needed and anticipated rain (25:14).

In sum, leaders are not called to become like islands, figuring out leadership on their own. Their strength of wisdom is in their willingness to humble themselves to observe, learn, pray, listen, collaborate—and then lead.

Wise Leaders Exhibit Self-Discipline and Self-Control

Command and restraint are the evidence of wisdom at work. These make for exceptional leaders, though not everyone agrees. In their book *Leaders Who Lust*, Kellerman and Pittinsky speak of a "symbiosis between lust and leadership" that causes some leaders to rise above others. "It is leaders who lust who mostly make history."[38] Ruled by their passions, they achieve a certain excellence. Leadership that seeks balance, control, and moderation tends to foster mediocrity.

---

38. Barbara Kellerman and Todd L. Pittinsky, *Leaders Who Lust: Power, Money, Sex, Success, Legitimacy, Legacy* (Cambridge: Cambridge University Press, 2020), 205.

The wisdom of God, however, does not associate powerful drives, insatiable appetites, and overpowering needs with discerning leadership. These are more consistent with folly. Those whose eyes are never satisfied rank right down there with death and destruction (Prov. 27:20). In contrast, wise leaders keep their desires in proper order and proportion.[39] They hold their temper in check (15:18). They set boundaries and steer clear of sexual temptations, knowing that the alternative is death (5:1–23). If they are prone to cave to their appetites, they put a knife to their throats (23:2).

Leaders are often out in front, so their words must be careful and cautious. The wise put a lid on their speech, knowing that the tongue has influence out of proportion to its size (James 3:5). Lips that open wide lead to ruin (Prov. 13:3). This requires a careful watch of the heart. The wise do a daily interior examination, looking for cracks. The springs of life flow from the heart (4:23 ESV). Small acts of folly lead to consequences. One simple misjudgment can ruin a lifetime of leadership (Eccl. 10:1).

The overwhelming message of Proverbs is that the shrewd stay in their lanes, within the boundary lines God has established (15:21). They take seriously the admonition, "Let your eyes look straight ahead; fix your gaze directly before you. Give careful thought to the paths for your feet and be steadfast in all your ways" (4:25–26). Giving oneself over to one's lusts might impress at first, but let's be honest: leaders driven by their drives tend to overreach, cross boundaries, and cover their discretions with dishonesty. Integrity and discipline, however, are what help a leader find one's way. They keep one from going out of bounds and caving to one's pleasures (11:3). People are counting on a leader not to compromise. Those who stay true to their calling will bring stability and flourishment, lifting a nation (29:4).

Let's pause and reflect. Given wisdom's poetic form, we need to do this often. So far we have discovered that God's wisdom is beyond us yet accessible. It is essential, as opposed to optional, to sound leadership. We

---

39. See Karen Swallow Prior, *On Reading Well* (Grand Rapids: Brazos, 2018), 51–68.

come to grips with life as it is. What we discover next is the most significant truth yet.

God's Wisdom Begins with a Holy Fear

The fear of God stands as the central thread tying the Wisdom Books together. It is the first and controlling principle of understanding (1:7; 9:10).[40] Holy reverence is the gate to gaining the ability to discern. It is the customs station before one can enter into the world of God's wisdom (Ps. 111:10).[41] Without a holy fear, we degrade proverbs to self-centered promises, tailoring them to our specifications without any room for trembling.

More than enabling a leader to acquire wisdom, the fear of God trains one for wisdom.[42] Proverbs declares, "The fear of the LORD is the instruction for wisdom" (15:33 NASB). We discover that the overwhelmingness of God is both the source and the substance, the cause and the effect, the first day's introduction and the curriculum for the course. It is the program of study for life. The fear of God is not a stage one passes through. It is both prerequisite and destination, theme and essence.

The writer of Ecclesiastes affirms the statements in Proverbs. For Qohelet, the fear of God is anything but an afterthought. The whole book is a journey to the conclusion that the fear of God is the essence of wisdom. The writer takes us down the road of life, following various narcissistic side paths that leaders fall prey to. This is the precursor to the book *Leaders Who Lust*, only the writer tells us these paths bring one to the end of oneself (Eccl. 2:1–11). James K. A. Smith describes the dead end this way: "The wandering, ravenous soul consumes everything and ends up with nothing: no identity, no center, no self.'"[43]

At the end of the line, only one thing counts: "Now all has been heard; here is the conclusion of the matter: Fear God and keep his commandments,

---

40. Fox describes the fear of God as "the sphere within which wisdom is possible and can be realized, the precondition for both wisdom and ethical behavior," *Proverbs 1–9*, 69.

41. Longman, *The Fear of the Lord*, 12.

42. Von Rad, *Wisdom in Israel*, 66.

43. James K. A. Smith, *On the Road with Saint Augustine: A Real-World Spirituality for Restless Hearts* (Grand Rapids: Brazos, 2019), 12.

for this is the duty of all mankind" (12:13). Fearing God is the end of the matter, the final resolution of life's complications. It is literally "the whole of man."[44]

These words underscore that the fear of God is the most important of all realities, the very soul of godliness, and the central, distinguishing mark of wisdom.[45] It is the essential skill of living—and leading. There is no beginning in the enterprise of wisdom without having the fear of God. There is no real leading without fearing God. The psalmist underscores this: "You kings, be wise; be warned, you rulers of the earth. Serve the Lord with fear and celebrate his rule with trembling" (Ps. 2:10–11).

What is claimed in Proverbs and Ecclesiastes was pointed out earlier in Job. To be wise is to fear God (28:28). It's notable that out of these words the book of Job then give one of the more exhaustive accounts of leadership wholeness (29:1–24). Among the attributes of a God-fearing leader are an intimate walk with God, a path drenched with cream, a life of honor in the highest places of leadership, a compassion for the poor, a life characterized by righteousness and justice, a fierceness to confront evil, and a determination to guide others (vv. 1–24). The chapter then closes with this summation of Job's leadership: "I chose the way for them and sat as their chief; I dwelt as a king among his troops; I was like one who comforts mourners" (v. 25).

Little wonder one commentator refers to this section of Job as "one of the most important documents in Scripture for the study of Israelite ethics."[46] Job 29 is the fear of God fleshed out and Job himself is the exemplar.

Again, stepping back, we have found in these sections that the wisdom that comes from God is different. It takes us beyond ourselves. It frames all of leadership. It tells us what true wisdom looks like in the life of an effective leader. But how does one gain this wisdom? This leads to the final discovery.

---

44. Derek Kidner, *A Time to Mourn and a Time to Dance* (Downers Grove, IL: InterVarsity Press, 1976), 107.

45. Other commentaries speak of the fear of the Lord as the basic datum in the wisdom enterprise, the most distinctive feature in theological wisdom, the central focus of wisdom, and the queen of all the rules of steering.

46. Francis I. Andersen, *Job* (Downers Grove, IL: InterVarsity Press, 1976), 230.

God's Wisdom Is Gained Only by a Divine-Human Partnership

There is an otherness to God's wisdom that makes it, at first, seem inaccessible. Job 28 describes God's wisdom as unsearchable; trying to obtain it is like being on a hike, never finding the trailhead, and ending up in a deep forest. The writer of the book of Job asks, "Where then does wisdom come from? Where does understanding dwell? It is hidden from the eyes of every living thing" (vv. 20–21).

Is there any hope of leaders finding divine wisdom? Do we stumble through life, happy to pick up scraps of wisdom here and there? Could it be this wisdom is too wild, incomprehensive, and deep, transcendent, before and above all things?[47] What is certain is that leaders who hope to be wise must be wise in the search.[48] There are rules, and the first rule is to kneel and ask (Prov. 2:3). Petitioning God to acquire wisdom is where the pursuit begins.

Wisdom comes to those leaders who are honest enough to admit that wisdom is not found on their own. They will have to humble themselves in holy fear and approach God in total dependence. Asking will demand a certain desperation. Leaders will have to "cry aloud" for wisdom (v. 3).

Leaders will have to be tenacious. The first nine chapters of Proverbs are a single sustained exhortation to seek the skill of living.[49] It will be an arduous, lifelong task (v. 4). There is no downloading of wisdom without strenuous effort.[50] The book of Job likens it to an expedition searching the deepest recesses of the earth for valuable ore.[51] Into the cavernous deep we dig, admitting the vastness of its depths (Job 28:12–22). It will require our best efforts, our greatest resources (Prov. 4:4–7).

Along the way, we find, however, that wisdom has also been searching for us. Crying out for us (9:3). This amazes me. It also shatters any illusion that the gaining of wisdom is one-sided, that it has been placed entirely

---

47. Bruce K. Waltke, *The Book of Proverbs: Chapters 1–15* (Grand Rapids: Eerdmans, 2004), 78.
48. Leithart, *1 & 2 Kings*, 77.
49. J. I. Packer, *Knowing God* (London: Hodder and Stoughton, 1973), 90.
50. Longman, *The Fear of the Lord*, 119.
51. James L. Crenshaw, *Old Testament Wisdom: An Introduction* (Louisville: Westminster John Knox, 1998), 48.

within the sphere of human effort.[52] The pursuit is less about personally grasping wisdom and more about opening our lives to receive what God wants to graciously give.[53] If we find divine wisdom, it is because God has chosen to intersect where other voices vie for our attention and share it with us. In the end, it is the Lord who gives wisdom; from his mouth come knowledge and understanding (2:6).

CONCLUSION

Any leader who hopes to lead—and lead well—must reckon with these words: "By me kings reign and rulers issue decrees that are just; by me princes govern, and nobles—all who rule on earth" (Prov. 8:15–16). Only by possessing divine wisdom does a leader have the necessary skills of statecraft, the expertise for earthy, hardheaded procedures and negotiations.[54] These are the rare leaders who instill confidence and compel people to follow.

Divine wisdom enables one to pilot one's soul in a world full of conundrums and mysteries that are well beyond the human capacity to lead. It regulates and balances all the other skills necessary for leading. It empowers a leader to discern reality, see the actual beyond the observable. With this wisdom a leader is able to conform to the created order, cope with enigma and adversity, tear down destructive strongholds, and enhance the lives of those they are summoned to lead.[55]

By divine insight, political leaders can see with greater precision the geopolitical landscape. Corporate heads can grasp where they are going. Generals can discern how things work in God's inscrutable deployment of creation.[56] Religious leaders are able to fit into the creative order as God intended. And explorers have realistic dreams. No wonder it is impossible

---

52. Von Rad, *Wisdom in Israel*, 57.
53. Waltke, *The Book of Proverbs: Chapter 1–15*, 223.
54. McKane, *Proverbs*, 347.
55. Waltke, *The Book of Proverbs: Chapters 1–15*, 77.
56. Walter Brueggemann, *Theology of the Old Testament: Testimony, Dispute, Advocacy* (Minneapolis: Fortress, 2005), 465.

to put a value on wisdom. Man cannot comprehend its worth. It cannot be bought for all the money in the world (Job 28:12–19).

Without the wisdom of God, one cannot lead well. In Strom's *Lead with Wisdom*, he compares leadership to the task of laying bricks. To hold the wall together, a leader needs the mortar of wisdom.[57] Wisdom, along with character, are essential to leading. Who wants to be led by an empty suit or, on the other hand, a mindless wag? We need both, though to be fully credible one also needs the particular skills (competence) to lead. This is where we go next. But first, a look at one of the wisest who ever lived.

ᘔᘔ SOLOMON ᘔᘔ

Solomon is an up-and-comer, surrounded by lickspittles and handlers who are both ambitious and ruthless. With their help, his authority as king is firmly established. Behind all of this political maneuvering is God. Solomon is his man (1 Chron. 29:1). Though it would appear Solomon successfully established himself, it is God who made him great (2 Chron. 1:1). This is true of all leaders.

Solomon will pour himself into numerous construction projects—a temple, a palace, a wall. International politics will be high on his list of priorities. Alliances are being formed, avenues of trade are being opened, and military liaisons are being created. He will lead Israel into a golden era. He will reach the apex of power.[58] Yes, taxes will be outrageous, and a military draft will be compulsory, but people will live in peace (1 Kings 4:7–20). After all, his name is linked with shalom. Under Solomon all the troops will come home.

But first things first. Solomon has an appointment with God—or rather God has a predetermined meeting with Solomon. Gibeon is the highest of the high places. It's where the people worship and where the political order takes shape. More important, it's the place of the tabernacle, where God is

---

57. Strom, *Lead with Wisdom*, loc. 6293 of 7127, Kindle.

58. Walter Brueggemann, *Truth Speaks to Power: The Countercultural Nature of Scripture* (Louisville: Westminster John Knox, 2013), 43.

and where God speaks to Solomon. Sometime in the evening, when it is just Solomon and God, God says, "Ask for whatever you want me to give you" (2 Chron. 1:7). It is the way of God—our asking shapes our receiving.

It does not take long for Solomon to answer. He is young and ready to take on the world. He has the right bloodlines, a great network, and a nation looking to him to lead. More than this, he has a sense that God is saying, "This is yours to do." But Solomon knows something he is probably hesitant to tell others—he is in way over his head. He does not really have it together. He can see his inadequacies and shortcomings, not to mention the temptations that are beginning to plague his darker side. He is aware that his life could fall into the dark side of leading, that he could become obsessed with money, power, and women. He has already made an alliance with Egypt, one of the world's superpowers, cementing it with a marriage to Pharaoh's daughter (1 Kings 3:1).

Like Moses, who said to God, "Who am I that I should go?" (Ex. 3:11), or Jeremiah, who admitted, "I do not know how to speak" (Jer. 1:6), Solomon expresses his own sense of inadequacy: "I do not know how to go out or come in" (1 Kings 3:7 ESV). It sounds almost childlike—because it is. More than anything, Solomon wants wisdom. Leading is a craft, an art, and Solomon needs to learn its skill. As Leithart put it, Solomon craves to be a "royal Bezelel," an artist who was earlier filled with wisdom to make artistic designs (Ex. 31:1–5).[59]

Solomon could have focused on the lesser things, immersing himself in the superficial trappings of kingship. But what does it matter to have too much to live with and too little to live for? What matters in this moment is that Solomon became what God had made him to be—a leader. What's required to govern is a listening ear, a discerning heart, and a judicious skill.

Wisdom is the royal virtue par excellence. It's what enables kings to discern reality and stay within the boundaries. Little wonder leaders from other realms began signing up to attend his leadership conferences and hear his wisdom. They discovered, like Solomon, a wisdom that surpassed the wisdom

---

59. Leithart, 1 & 2 Kings, 45.

of the world, a wisdom unique because it begins with the fear of God (Prov. 1:7; 9:10). Without it, leaders are senseless and reckless, lacking credibility.

Unfortunately, the benefits of wisdom were too much for Solomon. Success did him in. At some point in Solomon's leadership, his lust for power and wealth and women eroded his fear of God. His appetites lost all sense of reality. He no longer heeded his own warnings. Solomon exchanged wisdom for folly, forfeiting *shalom*, as well as a greater legacy he could have left.

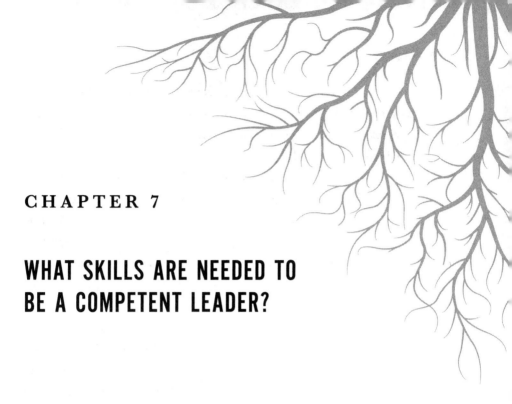

CHAPTER 7

WHAT SKILLS ARE NEEDED TO BE A COMPETENT LEADER?

Battlefields are unforgiving of mistakes.

—Jim Mattis

I think he's a man who clearly lacks self-awareness. I always said if he caught a glimpse of who he really is, his head would explode." These are Steve Carell's words, describing Michael Scott, the regional manager he once played in the TV show *The Office*.[1] Michael Scott is the archetypal boss who is totally incompetent and yet thinks he is a good leader. That this is played out in real life so often explains the show's popularity.

Most of us have had a season (or even a lifetime) under incompetent leadership. Here are some of my brushes with useless leaders: a supervisor who had no clue what his job was, a coach whose only competence was collecting a paycheck, a professor who never figured out how to teach the

---

1. Andy Greene, *The Office: The Untold Story of the Greatest Sitcom of the 2000s; An Oral History* (Hialeah: Dutton, 2020), 154.

course until it was over, a manager whose feedback went no further than my own self-analysis, and a boss who was a leader in title only. Some call this last example "absentee leadership" and refer to it as the most common form of incompetent leadership.

Liz Ryan is a workplace thought leader. She has studied leadership performance and has put together her own list. What makes for inept leaders prone to make mistakes? A leader out of touch with reality. A leader who blocks rather than unleashes energy. A leader who does your job instead of his own. A leader who no longer makes rational sense. A leader who is vacuous, having no ideas.[2] These are the leaders that cause society to wonder if we really need leaders.

Competence is becoming a rare quality. Even rarer is credibility—leaders who have all three attributes: character, wisdom, and competence. Each are necessary, coming to full expression when they work synergistically. What good is character if a leader is incompetent? What does it matter if one is skilled but lacking in moral weight? And who will follow if there is no evidence of sound judgment?

One of my closest friends is a successful financial planner. He is a graduate of Cornell University with an economics degree, as well as a graduate of a leading seminary. What sets him apart from others begins with impeccable character. People trust him with their financial future. He is also a shrewd manager of portfolios. He exercises prudence and sound judgment to handle each day's unpredictable forces. But there's one more thing. He is really good at what he does. He knows the systems like the back of his hand and delivers good results. In a word, he is also competent, which represents the third essential of credibility.

So what marks a capable leader? Let's imagine this question has been posed to a group of leaders gathered around a table. The conference "The Necessary Skills of a Leader" is in session. The figures are familiar. Some on the more academic side are puffing their pipes. Others can't seem to get

---

2. Liz Ryan, "Five Signs Your Boss Is Incompetent," *Forbes*, Dec 12, 2016, https://www.forbes.com/sites/lizryan/2015/12/12/five-signs-your-boss-is-incompetent/?sh=6ecd2dc43514.

disconnected from their smartphones. Everyone, however, is thinking about how their insights will match up. As we listen in, this is what we might hear:

General Jim Mattis, who has served at the highest levels of military and political leadership, might jump in first. After all, effective leaders are those who know there is no time to waste. Stewarding time, in his judgment, is an indispensable skill. A leader on the battlefield must be brilliant in the basics. In particular, one must be skilled at setting the pace. Pointing to his book, he would say, "Speed is essential, whether in sports, business, or combat, because time is the least recoverable factor in any competitive situation."[3] Competent generals know how to read the clock.

Next in turn, Peter Northouse, an educator who has written an industry standard work on leadership theory, would affirm the importance of competencies. Turning to his chapter "Developing Leadership Skills," he would state that there has been a needed shift of emphasis from leadership traits to leadership skills.[4] Using three charts, he would divide leadership competence into three categories: administrative (able to manage resources), interpersonal (able to demonstrate emotional intelligence), and conceptual (able to create a vision). Employing these skills is what gives a leader the capacity to influence others.

Bernice Ledbetter, a lecturer on organizational theory and management, would also break down the essential skills of a leader into three categories: leaders need to have expertise in the technical (competent to deal with financial matters), relational (competent to recruit and build professional relationships), and conceptual (competent to solve problems). They must also be adept at communicating a set of values.[5]

John Gardner, after sharing a story or two from his years with Lyndon Johnson, might speak to skills particularly important to political leadership. He would begin with the relational. A leader must be proficient at building consensus. One must be able to create trust, work through

---

3. James Mattis, *Call Sign Chaos: Learning to Lead* (New York: Random House, 2019), *238*.

4. Peter G. Northouse, *Introduction to Leadership: Concepts and Practice* (Thousand Oaks: SAGE, 2015), 123–47.

5. Bernice M. Ledbetter, Robert J. Banks, and David C. Greenhalgh, *Reviewing Leadership: A Christian Evaluation of Current Approaches* (Grand Rapids: Baker, 2016), 114–24.

conflict resolution, and be really good at networking. Competent leaders must also know how to exercise nonjurisdictional power, meaning they know how to work on numerous fronts with groups in which they have no authority. Finally, they must be flexible, able to adjust and adapt to a rapidly changing world.[6]

James Baker, another politico, one who dominated American politics and policymaking for thirty years, would speak to the skill of preparation and getting things done. These drove him with a ruthless focus. His advice would be precise: "Competent leaders live by the mantra, 'Prior preparation prevents poor performance.'"[7] Those leaders who are most capable are fanatically well-organized. Systematic organization and attention to detail are what creates order out of chaos.

James Kouzes and Barry Posner, who have written numerous books on leadership development, would pass around the research they have captured in their book, *Leadership Challenge*. It reveals that leaders who are skillful know how to guide people toward a common set of shared values and a mutual vision. Leaders who are competent have the ability to challenge and disrupt the status quo, guiding an organization in the direction it needs to go.[8]

After lunch, Warren Bennis would sum up his years of teaching leadership, observing that leadership is like beauty: it's hard to define, but you know it when you see it.[9] He would then highlight several essential skills. First, one has to be able to adapt. There will be adversity, and skilled leaders know how to handle the chaos. Second, a leader is good at engaging others in shared meaning and getting people on their side. Those good at leading know how to create strategic alliances and partnerships. Third, the competent leader has developed a distinct and compelling voice. True leaders possess the "Nobel Factor." They communicate optimism, faith, and hope.[10]

---

6. John W. Gardner, *On Leadership* (New York: Free Press, 1993), 119–20.

7. Peter Baker and Susan Glasser, *The Man Who Ran Washington* (New York: Anchor, 2021), 24.

8. James M. Kouzes and Barry Z. Posner, *The Leadership Challenge* (San Francisco: Jossey-Bass, 2007), 161–220.

9. Bennis, Warren G. *On Becoming a Leader* (New York: Addison-Wesley, 1989), 1.

10. Warren G. Bennis and Robert J. Thomas, *Geeks and Geezers: How Era, Values, and Defining Moments Shape Leaders* (Boston: Harvard Business Review Press, 2002), 121. See also Bennis, *On Becoming a Leader*, 196.

What Skills Are Needed to Be a Competent Leader?

Michael Useem, after years of scrutinizing people in their leadership moments, would tell a number of stories. In looking at abilities that leaders like Eugene Kranz, Clifford Wharton, and Arlene Blum had in common, he would say that a leader has to be good at decision making, communication, team development, reading people, leading change, and reconciling diverse opinions. Most of all, leaders need the skills to recognize and seize their moments.[11]

Finally, leadership columnist Sam Walker would demonstrate from his research in the world of sports that tier-1 captains, skilled as they are, are not necessarily glamorous; they only need a knowledge of what a successful effort looks like. On the field of competition, they sound the right notes. They demonstrate the ability to focus, play to the edges and test the limits, work in the shadows in such a way that makes the team depend on them, motivate players with passionate nonverbal displays, and keep emotions under control.[12] If you want to win, this is what you do.

As the afternoon comes to a close, these leadership experts might pause to reflect on their differences regarding which skills are most important. Because context plays a significant role, everyone will have their own priorities, and this is okay. What all would likely affirm is that it is not enough for a leader to have character and sagacity. Important as these are, a leader who is credible has to demonstrate basic leadership competencies. True, leadership cannot be reduced to skills and techniques, but it cannot be successful without them.

Since we are imagining, let's suppose a theologian is also invited to be part of the conversation. It is now this person's turn to weigh in on the subject of leadership competence. Does God have anything to say on the subject? How does God see it? In a secularized age, in which religious thinking, practices, and institutions have lost social significance, some at the table might question a theologian's competence to speak on competence.

---

11. Michael Useem, *The Leadership Moment* (New York: Three Rivers, 1998), 3.

12. Sam Walker, *The Captain Class: A New Theory of Leadership* (New York: Random House, 2017), 90–91.

But those who would listen might be surprised to find that one who invests in the study of God has much to contribute to the subject.

GOD'S VIEW ON LEADERSHIP COMPETENCY

Like the other sciences represented at the table, theology is its own discipline with its own rigors. As noted in chapter 1, with every other inquiry, theology proceeds with postulates out of which its data gathering and induction of facts proceeds.[13] But the knowledge here is ectypal; the theologian is not seeking to be original.[14] What is shared can come only by divine revelation, not one's own imaginings.

Theology also works by its own methods, its own inner working. We cannot understand unless God enables us to understand. Faith is the starting point, and it is faith that leads to understanding. Finally, though obligated to speak of God, this theologian might once again admit one's inability to speak fully of God. How, after all, can one speak of that which is ultimately unknowable?[15]

After this introduction, sure to bewilder some, the theologian would make the case that Scripture does speak to leadership competence, but one will have to connect certain dots. There is no systematized list. There are, however, stories. Ironically, most are narratives of incompetence. The patriarchs demonstrated flashes of leadership failure, the judges were a disaster, and the stories of the kings were a remarkable mix of lackluster and botched leadership accounts. Few evidenced any virtues like integrity, courage, temperance, and faith. Only one seems to have laid hold of true wisdom, and after him it all but disappeared. What success stories there were, were more the exception than the rule. In the end much of their leadership incompetence led to severe judgment.

---

13. Thomas C. Oden, *The Living God: Systematic Theology* (New York: Harper & Row, 1987), 1:17.

14. Kapic, *A Little Book for New Theologians: Why and How to Study Theology* (Downers Grove, IL: InterVarsity Press, 2012), 31.

15. Galli, *Karl Barth: An Introductory Biography for Evangelicals* (Grand Rapids: Eerdmans, 2017), 182.

This is not to suggest that competence for leading doesn't matter to God. Not only does able leadership matter; it is essential to his purposes. Despite our propensity to be clumsy in our leading, God has made us to do things thoroughly, carefully, and skillfully. If we are running a race, his Word exhorts us to run with skill to gain the prize (1 Cor. 9:24). When you sow, don't do it sparingly (2 Cor. 9:6). Once you have discerned God's purpose for your existence, give your whole life to laying hold of it (Phil. 3:12). Whatever talent you have received, do not neglect it. Do not be inattentive to how God has gifted you (1 Tim. 4:14).

If one has been given the gift of leadership, what Scripture refers to as a "manifestation of the Spirit" (1 Cor. 12:7; cf. v. 28), God says, "Do it diligently" (Rom. 12:8). Behind the word *spoudē* is the idea of haste, zeal, industry, effort, and pain (2 Tim. 4:9).[16] The antithesis is sloth and sloppiness (Rom. 12:11). If your talent is leading, Paul is exhorting, "Get on with it! Do it with competence!" And those who do it well, God says, should be accorded double honor (1 Tim. 5:17).

God requires competence for leadership because leaders are summoned to ultimately serve him and his purposes. In this there is no room for ineffective leading. What, then, are the specific skill sets required of a capable leader? What evidences the gift of leadership? How does it compare and contrast with what has already been said? If we look in Scripture, the following competencies stand out.

Able to Follow

A general maxim of leadership states, "He who cannot be a good follower, cannot be a good leader."[17] To go before, one must learn to follow after. This is true in most any leadership context. Before leaders can be

---

16. Wolfgang Bauder, "zeal," *The New International Dictionary of New Testament Theology* (Grand Rapids: Zondervan, 1978), 3:1168.

17. The quote is attributed to Aristotle. See Bernard Schroeder, "To Be a Great Leader Learn How to Be a Great Follower: The Four Rules of Following," *Forbes*, December 5, 2019, https://www.forbes.com/sites/bernhardschroeder/2019/12/05/to-be-a-great-leader-learn-how-to-be-a-great-follower-the-four-rules-of-following/?sh=282dea9c7325.

proficient at leading, they have to be adept at learning, and learning begins with getting behind God.

Humanity was formed out of the ground, and its first mandate was to get in step with God's purposes and stay within his boundaries (Gen. 1:28; 2:16–17). It continues throughout life. God is saying, "Listen. Observe. Always stay on my path, the one that is narrow." Do not swerve to the right or the left (Prov. 4:27).

Following God is not a skill that would-be leaders pick up easily. We have a propensity to get ahead of God. It's in our nature to trespass, and this goes back to Adam (Gen. 3:1–7). Almost every leadership story illustrates the need for leaders to first follow. Moses led Israel in the wilderness only after he spent forty years following God in the desert. David was a man on the fast track to leadership, but he was not crowned before he spent time in the desert learning to seek God's ways and move off his own. Jesus did not send his disciples out to lead without first calling them to follow (Matt. 9:9). Paul's leadership enabled the early church to flourish, but not before he spent time in the desert learning to follow God (Gal. 1:13–17).

Learning to follow God's lead is a sine qua non of leadership.[18] We learn to die to our priorities and live for his (Luke 9:57–62). In following we discover that we are not in control. We begin to see that leadership is about summons and servanthood and submission.

Followership begins with God, but it also includes getting behind seasoned leaders. Before God said to Joshua, "Be strong and courageous, because you will lead these people" (Josh. 1:6), he placed him under Moses as an understudy. Samuel would lead one day, but he first served as an apprentice to Eli. Elisha had generals waiting at his door, but not before he learned to wait at Elijah's (1 Kings 19:21). What Paul learned, he passed on to the church's future leaders. He called men like Silas and Timothy and showed them that leading begins with following his example (2 Tim. 1:13).

---

18. Tod Bolsinger, *Tempered Resilience: How Leaders Are Formed in the Crucible of Change* (Downers Grove, IL: InterVarsity Press, 2020), 61.

Following is its own skill. It requires discernment. What should I emulate, and what must I avoid repeating once the mantle of leadership shifts? An able follower is quick to hear, slow to speak, and slow to frustration (James 1:19). In the early days of following, one is aware of just how far one can see. A skilled follower knows the difference between loyalty and becoming one's sycophant. Competence also includes the ability to discern when it is time to move from understudy to leader.

Able to Think

Competent leaders give themselves to learning how to think well. How can one hope to be an effective leader if one tends to leave the brain dormant? Especially in today's world. In a *Harvard Business Review* article, Helen Tupper and Sarah Ellis write, "Our capacity for learning is becoming the currency we trade on in our careers. Where we once went to work to learn to do a job, learning now *is* the job. Adaptive and proactive learners are highly prized assets for organizations."[19] This is one of their core skills.

Learning requires thinking, and thinking requires intentionality. Mindfulness is not automatic. A leader must develop the art. Followers cannot afford to settle for leaders who are small-minded, incurious, and intellectually lazy. Who wants to follow someone who is quiet not because he is thinking some deep and important thoughts but because he is thinking of nothing at all? And yet we live in a day one of society's most egregious conceptual gaps is the way we train future generations of leaders how to think. We have grown incurious about new ideas—even intolerant—leading to what one describes as "a leadership culture that is rotten."[20]

Leaders who are careful thinkers learn from others, experiment with ideas, unlearn the safe and familiar, relearn and reassess, and ask propelling questions. Such queries, according to Tupper and Ellis, reset the status quo. Here are some critical questions to think about:

---

19. Helen Tupper and Sarah Ellis, "Make Learning a Daily Part of Your Routine, *Harvard Business Review*, November 4, 2021. https://hbr.org/2021/11/make-learning-a-part-of-your-daily-routine.

20. Joe Lonsdale, "America's Leadership Culture is Rotten. That's Why We Need the University of Austin," *Washington Post*, November 22, 2021. https://www.washingtonpost.com/opinions/2021/11/22/joe-lonsdale-university-of-austin/.

- Imagine it's ten years from now. What three significant changes have happened in your profession?
- How might you divide your role between you and a robot?
- Which of your strengths would be most useful if your organization doubled in size?
- How could you transfer your talents if your industry disappeared overnight?
- If you were rebuilding this business tomorrow, what would you do differently?[21]

Skillful leaders are those who keep refining, keep giving some of their best time and energy to stretching their thoughts, sharpening their arguments, and expanding their imaginations. Otherwise, in the marketplace of ideas they become shoplifters rather than contributors. Goodwin describes this effort to think as a fierce, almost irresistible, compulsion to understand the meaning of what one hears or reads.[22] Those who do not make such effort reduce their leadership to small ideas. They become imaginatively gridlocked.[23] Their leadership will be ruled by feelings and impressions and swayed by mindless opinions. This will lead to flawed decision making and follow-through.

Theology affirms this skill, though underscoring that thinking begins with the right motives. It's not about knowing for the sake of being known as a leader who knows. Pursuing knowledge isn't in order to get noticed, wield power, or be seen as smart.[24] It is about processing important questions, unlearning and relearning how to think. In Philippians 4:8, Paul's admonished his readers to focus their minds on things that are excellent, that answer the following::

- What is true?

---

21. Tupper and Ellis, "Make Learning a Daily Part of Your Routine."

22. Doris Kearns Goodwin, *Leadership: In Turbulent Times* (New York: Simon & Schuster, 2018), 5.

23. Tod Bolsinger, *Canoeing the Mountains: Christian Leadership in Uncharted Territory* (Downers Grove, IL: InterVarsity Press, 2018), 32.

24. Smith, *On the Road with Saint Augustine*, 144.

- What is noble?
- What is right?
- What is lovely?
- What is admirable?
- What is excellent?

Those who intend to lead in service to God must come with a mental resolve, minds alert and fully sober (1 Peter 1:13; 3:15; 4:7). In his chapter "Transforming the Mind," Dallas Willard speaks to this priority: "Bluntly, to serve God well we must think straight."[25] Thinking straight involves a daily renewal of the mind. This begins with a daily process of getting one's thoughts about God in line with who God is. Exposing oneself to God's Word. Tozer's statement deserves careful pondering: "What comes into our minds when we think about God is the most important thing about us."[26] It's the most important thing about leadership.

When minds are renewed, leaders are transformed and equipped to test and approve what the will of God is and how to carry it out (Rom. 12:2–3). Clear and perceptive thinking is what awakens and strengthens faith.[27] It's what elevates the stature of a leader. They are thinking at the highest level, processing, reasoning, and exhorting others to do the same. They burn with new thoughts, asking, "Where should we go next? If what got us here won't get us there, what do we need to discover? Is there a better strategy? What are the opportunities in front of us? How might God use me in a next leadership assignment?"

Finally, this is a skill requiring vigilance. Wrong ideas are always seeking to lay hold of the heart. Getting control is imperative, but we cannot do this on our own. Competent leaders take every thought captive to make it obedient to Christ (2 Cor. 10:5). We have to give him charge. The mind is where the battle is won or lost (4:4). If we are not

---

25. Dallas Willard, *Renovation of the Heart: Putting On the Character of Christ* (Colorado Springs: NavPress, 2002), 106.

26. A. W. Tozer, *The Knowledge of the Holy* (New York: HarperCollins, 1961), 9.

27. John Piper, *Think: The Life of the Mind and the Love of God* (Wheaton, IL: Crossway, 2011), 67.

managing things, we will not be able to marshal good arguments. Worse, we will allow unwelcome visitors to enter the mind, where they can soon become permanent tenants.

Able to See

We can see only so far, and this is to our disadvantage. As one philosopher put it, "We lead telephoto lives in a wide-angle world."[28] Nonetheless, leaders have to develop the skill of seeing from multiple angles. They cannot afford to be myopic, choosing to see only what they want to see. The world and the people whom God has made are too complex. Organizations we lead are too multifaceted.

Books like *Reframing Organizations* provide a helpful approach to seeing the frames that are before us. Smart leaders need to see the social architecture (the flowcharts), the politics (the tribes and coalitions), the symbolism (the story), and the people (the hearts).[29] Seeing through multiple frames at the same time enables leaders to see the bigger picture.

Theology points us to an even larger picture, one that sees through a divine frame. People in God's sight are far more than units and accomplishments, names and qualifications, history and stories. Beyond the flesh and blood are hearts and souls made in the image of God. Capable leaders see this, and it informs their leading. They make it a priority to treat their followers with dignity.

Those with the greater competence can see that God is at the top of the flowchart. Whatever decisions that have to be made must conform to his (Ps. 2:2–6). Any power that coalitions hope to accumulate is secondary to God's. Politics will often come into play, and while a leader needs to adjudicate, see the issues, and discern the tribal factions and interest groups, the able leader sees through a larger lens. We observe this in Acts 15, where skillful leaders were able to confront the sectarian strife

---

28. Eric Weiner, *The Socrates Express* (New York: Simon & Shuster, 2020), 91.

29. Leo G. Bolman and Terrance E. Deal, *Reframing Organizations: Artistry, Choice, and Leadership* (San Francisco: Jossey-Bass, 1996).

and bring about unity because they could see the larger redemptive story God was writing (vv. 7, 12).

Those with the greatest skill at seeing were the Old Testament and New Testament prophets. They were seers by trade who could see what others could not. With their prophetic imaginations, they perceived an alternative to the existing culture.[30] This is a necessary and missing task of leaders today. We overlook that at Pentecost God poured out his Spirit, empowering us to be sons and daughters of the prophets (Acts 2:17). Leaders who take the prophetic work of God seriously recognize they are called and equipped to lead with a prophetic imagination. Like prophets of old, they stand up and expose the lies, revealing a better future. They see through a larger frame and gain a glimpse of where history is going.

Seers like Nathan, Elijah, Micaiah, Isaiah, and Jeremiah spoke with courage and boldness. In the process they took center stage. Their ability to see and frame things caused the kings of the world to recede into the background.[31] One can't help but ask, "Where are the prophetically skilled leaders today?"

Able to Shape

Effective leaders make leaders. It is a skill, one that can be done well or done poorly. Business leaders like Noel Tichy make the case that future leaders are an organization's "leadership engine."[32] The best organizations give priority to skillfully pouring into their emerging leaders. These in turn drive the future.

Building into lives, however, is more than a business strategy. It goes back to God and his design. Throughout Scripture shaping lives is seen as the key to having future leadership. It is God's mandate for leaders. Paul commanded Timothy, "The things you have heard me say in the presence

---

30. Walter Brueggemann, *The Prophetic Imagination*, 2nd ed. (Minneapolis: Fortress, 2001) 3.

31. Peter J. Leithart, *1 & 2 Kings* (Grand Rapids: Brazos, 2006), 18.

32. Noel Tichy, *The Leadership Engine: How Winning Companies Build Leaders at Every Level* (New York: Harper Business, 2002), 57.

of many witnesses entrust to reliable people who will also be qualified to teach others" (2 Tim. 2:2).

This continues a tradition going back to leaders like Moses, who poured himself into Joshua (Ex. 17:14). Elisha had his company of prophets (2 Kings 2:5). Paul invested his time in Timothy, preparing him to lead the church in Ephesus (1 Tim. 1:3). And so it goes, from one generation to the next. It is what the best leaders do.

What does the skill of formation look like? In the secular world, books like Paul Hersey's *Situational Leader* give a helpful process.[33] His seminars train leaders to match their leadership styles with follower readiness. When a person is unable and unwilling, a leader will need to be more directive and less relational. As a follower becomes more able and willing, a leader becomes less directive and more personal.

Sadly, some leaders are like aging athletes who never yield to the next generation because they are too deeply attached. In some cases they do not prepare the next-generation leadership, either because they are sure no one can replace them or because they do not see shaping as a priority. Could one of these be the explanation for Joshua's failure to mold a future leader? He left a nation asking, "Who of us is to go up first to fight against the Canaanites?" (Judg. 1:1).

When it comes to skillful shaping, Jesus is the model par excellence. He took incompetent men and transformed them into world changers. When he met resistance or heard excuses, Jesus did not compromise his demands (John 3:1–10; Luke 9:57–62). When faithlessness reversed the readiness of those who signed on, Jesus knew how to be severe without being abusive (Matt. 8:26; 17:17). As his followers matured, Jesus challenged them to reach to the heights. He pointed them to possibilities they never imagined (John 14:12; cf. Eph. 3:20–21). He opened the world to them and commissioned them to go to the farthest reaches (Matt. 28:16–20; Acts 1:8). And then he passed the baton (John 20:21).

---

33. Paul Hersey, *The Situational Leader* (New York: Warner, 1985).

Able to Communicate

It's clear in the biblical narrative, as well as the world outside of it, that gifted leaders are skillful with their words. They are able to connect with those they lead. When there is a disconnect, when a leader's voice is weak when it needs to be strong, or harsh when it needs to be soft, leadership falters (1 Kings 12:1–17).

A leader cannot be conspicuous by his silence. A person may want to be known as one of few words; what matters is that one's words are measured. As one of the colleagues at the table, Michael Useem, writes, "Being a person of few words may be fine in a technical position, but it is a prescription for disaster in a position of leadership."[34] Being a leader with the right words in the right moment—this is the competency that can lift people and change everything.

As with the other skills, theology not only affirms the necessity of communication but takes us into the world of God, where such abilities take on otherworldly dimensions. Speaking well is not simply about practicing in front of a mirror. One must first cultivate the skill of listening, and all listening begins with hearing the voice of God. This centers all of our speaking. It is God's nature to speak, and he does it in multiple ways, be it through nature (Ps. 19:1–2), his Son (John 1:1), or his written revelation (2 Tim. 3:16). God revels in self-expression. When Jesus gathered his core leaders and took them to the mountain, the mandate they were left with was, "Listen to him!" (Matt. 17:5).

The lesson from theology is that effectual leadership takes advantage of this divine voice. It understands that communication is more about the skill of the ear than the competence of the tongue. Our authority to speak is rooted in our ability to remain silent and listen, waiting with expectation for God to speak. God always has the first word. If a leader's ultimate aim is to serve a divine purpose, one will need to enter the silence and let God break it (Jer. 23:18).

A discerning leader also knows when God has placed something on his

---

34. Useem, *The Leadership Moment*, 275.

heart—something that must be said. When leaders hold back from speaking, it can—it should—feel like a fire shut up in the bones, a flame that can wear one out (Jer. 20:9). This is because everything changes when God speaks. A mere whisper from God can twist the oaks and bring down a forest (Ps. 29:5, 9). Imagine what happens when God raises his voice! The psalmist bears witness to his occasional blasts, which send terror (18:13–14). Part of competence is speaking with a divine-inspired intensity.

God often speaks through people, and leaders who listen to those they lead are better able to speak into their lives. Effective listening to the world around them is one of a leader's great skills. It requires slowing down. Just as leaders must look for a long time before they can see, so they must listen for a long time in order to hear (James 1:19). Only after listening well can a leader speak.

Moments will call for leaders to inform, teach, inspire, correct, and direct. They will need to articulate the fears and aspirations of those they lead. At other times a more muscular voice will be needed, one that goes beyond measured tones. Leaders will need to call out and exhort. If they are listening to God, they will speak with words that "limit and permit the reality which society lives."[35] In certain moments, their anointed speech might even shatter old worlds and evoke new ones.

Able to Manage

This is a skill that needs particular unpacking. Leaders tend to give their best attention to the broad scope, leaving the less glamorous administrative details to someone else (a.k.a. a manager). It's a common assumption of most leadership books. Gardner describes leaders as those who think longer term, grasp larger realities, emphasize intangibles (vision, mission, values), and think in terms of renewal.[36]

Administration, however, is not an addendum to the real work of leading. The theologian might bring out the fact that the word *administer*

---

35. Walter Brueggemann, *Like Fire in the Bones: Listening for the Prophetic Word in Jeremiah* (Minneapolis: Fortress, 2006), 7.

36. Gardner, *On Leadership*, 4.

literally means "towards ministry" or "an intensification of ministry."[37] Part of this involves taking responsibility for organizational processes. Who wants a leader so disjointed he or she can't organize a two-car funeral? Leaders can ill afford to ignore the organizational architecture. They must make sure that tactics align with strategies, and budgets line up with operational plans. Inattentiveness to this generally spells disaster.

From the perspective of theology, leadership is a work of oversight and details. God placed Adam in the garden to both oversee and work the soil (Gen. 2:15). Breadth and depth. The same language is used in other leadership settings. The priest was to keep guard as well as to do the day-to-day work of the tent of meeting (Num. 18:5–6). The prophet stood and gave his sweeping announcements, but he was also sent to do the menial work (like providing daily food for widows (1 Kings 17:1–16). This is the nature of leading—overseeing as well as getting one's hands dirty.

God serves as our model. This is no absentee, deistic God, who has delegated and moved on. God oversees and manages. He casts an eternal vision, one that flows out of his overarching mission, yet is attentive to the details. The God who sets the sun and moon on their courses clothes the short-lived grass with unspeakable beauty (Matt. 6:28–30). He stops to measure out the waters, weigh the mountains on a scale, and call the stars by name (Isa. 40:12–26). He knows every bird in the mountains and every creature that moves across the fields (Ps. 50:11).

The God who is above and beyond is in the here and now. He pays attention to things to which we give little to no thought. I may overlook a parishioner's grief, but God records every tear (56:8). He even numbers the hairs on our heads (Matt. 10:30). What a strange thought. But what a comforting thought. Nothing goes unnoticed in his kingdom.

The idiom "The devil is in the details" has it wrong. It is God who is in the details. This is the nature of God—he cares about naming, managing, and preserving. He expects this of his leaders. What are some of those details?

---

37. Thomas C. Oden, *Pastoral Theology: Essentials of Ministry* (New York: HarperOne, 1993), 153.

The Resource of Time

Most leaders recognize that time management is a necessary skill for successful leadership. It's reflected in the endless time management seminars.

God also affirms that managing time is an important detail. This begins with understanding the times, something some in Scripture were especially known for (Est. 1:13; 1 Chron. 12:32). As quickly as a leader's moment comes, it is gone (James 4:14; 1 Peter 1:23). Effective management of time begins with numbering one's days (Ps. 90:12). There is no time to waste. Whatever is available needs to be bought up and used up (Eph. 5:15–16).

From a divine perspective, time is all we have in order to serve the purposes of God. How we use it will have consequences that last through eternity, consequences that include rewards and positions. Participants at the conference might begin getting nervous here. Let's move on.

The Resource of People

Stewarding people occupies most of a leader's time. With Northouse, the theologian affirms, "Few leaders can do without the skill of being able to manage people."[38] Can *any* leaders do without this skill?

A divine perspective, however, adds that all of us are broken and in need of repair (Eph. 4:11–12). Leaders are sent to do the mending and the managing, helping people to do their necessary work. It goes beyond utilitarian outcomes to something far greater. Skillful managing gives attention to the healing necessary. It gets into the details of a person's life, envisioning what God has designed this person to become. Effective leaders work at maximizing a follower's strengths rather than focusing on their weaknesses. They position them to complement one another. In the end great leaders release followers to do what they have always dreamed of doing, with the aim that each person looks more and more like Jesus (v. 13). This is our theological imperative.

Managing people involves managing teams. It is a critical skill, though

---

38. Northouse, *Introduction to Leadership*, 125.

all too many give little attention to refining it. This is reflected in ineffective meetings and low morale. The most effective leaders pay careful attention to staff and board. Moses, David, Nehemiah stand out as team builders. Building a cohesive leadership team is an organizational imperative.[39] Good teams provide needed counsel and correction. Healthy teams have one another's backs. They press each other to accountability.

The Resource of Wealth

A competent leader cannot simply delegate financial matters to others. One must have a keen awareness of the availability of resources and how to steward them. Underspending during a fiscal year might impress board members, but it might also be a sign that diligence and faith were lacking. Overspending, on the other hand, can mean a leader has been inattentive—or worse, reckless. Part of this begins with learning how to manage things at home, learning how to read checkbooks so that one can read spreadsheets and financial reports (1 Tim. 3:4).

From a theological perspective, one of the marks of a sound manager of resources is a recognition that God owns everything (Prov. 8:18). This is the most elemental claim the Bible makes about wealth. Management has less to do with running a sound budget and more to do with honoring God's ownership. Everything comes from his hand (Deut. 8:17–18).

Skillful managers are also shrewd managers (Luke 16:8–9). God rewards those who view life as an investor, stepping out and taking risks (Matt. 25:14–30). In the end the very best managers are those who know not only how to generate capital and spend carefully but also how to give it away (1 Tim. 6:17–18).

In the end, most critical to effective management is a recognition that everything comes from God—time, people, resources. This includes one's very position of leadership. Management begins with presenting oneself before God for service (Isa. 6:8). This means keeping things in order without getting bogged down in the minutia, knowing the difference between

---

39. See Patrick M. Lencioni, *The Advantage: Why Organizational Health Trumps Everything Else in Business* (San Francisco: Jossey-Bass, 2012), 15–71.

managing and micromanaging, and knowing how to be efficient without becoming rigid. In the end leaders who are competent to manage create the kind of environment where people flourish.

Able to Implement

So far, the theological voice at the table has highlighted six competencies: the ability to follow, think, see, shape, communicate, and manage. All take on different realities when seen through God's lens. But none matter if one is unable to bring a dream to reality. One must be able to move objectives off the drawing board and into action. This involves the following:

Deciding

Nothing will ever get done until decisions are made. Most everyone gets this. At strategic moments, leaders face a go or no-go point. Even though human knowledge is provisional, partial, limited, fragmented, error ridden, and vaporous, leaders have to decide.[40] If we remain fixed on waiting—watching the wind or looking at the clouds—we will neither sow nor reap. This is the observation of Qohelet (Eccl. 11:4).

Scripture warns that decisions must be made, but those made apart from prayer usually lead to poor judgments. Consider David's decision to take a census (1 Chron. 21:1–4), Asa's decision to make a treaty with Syria (1 Kings 15:18–19), Hezekiah's choice to receive pagan envoys (2 Kings 20:13), Uzziah's determination to enter the temple (2 Chron. 26:16), and Josiah's decision to confront Necho (2 Chron. 35:20). In each of these situations, the leader decided but failed to seek to discern God's mind, leading to dreadful ends.

In almost every case a season of waiting will be required. God often speaks through his Word, but one must have a humility to hear what God is saying. Unfortunately, the Scriptures are sometimes used to confirm what a leader has already decided. Texts can be treated like soft wax that can be molded as one likes.[41]

---

40. Peter J. Leithart, *Solomon among the Postmoderns* (Grand Rapids: Brazos, 2008), 99.
41. Ibid., 86.

Adjusting and Adapting

Once decisions are made, things can go wrong. Unexpected conflict with difficult people, turnover of staff, budget constraints, and unforeseen global events—like a pandemic—may require a change of course.

Skillful leaders prepare for curves. This is true no matter the context one leads from. Jim Mattis, after serving at the highest levels of leadership militarily and politically, might interrupt and add, "If you don't like problems, stay out of leadership."[42] Problems come with the territory. It's the story of life. It is also the testimony of Scripture.

In the journey to the execution of plans, God often changes things up. God's purposes often play out differently than we imagined. Abraham was promised a seed, but the years of waiting forced him and his wife to constantly adjust their expectations (Gen. 16:1–4). Moses had to rearrange his promised land expectations and travel forty years in the desert (Deut. 1:34–36). On his way to implement the takeover of the land, Joshua faced defeat (Joshua 7). Like Eli's sons, Samuel's sons went off the deep end, changing everything (1 Sam. 8:1–5). He was forced to accommodate a theocracy-monarchy shift. Saul's army lost confidence (1 Sam. 13:6). David was constantly putting out fires started by the sons of Zeruiah (2 Samuel 2–4).

Change happens; it is impossible to stop it (that's the definition of death).[43] Leaders who are good at completing things know they will face setbacks. They will have to rethink, redecide, adjust schedules, and adapt. Adaptive capacity is part of a leader's competence.[44] The best live by faith, not just by sight.

Executing

Getting to a decision and adjusting when changes call for alterations are critical steps, but it does not necessarily mean anything has yet happened. At some point there has to be execution. Otherwise decisions and adjustments can be empty gestures. Gardner might interject and warn,

---

42. Mattis, *Call Sign Chaos*, 158.

43. Leithart, *Solomon among the Postmoderns*, 103.

44. Bennis and Thomas, *Geeks and Geezers*, 91.

"The announcement of goals without a proposed program for meeting them is a familiar enough political phenomenon—but not one that builds credibility."[45] A proposed program has to eventually be an implemented program.

In their book *Execution*, Bossidy and Charan define it this way: "Execution is a systematic process of rigorously discussing hows and whats, questioning, tenaciously following through, and ensuring accountability."[46] It will require strength of character, as well as the kind of wisdom that faces things as they are. Realism is the heart of execution.[47]

If anyone modeled execution in Scripture, it was Paul. In strategic moments he declared that leadership is about finishing, and finishing well:

- "I consider my life worth nothing to me; my only aim is to finish the race and complete the task the Lord Jesus has given me—the task of testifying to the good news of God's grace" (Acts 20:24).
- "Do you not know that in a race all the runners run, but only one gets the prize? Run in such a way as to get the prize" (1 Cor. 9:24).
- "Not that I have already obtained all this, or have already arrived at my goal, but I press on to take hold of that for which Christ Jesus took hold of me" (Phil. 3:12).

Like any competent leader, Paul visualized a path to the goal. This requires discipline and courage, the kind that takes on and defeats procrastination, distraction, and the need to be liked. It's hard, hard work. Collins likens it to pushing a giant, heavy flywheel, turn upon turn, until momentum leads to breakthrough.[48]

This is a harsh but true statement: without implementation leadership is a waste of time. David did not sleep until he "served God's purpose

---

45. Gardner, *On Leadership*, 15.

46. Larry Bossidy and Ram Charan, *Execution: The Discipline of Getting Things Done* (London: Random House, 2011), 22.

47. Ibid., 67.

48. Jim Collins, *Turning the Flywheel: A Monograph to Accompany Good to Great* (New York: Harper-Collins, 2019), 33.

in his own generation" (Acts 13:36). Nehemiah executed a plan and completed the wall (Neh. 6:15). Jesus fulfilled his purpose, completing the work the Father gave him to do (John 17:4). Leadership that matters sees things through.

Measuring

Deciding, adjusting, and executing. Now that plans are implemented, leaders must ask themselves if the outcomes aimed for and achieved have amounted to success. One must determine the yardsticks of performance, and this takes skill. It requires a broader perspective.

A leader seeking to conform to God's purposes will approach outcomes differently. This is the leader who asks if the assumed success is consistent with how God measures it. We all will one day stand and be measured by him for the things done in the body, whether good or bad (2 Cor. 5:10). Good leadership or bad leadership will be examined, and leaders will be held accountable for how they led (Heb. 13:17). More squirming at the table.

Theology reframes the standards by which we measure outcomes. God's instruments for measuring are different than the world's. It's less about numbers and profits and size. Whether one makes *Forbes'* list or builds empires doesn't much matter to God. These are questions he will ask:

- Was a leader faithful, with an eye toward being fruitful as God defines it (1 Cor. 4:1–2)?
- Was leadership an act of servanthood, done with a heart of humility (Num. 12:3)?
- Was a leader devoted to truth (2 Tim. 2:15)?
- Did a leader fulfill the purpose for which he was called (Phil. 3:12)?
- Did a leader enable the lives of their followers to flourish (Heb. 13:17)?
- Were the accomplishments aimed to bring glory to God (1 Cor. 10:31)?

CONCLUSION

Theology, it turns out, has an important contribution to make at this imaginary session. Though there is intersection at numerous points, theology goes further into uncovered territory. It takes the risk of telling others at the table what some do not want to hear, which is okay. A prudent theologian knows that accommodating to the world's demands is a fool's errand.[49]

The skills noted are not exhaustive, but they do represent *the* core proficiencies. If one is incapable of acquiring these seven basic skills—following, thinking, seeing, shaping, communicating, managing, and implementing—one might consider pursuing another line of work.

When moral character and godly wisdom and competent leadership intersect and define a leader's life, the potential for greatness is at hand. One's leadership is nothing less than credible. But credible for what? What is the leader's task? This takes us to the next chapter. But first a look at a leader who was really good at leading.

NEHEMIAH

Nehemiah was skilled where it counted . . . wine tasting (Neh. 1:11). He knew just when the king wanted a merlot or a cabernet sauvignon. Punctual, organized, having it all together. Everyone could see that this underling, having access to the king, had a potential that was both realized and untapped. His skills were used yet wasted on serving the pleasures of a pagan king vacationing in his winter palace. It was November, the twentieth year of Artaxerxes's lifetime term.

It's not as if cupbearers had to earn a terminal degree to master the fine art of sipping. But in fairness to those in the guild, the job came with some risk. If someone wanted to poison the suzerain, the wine taster would be the

---

49. Trueman, "The Failure of Evangelical Elites," 101.

one taken out. These were the expendable eunuchs. And Nehemiah could have been lost in the shuffle, a no-name that no one would have missed.

God, however, notices. Nothing goes unseen in his kingdom. One day this high-class slave was visited by a few men returning from Jerusalem. They came to tell Nehemiah how things were back home. Behind it all, heaven was at work. Nehemiah was being summoned for something far bigger than sampling vino. God was looking for someone willing to enter into the epicenter of divine activity. There was a wall to be built, and it required a skilled leader. Someone who, in his own Solomonic moment, would hear the question, "What do you want?" Nehemiah knew. He wanted his life to matter. He wanted to maximize his abilities. He wanted to rebuild (2:5).

Nehemiah's life checked every one of the items on the list of competencies we've discussed. It's as if he was made for this—because he was. Receiving the news of broken walls and boarded-up windows and life in general disarray, Nehemiah wept. More, he prayed and planned (chap. 1). He would be ready when his moment came. This is what capable leaders do. Nehemiah sorted out the logistics required for a thousand-mile journey. He knew the papers he would need to ensure a safe expedition. He mapped out the materials necessary for the gates. James Baker would be proud. There was a boldness in his ask. The king was so impressed, he sent army officers and calvary to accompany Nehemiah (2:6–9).

Few knew it, but behind the garment of servitude was an administrative genius, a skilled strategist, a capable tactician. He mustered a task force and inspired commitment from a populace that had been stuck in desolation and despair (vv. 11–17). Governors and mayors and do-nothing councils were too self-absorbed to address the squalor. It left a populace filled with shame. Someone with competence needed to come in, survey the scene, and mobilize the will to rebuild. That someone was Nehemiah.

Moving from gate to gate, Nehemiah did his due diligence. For all of his speed and drive, he was also a leader of detail.[50] He knew that if he did not grasp the enormity of the task and its costs, his ideas would be half-baked

---

50. Derek Kidner, *Ezra & Nehemiah* (Downers Grove, IL: InterVarsity Press, 1979), 82.

and his plans half-formed. Like every competent leader, he spoke with an authoritative voice—but it was more. He identified with the need. When he gathered the officials and the priests, he said, "You see the trouble we are in" (v. 17). Their despair was his despair, their disgrace his disgrace. A shame had hung over this place like a deep fog, but it was about to lift. This is what skillful leaders do.

The people responded with, "Let us start rebuilding" (v. 18). They could see Nehemiah was a man with the hand of God on him. They saw something they had never seen in their lifetime—a competent leader with a vital sense of God's presence. Nehemiah was all business. Everyone was assigned a task and worked under careful order (chap. 3). This leader was tenacious when it came to completing the task. As history would reveal, he could be remarkably humble, but when the times required, he could border on scary.

During the rebuild, Nehemiah had no patience with ungodliness, and no hesitancy to pray down judgment, call down curses, and even pull the hair out of those who did not walk the line (13:19–25). This was no leader with a jellyfish mentality—having no bones, no frame, no convictions, no edge, no point. It's not hard to imagine him praying both psalms of praise and imprecatory psalms.

Nehemiah's competence as a leader was more than ferocious resolve and holy indignation. There was wisdom. There was competence. There was credibility. There would be obstacles and enemies, lots of them, but timidity was accorded no space in Nehemiah's calendar. He would stay on course until the project was finished. Stone by stone, Nehemiah carried his weight—and more. He was part contractor, part builder, part military commander, part governor, and part spiritual leader. Fifty-two days later—under budget and ahead of schedule—the wall was completed. It was a remarkable feat of organizational leadership.[51] It would take another eleven years to rebuild community, and this would require its own skills. Like the wall, the well-being of the people had been reduced to rubble. But this was okay. If Moses was the first founder of Israel, Nehemiah was good with being the second.

---

51. H. G. M. Williamson, *Ezra-Nehemiah* (Grand Rapids: Zondervan, 2015), 211.

What Skills Are Needed to Be a Competent Leader?

Like all proficient leaders, he was ultimately concerned with meeting his core outcome. Ironically, it wasn't the wall. His prayer to God was that he would be remembered for something far greater—for the house of worship and its services—which a completed wall allowed (v. 14).

All of this was recorded—not to fill space in the biblical narrative but to underscore that skillful leadership is a leadership duty. A number of essential skills are found here. Wise are the leaders who review their checklists regularly.

CHAPTER 8

WHAT TASKS MUST EVERY LEADER CARRY OUT?

The single defining quality of leaders is the capacity to create and realize a vision.
—WARREN BENNIS

Roy Vagelos faced a dilemma. Africa was afflicted by a pandemic. A species of flies was transmitting a pathogen that led to visual impairment in humans. In some regions of the continent, half of the residents became blind. Someone needed to step up and help.

Vagelos had recently become the chief executive officer of one of the world's largest pharmaceutical companies, Merck. As with any CEO, it was his responsibility to ensure that the firm was profitable. This meant investing only in those drugs that reflected a judicious use of investors' equity. One of the choices was an antiparasitic drug, one that had been proven to inhibit the spread of parasites and the progressive blindness occurring in regions of West Africa. But victims were too poor to pay, and delivering the drug would cost millions. It came down to health or wealth.

Michael Useem, who tells the story in his book *The Leadership Moment*, comments, "Achieving an organization's imperative is a leader's calling."[1] Vagelos answered the call. He went back to the mission, one dating back to Merck's inception in 1668: "We are in the business of preserving and improving human life." Vagelos decided to provide the drug for free to West Africa until the pandemic was under control. Strategies and procedures were set in motion to guarantee successful distribution. Over the next two decades, fifty-five million doses were dispensed, ending the health crisis.

Leaders like Roy Vagelos exemplify the tasks of a leader—to be missional, to envision a better future where humanity flourishes, to be strategic in the planning and tactical in the implementation. These are the tasks leaders are called to carry out. These are what the most successful give themselves to doing. All of these, however, must be rooted in something deeper than earthly profits or humanitarian concern. Theology takes us there. Let's unpack each one.

MISSIONAL TASKS OF A LEADER

When a person is summoned to lead, one of the immediate priorities is to get clarity and buy-in regarding the mission. Gathering a team, a leader must ask central questions such as, "What is our purpose? Why are we here at this moment and in this place?" Most leadership contexts affirm the importance of carrying out the missional task, no matter the setting. After working with four American presidents (Nixon, Ford, Reagan, and Clinton), David Gergen concluded that those most effective had a central and compelling purpose, one rooted in the organization's values.[2]

Addressing the business world, Peter Drucker also underscores the missional imperative. The mission is not only a critical task; it is the "first

---

1. Michael Useem, *The Leadership Moment* (New York: Three Rivers, 1998), 34.
2. David Gergen, *Eyewitness to Power: The Essence of Leadership; Nixon to Clinton* (Boston: GK Hall, 2001), 347.

task" of a leader.[3] A mission provides some sense of meaning, hope, and identity.[4] When there is a lack of clarity as to why an organization exists, a leader and his or her followers betray their fundamental task, and people are uncertain as to what they are asked to do.

Leaders on the field of battle must also be certain about their mission. For them to be effectual, it must also reflect a collaborative effort. Early in his military experience, General Mattis found that if a leader defines the mission as the leader's responsibility alone, that leader has failed.[5] While effective leaders seek to infuse meaning and purpose into the organization, it has to become a corporate task. An organization must collectively ask, "What is our purpose?" There cannot be ambiguity at any level.

Only when the mission is determined will an organization realize what it is tasked to do. Establishing credibility, determining the reason for existence, is the first and most vital undertaking.

GOD'S VIEW ON THE MISSIONAL TASKS OF A LEADER

Leaders dare not get too caught up with their "missionalistic" thinking without considering God's. God is missional. Everything God does derives from his purposes. Those he summons to lead find their ultimate meaning here. It's not about whether God fits into our mission but whether our mission fits into his. Leaders who matter first grapple with this question. Writers like Christopher Wright underscore that any mission in which we invest our vocation, gifts, and energies needs to align with, participate in, and flow out of this larger reality.[6] Anything less is—well—less.

The mission has to be bigger than our earthly ventures. In 2020 Apple became the world's first company to record a market capitalization of

---

3. Quoted in Warren G. Bennis, *On Becoming a Leader* (New York: Addison-Wesley, 1989), 192.

4. Stanley McChrystal, *Leaders: Myth and Reality* (New York: Portfolio/Penguin, 2018), 397.

5. James Mattis, *Call Sign Chaos: Learning to Lead* (New York: Random House, 2019), 16.

6. Christopher J. H. Wright, *The Mission of God: Unlocking the Bible's Grand Narrative* (Downers Grove, IL: InterVarsity Press, 2006), 531.

$1 trillion. Behind this historic achievement was a mission, which continues to capture the world: "To bring the best user experience to its customers through its innovative hardware, software, and services." On the surface it's an inspiring mission. When founder Steve Jobs approached John Sculley of PepsiCo to join his leadership team, Jobs came back to Apple's mission and compared it to a company dedicated to providing the consumer with a delicious beverage. He asked Sculley, "Do you want to spend the rest of your life selling sugared water, or do you want a chance to change the world?"[7]

One sensitive to a missional God might ask it differently of *both* men: "Do you want to spend the rest of your life carrying out a mission that goes no further than the here and now?" If it's a matter of simply shifting from one consumer product to another, is it worth giving one's best energies? Does your mission go no further than your grave? These are the questions theology forces us to ask.

In many of the stories of Scripture, God is summoning leaders to serve his mission. His purposes go beyond products and profits and personal happiness. Jeremiah, like so many other leaders, was sent on a divine mission to change the world: "Before you were born I set you apart; I appointed you as a prophet to the nations" (Jer. 1:5). As Brueggemann puts it, he was *"sent/commanded/set* for the sake of a mission . . . to shatter and form worlds by his speech"[8] And like all of us, his mission came from a God who has an overriding and tenacious commitment to his own purposes.[9]

God's mission has multiple dimensions. It is first redemptive, a thread running from beginning to end of Scripture. Seeing Israel's plight, God declared to Moses, "I have come down to rescue them . . . and to bring them up out of that land into a good and spacious land. . . . So now, go. I am sending you" (Ex. 3:8, 10). God gave his one and only Son to bring salvation to those who believe (John 3:16), and Jesus sent his disciples on a

---

7. Quoted in Walter Isaacson, *Steve Jobs* (New York: Simon & Schuster, 2011), 154.

8. Walter Brueggemann, *Like Fire in the Bones: Listening for the Prophetic Word in Jeremiah* (Minneapolis: Fortress, 2006), 5, italics in the original.

9. Ibid., 6.

divine mission to save the world (Acts 1:8). A leader must ask oneself, Is the mission I am giving myself to helping to bring life?

God's mission is also about restoring his kingdom. Extending God's rulership should be at the heart of our mission and reflected in our work. This too is underscored in both testaments. David was called from the field to embody the reign of God: "I took you from the pasture, from tending the flock, and appointed you ruler over my people Israel" (2 Sam. 7:8). Jesus came to reclaim God's rule in the world (Mark 1:15), and he calls us to join his purpose.

Fulfilling the missional task requires coming to grips with the person of God. Only then can we be certain of our purpose. McKnight describes the sequence this way: "We need to reclaim a more robust Christology, and let it work its way through us into mission. We must begin, then, with Jesus and not with our social visions as our grandest ideas."[10] Knowing Christ and his will for this world centers us and our endeavors. We are then compelled to join with him in his mission to give life and advance his kingdom. Our daily prayer becomes a missional prayer: "Your kingdom come" (Luke 11:2).

Beginning with God, we come to find that his mission is not only about our redemption and his kingdom; it is about worship. The deeper our journey into knowing God, the more the worship of him becomes the purpose and goal of our existence.[11] This becomes a leader's bottom line. It doesn't matter if one leads a ministry, a branch of the military, a corporation, or a political organization—whatever we do is to bring glory to God (1 Cor. 10:31). This is our chief and highest end. Nothing operates outside of this. This is our reason for existence. This is what we do.

Mission—God's mission—is the critical first step in a leader's task. When the mission of God is at the center of our existence, it is disturbingly seditious to the ways of the world. It moves us to the kind of leadership that goes

---

10. Scot McKnight, *Kingdom Conspiracy: Returning to the Radical Mission of the Local Church* (Grand Rapids: Brazos, 2014), 134.

11. Michael F. Bird, *Evangelical Theology: A Biblical and Systematic Introduction* (Grand Rapids: Zondervan, 2013), 756.

beyond our egocentric purposes. We give ourselves to that which will allow divine grace to seep into and infiltrate the cracks and crevices of society. We help people see their true brokenness and need for God. We look at the mission in the place where we work and ask, "Will it provoke people to live a more flourishing life?" "Will this mission draw people to love rather than hate?" "Will my undertaking lead people beyond the worship of things to a better worship?" "Will God's majesty become more pronounced?"

VISIONARY TASKS OF A LEADER

The leadership task begins at the missional level, but this is only the start. Leaders also have a visionary work to do. They not only address the "Why are we here?" question; they seek to answer the "Where are we going?" question. Part of leadership is drawing people into the future, and the future looks different for people and organizations. We might have the same mission but have a different dream. A vision is more personal; it is what particularizes the mission.[12]

Not everyone wants to think out into the future. In a day of global pandemics, stock mobs, technological advancements, and conspiracy theories, the future can be a scary thought. Consider this example: Some are predicting that within the next ten to twenty years, billions of people will become economically redundant.[13] Humans have always maintained an edge over machines in cognition, but this is changing. AI is poised to hack humans, finding and manipulating vulnerabilities in all sorts of social, economic, and political systems. The eventual aim is to outperform us. Connectivity and updatability are giving machines an edge. With this outlook, who wants to think about tomorrow?

More than ever, organizations will need leaders who are intentional to read, think, and plan. Followers will look for leaders who will inspire hope,

---

12. George Barna, *Leaders on Leadership: Wisdom, Advice, Encouragement on the Art of Leading God's People* (Grand Rapids: Baker, 1998), 39.

13. Yuval Noah Harari, *21 Lessons for the 21st Century* (New York: Random House, 2018), 19.

confront the present, and craft a "visceral sense of the possible."[14] While the mission provides the meaning, the vision provides the direction. Visionary leadership averts a crisis by anticipating and preparing for it (think Elon Musk, Jeff Bezos). Those who are stuck in the past, married to obsolete ideas, and fearful of change end up in ruin (think Kodak, Sears). Visionaries are willing to see around the bend to what are the upcoming opportunities and threats. Some call it "upstream leadership."

Most leadership books testify to the value of a visionary leader:

- It is the leader's calling to imagine a future (Kouzes and Posner).[15]
- It is the leader's task to arouse the imaginative abilities that lie within one's soul (Hirsch).[16]
- It is the core and essence of leadership (Gardner).[17]
- An effective leader creates compelling visions that guide people's behavior (Northouse).[18]

Organizations that prepare for the possible threats and are deliberate to avoid the normal course of atrophy look for such leaders. They seek those who spend a portion of their time gazing out into the realm of possibilities. Gaining a mental picture of what could be, these leaders are fueled by the conviction that it should be.[19]

Like the missional task, a visionary undertaking is a shared responsibility. A vision might begin as a monologue, but it must eventually expand to a dialogue. No matter the differences various members of the team might have, the vision process will require collaboration. Together a team must look backward and ask, "What does our past tell us? Where have we

---

14. McChrystal, *Leaders*, 395.

15. James M. Kouzes and Barry Z. Posner, *The Leadership Challenge* (San Francisco: Jossey-Bass, 2007), 105.

16. Alan Hirsch, forward to *God Dreams: 12 Vision Templates for Finding and Focusing Your Church's Future* by Will Mancin, (Nashville: B&H, 2016), loc. 261 of 4740, Kindle.

17. John W. Gardner, *On Leadership* (New York: Free Press, 1993), 21.

18. Peter G. Northouse, *Introduction to Leadership: Concepts and Practice* (Thousand Oaks: SAGE, 2015), 149.

19. Andy Stanley, *Visioneering: Your Guide for Discovering and Maintaining Personal Vision* (Portland: Multnomah, 2005), 18.

been? What are the overarching patterns?" Churchill, like most visionary leaders, was schooled in history. He studied patterns in the past; hence his decisions reflected a prescient spirit.[20] It's called the Janus effect: the further back you look, the further you see into the future.[21]

A leader and his team must also live in the present with a curiosity that asks, "What are our times telling us?" Leaders cannot dream forward until they have some grasp of present realities. "What are our present strengths? Where are our weaknesses? What is hurting our morale?" It might be a gradual decline of an organization, or an ongoing dissension that is killing the team. "What opportunities are staring us in the face? What are the threats? What is it about the present times that we can ill afford to miss?" Often, to miss the here and now leads to a misperception or a skewed perception of what could be.[22]

Finally, a leader and team bring others into the future, though it can, as noted, be scary. Futurist Peter Schwartz writes, "Peering at what's next is invariably a risky proposition."[23] There will be misreads. Things are constantly changing. It's important to compare notes. There are occasional black swan (unforeseen) events. Teams that are thinking out into the future will need to do scenario thinking. They will have to identify relevant probabilities, acquire the best information, invite a diversity of views, and think together about contingencies if things go in an unexpected direction.

GOD'S VIEW ON THE VISIONARY TASKS OF A LEADER

Casting a vision is more than an organizational priority; it is a theological mandate. God is not only God of the past and God of the present, but God

---

20. Ibid.

21. Kouzes and Posner, *Leadership Challenge*, 107.

22. Dave Fleming, *Leadership Wisdom from Unlikely Voices: People of Yesterday Speak to Leaders of Today* (El Cajon, CA: EmergentYS, 2004), 74.

23. Peter Schwartz, *Learnings from the Long View* (Scotts Valley, CA: Create Space, 2011), loc. 36 of 1033, Kindle.

of the future. So much of what he has revealed points to a coming age. From Genesis 3:15 to Revelation 22:20, God is envisioning an eternal future. It is anything but an afterthought to him. Constructing a way forward—even structuring a theology—must be mindful of our future hope. The yet to come gives meaning to every dogma, every creed, and every plan.[24]

The task of creating a God-shaped vision is necessary, but it will not be easy. Leaders will have to get beyond their own imaginings. If a vision does not grapple with God and his future, a vision retreat may represent little more than *our* ideas and *our* plans. The challenge is to discern God's plans and his purposes, perceive where he is leading and where he is taking us. There is a grander eschatological (last things) perspective that guards visionary leaders from stopping with small, temporal, and—in some cases—hedonistic goals. A glimpse of God's eternity provides a necessary context for everything we dream.

If we become immersed in our aspirations for the organization, we may end up like David, a leader caught up with his own building projects and futuristic plans. Somewhere in the process, his dreams got out of sync with God's (2 Sam. 7:1–5). Sometimes leaders need to begin by sitting down and asking, "Who am I, Sovereign Lord?" (v. 18). The future that God is shaping is not what a leader does for God but what God does through a leader.[25]

Casting a vision that sees beyond the immediate and out into God's future will also encounter resistance. I have discovered that it is a formidable challenge to get people to consider what their lives, or the organization's, could look like in five or ten years. Some of it is fear. Complacency can be part of the reason, but it might also be intransigence. Some have a tendency to live in the past, while others prefer to stay bound to the present.

The challenge is to help people get beyond their short-sightedness and see that there are advantages to becoming visionary, to thinking out and beyond the immediate and into God's future. Here are some:

---

24. Bird, *Evangelical Theology*, 235.
25. Eugene H. Peterson, *Leap Over a Wall: Earthy Spirituality for Everyday Christians* (New York: HarperCollins, 1997), 160.

A Divine Vision Allows Us to Live with Direction

When a life has no sense of future, it tends to simply exist. Things drift, even become chaotic. One can end up going in circles. The same holds true for organizations. A vision creates a straight line. It liberates a group from becoming chained to the present and bound to the past. Having a vision provides a sense of destination, one that frames our weekly agendas.

A Divine Vision Allows Us to Live More Expansively

A leader's task is to move the imagination, enlarge one's curiosity, and help one see into tomorrow. People need a guide who walks with God and dreams with God and emerges to give hope.

Leaders who capture something of God's future see the possibility of a more sizable life. They speak in five- and ten-year goals, as well as ones further out into eternity. This enables followers to rise above the temporal sphere (this fiscal year or even this civilization). Prayers and hopes move beyond the ordinary to the extraordinary. We determine to build with materials that go further than ourselves, the kind that will stand the test of eternity (1 Cor. 3:10–13). We frame decisions so that in the end we will not find ourselves with the writer of Ecclesiastes, declaring, "Meaningless! Meaningless!" (Eccl. 1:2).

Something draws people to identify with Jabez, a nondescript person who emerges out of a forgettable genealogy, an account that goes for pages in Chronicles. He wanted to leave the seeming fate of his name's meaning (pain and confinement) to a life of blessing and enlarged borders (1 Chron. 4:9–10). He envisioned an expansive life, so he prayed, and God granted his request. Some make it a daily prayer today. I do. Why not? It presses us to consider future possibilities.

Jesus entered this world with the same challenge to move beyond the immediate. His kingdom introduced us to something *new* vis-à-vis the given world, something that "inaugurates its total renewal."[26] Whatever

---

26. Eberhard Busch, *The Great Passion: An Introduction to Karl Barth's Theology* (Grand Rapids: Eerdmans, 2004), 280.

our endeavors, God's future has invaded the present, pointing us to a future far beyond what one we can imagine (Luke 17:10–21). His kingdom is here, the heavens have opened, and those who believe can do greater things than he did (John 1:51; 14:12). Think big. Set daring goals, so long as they point to his.

One day what has been inaugurated will be consummated, so God would have us think future, think eternal. Think about what will last. Guard against settling for bread alone, always the temptation of the devil (Matt. 4:1–4). When we cave, we fail our humanity.[27] We misjudge and live for less. Jesus's question must always haunt us: "What good will it be for someone to gain the whole world, yet forfeit their soul?" (Matt. 16:26).

A Divine Vision Enables Us to Get In Step

In carrying out the visionary task, leaders are on solid footing. From Genesis to Revelation, God pointed men and women toward his future. To Abraham, God gave a vision of a great nation (Gen. 12:1–3). It was a futuristic picture of a new world, a rescued world, where humanity would once again flourish and beauty would triumph over ugliness. To Joseph he revealed a picture of a more prominent life—a future leadership that would have its way and go well beyond his life (Gen. 37:5–7). To Moses God revealed a future in which Israel would be rescued and enter a spacious land, one that would serve as a foretaste of our eternal rest (Ex. 3:8; Heb. 4:8–9). To David God pictured a future in which his royal house would continue forever (2 Sam. 7:9–16). To the prophets God gave a vision of both an immediate and a long-term glorious future (Isa. 2:2–4; 11:1–9; 65:17–25; Jeremiah 30–31; Daniel 12). To Paul (as we will see) God gave a vision of a much wider reach of the gospel (Acts 15:12). To us God points to the future and the possibilities and invites us to revise and expand our journey (Eph. 3:20–21).

---

27. Miroslav Volf and Matthew Croasmun, *For the Life of the World: Theology That Makes a Difference* (Grand Rapids: Brazos, 2019), 34.

A Divine Vision Causes Us to Have a Greater Awareness of Time

Leaders who point people into the future move them out of their complacency and into a greater consciousness of time. When leaders challenge us to look further out and consider the possibilities, we tend to approach life with greater exigency. We become more aware that moments are going as quickly as they come (Ps. 39:5). There is no time to waste. We must number our days and run our race, for if there is a future, we must seize it now (Ps. 90:12; Phil. 3:12; Heb. 12:1–3).

Leadership theorists tell us that this is an essential task of leadership—to create a sense of urgency. Without urgency and determination, the visionary task may become stillborn.[28] Theology drives us to see from a deeper, eternal perspective. We are called to move at God's velocity, but that is not so easy to track. It cannot be measured like one uses a radar gun to track the velocity of a pitch. God's movements can be both red-hot and glacial. We are, after all, working within the conditions of sin and alienation to behold the providential activity taking shape in its own way and time.[29] In God's kingdom, and into his future, things move at a divine pace (1 Cor. 3:6).

A Divine Vision Causes Us to Have a Greater Awareness of Our Dependency

Leading a vision process requires complete reliance on God. Only God knows the future, and he alone owns it. He is not like some Wall Street speculator hedging his bets, uncertain of what the future will bring. God sees the future as clearly as he sees the present and the past. We have our ideas, but in truth we are feeling our way in the dark. The future is not ours to control.

Visionary leaders who are wise understand this. They can claim no certainties except those that rest in God and his timing. James 4:13–14 in Peterson's *The Message* makes the point: "Now I have a word for you who brashly announce, 'Today—at the latest, tomorrow—we're off to such

---

28. See John P. Kotter, *A Sense of Urgency* (Boston: Harvard Business Press, 2008).
29. Thomas C. Oden, *Classic Christianity: A Systematic Theology* (New York: HarperOne, 2009), 162.

and such a city for the year. We're going to start a business and make a lot of money.' You don't know the first thing about tomorrow." Only God does.

There is a name few remember today, but at one time it was national news. The name is Joseph Hazelwood. Here was a man with incredible self-confidence. His motto in his high school yearbook read, "It will never happen to me." And why not? His future was bright. He set off for maritime college, excelled, and became part of an elite group selected to drive mighty ships for a major corporation. Others marveled at his near-perfect instincts to guide huge vessels. He could smell an approaching storm out at sea, while others were oblivious. At thirty-two he became the youngest skipper in the corporation's fleet. But it did happen to him. One fateful night, March 24, 1989, Hazelwood's ship, the *Exxon Valdez*, sailed out of an Alaskan port and hit Bligh Reef. Eleven million gallons of crude oil spilled, obliterating life along twelve hundred miles of pristine coastline. It was one of the worst ecological disasters in modern times.

There's a bit of Joseph Hazelwood in all of us. It assumes we know something of tomorrow, own something of the future. Theology reminds visionary leaders that they can see only as far as the present. We know only what we presently know. While our minds look backward in time until the dim past vanishes, then turn and look into the future until thought and imagination collapse from exhaustion, God is at both points, unaffected by either.[30] He is from everlasting to everlasting (Ps. 90:2). He is the one "who is, and who was, and who is to come" (Rev. 1:8). God stands above the limitations of temporal sequences and beyond the limitations of successive moments.[31] We pray, set a course, and depend completely on him.

Reliance includes trust. We are exiles living in transition, and we do not know what will come next. The future and God's paths are "beyond tracing out" (Rom. 11:33). But we press on by faith, urging those we lead to step out and resist stagnancy. We must keep walking—walking in the

---

30. A. W. Tozer, *The Knowledge of the Holy* (New York: HarperCollins, 1961), 45.
31. Bird, *Evangelical Theology*, 128.

Spirit, walking in the truth, walking in the light. Theology, in a centering way, helps us see we are made for a different future, a future of God's making. A future driven by faith.

Something of this spirit might explain the reason why the early church was referred to as the Way (Acts 9:2; 19:9, 23; 22:4; 24:14, 22). The Christian community was not referred to as the Idea or the Ideal or the Doctrine or the Place. "The Way" underscored that Christianity is not a set of doctrines to master but a path to travel.[32] One of Jesus's first commands was, "Come, follow me" (Matt. 4:19). Jesus was inviting people into a more expansive future, for he is the Way (John 14:6).

Following the missional task, inviting people into God's future is the second responsibility of a leader. When it is done well, people have a clearer heading, a more flourishing life, and a greater sense of urgency. The future belongs to God alone, and unless we discern his will, we will lead people astray. But none of this happens without a plan.

STRATEGIC AND TACTICAL TASKS OF A LEADER

Visions are birthed out of dreams, and with dreams come responsibilities. One of the first is to develop a way forward—a strategy. Like the mission and the vision, the strategy has its own question: "How are we going to get there?" As the authors of *Execution* note, if strategy does not address the hows, it is a candidate for failure.[33]

Strategic thinking is one of the most important skills, and carrying it out is one of the core tasks. The irony is that few leaders think strategically. Most prefer to react, preserve, and buy time rather than pay the costs of strategic reforms. But lacking a grand strategy ultimately leads to inaction.[34]

---

32. Mark Buchanan, *God Walk: Moving at the Speed of Your Soul* (Grand Rapids: Zondervan, 2020), 24.

33. Larry Bossidy and Ram Charan, *Execution: The Discipline of Getting Things Done* (London: Random House, 2011), 141.

34. Tom McTague, "What Joe Biden's Global Legacy Might Be," *The Atlantic*, November 2, 2021, https://www.theatlantic.com/international/archive/2021/11/joe-biden-g20/620580/m.

Some of this reflects poor training, even at the most basic level. Leadership consultants like Lencioni find that *strategy* is "one of the most widely employed and poorly defined words."[35] In the opening words to his chapter, "Thinking Strategically," former Secretary of Defense Donald Rumsfeld used the adjectives *overused* and *misused*.[36] Given these assessments, it's no surprise few leaders have an integrated plan for carrying out the mission and the vision. Strategic retreats tend to devolve into confusion and aimless discussions. I know. I have participated in these.

There are not many books devoted to strategic thinking, but those that speak to it argue that having a strategy is necessary to achieving the mission. It's the road map of the shortest route to the destination (one that is lightly filled in to give room for maneuvering).[37] Lencioni, in studying those organizations that have an advantage over others, concludes that a good strategy is a leader's plan for success.[38] Other business leaders agree, stating that without a strategy the vision will lack credibility and remain an illusion.[39]

In the corporate world, strategic organizations intent on acquiring market share focus on what they do best. They create a plan that will win the customer's preference and create a sustainable competitive advantage.[40] They pay close attention to their competition, asking, "What are *their* strategies and *their* weaknesses?" They set goals, and these are typically embedded in their strategy.[41]

It's the same in the political realm. Political strategists plot out which areas need the most investment of time and resources. They raise strategic questions: How do we obtain and sustain formal power?" "How can we harness the public mandate?" "What's our plan for keeping political

---

35. Lencioni, *The Advantage: Why Organizational Health Trumps Everything Else in Business* (San Francisco: Jossey-Bass, 2012), 107.

36. Donald Rumsfeld, *Rumsfeld's Rules: Leadership Lessons in Business, Politics, War, and Life* (New York: Broadside, 2013), 64.

37. Bossidy and Charan, *Execution*, 185.

38. Lencioni, *The Advantage*, 107.

39. Leo G. Bolman and Terrance E. Deal, *Reframing Organizations: Artistry, Choice, and Leadership* (San Francisco: Jossey-Bass, 1996), 215.

40. Bossidy and Charan, *Execution*, 178.

41. Ibid., 65.

opponents on the defensive?" They strategize how to maximize the first hundred days, knowing the first three to four months define a president's leadership. They do this because, in most cases, power does not grow over time. It evaporates quickly.[42]

In the military world, few battles are won apart from a stratagem, a scheme. It has to be right. Quoting naval strategist Alfred Mahan, Mattis writes, "If the strategy be wrong, the skill of the general on the battlefield, the valor of the soldier, the brilliancy of victory, however otherwise decisive, fail of their effect."[43] A strategic plan also has to include alternatives. Given the unpredictable twists and turns of war, military leaders need multiple courses of action. This is the strategic advice of Jim Mattis: "Always build shock absorbers."[44]

Like the other leadership responsibilities, developing strategy is a shared task. Strategic thinking is not for lonely heroes. A leader helps to articulate the vision and initiate a strategy, but the plan has to be constructed and owned by those who will execute it.[45] Part of getting buy-in is putting heads together to assess where things stand, using a tool like a SWOT analysis, which looks at strengths, weaknesses, opportunities, and threats. This tool helps an organization ask, "How can we apply strengths against weaknesses? What are the critical factors the organization is facing, and how can we design a way of coordinating and focusing actions to deal with those factors?"

If such strategizing is done well, a coherent plan of action will emerge. The challenge in working together is to keep the strategic plan concise. Too many strategic initiatives, and people get overwhelmed. Too many goals, and things become "a scrambled mess of things to accomplish."[46] The book *The 4 Disciplines of Execution* underscores the importance of developing one

---

42. Gergen, *Eyewitness to Power*, 350.
43. Mattis, *Call Sign Chaos*, 233.
44. Ibid., 217.
45. Bossidy and Charan, *Execution*, 185.
46. Ibid., 52.

or two goals at best, one(s) that establish the strategic priorities.[47] Staying with one or two and not adding more will ensure focused energy. Focusing on less enables a team to achieve more.

In the end, everyone needs to be clear as to what matters most. If you can't corporately describe it, you can't implement it. The team must be united around a good plan. Bad strategies are thoughtless statements drawn up to please. They end up as little more than popular slogans, superficial statements that say the obvious.[48] Worse, they can be impractical concepts that no one understands.[49]

In sum, a leader's task is not completed until the organization's imperative (mission) is carried out. This requires a clear direction (vision), a solid plan (strategy), as well as skillful objectives (tactics). In this final task, the road map begins to fill in. The leader is now asking, "Who will carry this out?" and "When will this be completed?"

Prioritization in these becomes critical. Bossidy and Charan remark, "A leader who says, 'I've got ten priorities' doesn't know what he's talking about—he doesn't know himself what the most important things are."[50] In the end accountability is the difference maker. It is the final part of the leadership task, and it is one that leaders sometimes avoid. Keeping everyone's feet to the fire is not easy. Confronting is not popular. There will be excuses. Pushback. But ultimately, answerability is what leads to execution.

It all sounds so corporate for some. For religious leaders, strategy and tactics might even seem irrelevant. Leave it to businesses. Aren't faithfulness and fruitfulness the bottom line for those in ministry? There's more than enough to do in leading people into worship, ministering the Word, and caring for souls. Do these other things really matter to God?

---

47. Chris McChesney, Sean Covey, and Jim Huling, *The 4 Disciplines of Execution: Achieving Your Wildly Important Goals* (New York: Free Press, 2012), 10, 300.

48. Richard Rumelt, *Good Strategy/Bad Strategy: The Difference and Why It Matters* (New York: Crown Business, 2011), 276.

49. Ibid., 32.

50. Bossidy and Charan, *Execution*, 69.

GOD'S VIEW ON THE STRATEGIC AND TACTICAL TASKS OF A LEADER

Everything God does is strategic. Think about it for a moment. Is there any initiative God carries out that has not been planned with precision in eternity past? From Genesis to Revelation, we are told that God is working out everything according to his plan. The sage observes all this and writes, "The LORD works out everything to its proper end—even the wicked for a day of disaster" (Prov. 16:4).

Behind our plans are God's. In the midst of our schemes lies a greater scheme, a greater strategy. In the end all our endeavors must coincide with his (v. 9). Regardless of our initiatives, God's stratagems will stand.

To the superpowers of Isaiah's day, those who assumed that their forces were impenetrable and their strategies formidable, God declared, "Surely, as I have planned, so it will be, and as I have purposed, so it will happen" (Isa. 14:24). In Isaiah 46:10 God once again states, "My purpose will stand, and I will do all that I please." Every strategic initiative coheres to reality. Behind every plan and every purpose is careful design, undistracted focus, perfect timing, and unimpeded follow-through.

Behind his saving work is a strategy. God set it in motion when the times reached their fulfillment, and it all worked according to plan (Eph. 1:4–11). Nothing is random in God's world, especially when it comes to making us whole. Everything is planned and executed by God "for the praise of his glory" (v. 12).

Atoning for sin and reclaiming his rule is a work that was set into motion back in Genesis 3:15. Jesus came "when the set time had fully come" (Gal. 4:4). Not a day too early and not a day too late. Though the Adversary attempted to counter God's plan—tempting Jesus to sell his soul (Matt. 4:8–9), trying to replace his kingdom ministry with a healing rally (Mark 1:32–37), and trying to dissuade him from the cross (Matt. 16:22–23), Jesus remained resolute: "The Son of Man came to seek and to save the lost" (Luke 19:10). Nothing gets in the way of God's strategic initiatives.

Strategy is also behind the advancement of God's kingdom. Jesus selected a core of disciples, poured himself into them, and sent them out. This is how the kingdom of God grows. He directed the Spirit to come at the right time to the right people for the right purposes (John 16:7; Acts 1:4–7; 2:1–4). He gave the disciples an overall strategy: begin local and go global (Mark 3:13–15; Luke 10:1–16; Acts 1:8).

In sending us into the world, he calls us to think strategically. It may not get the world's notice. Much of God's strategic initiatives are subversive, underground where things are rooted (Matt. 13:31–33). We are to be salt and light, using the unobserved tools of Word and prayer (5:13–16). For the church to be strong and mature, within which saints become the measure of the stature of the fullness of Christ, God sends gifted leaders with a strategy—not to do the ministry themselves but to equip the saints for the work of service (Eph. 4:10–16). Neglecting this explains much of the church's present ineffectiveness. Saints are passive observers, while pastors assume a role that misses God's plan.

If we step back, it is clear nothing God does is nonstrategic. He expects nothing less of his leaders. Those who imitate him are calculating because he is calculating. They see the priority of strategic retreats. They look at the mission and vision and regularly ask, "What is our game plan?" If God is this intentional, we dare not be careless or sloppy or unintentional. Why would the church be any less strategic than a corporation like Apple or Amazon? Strategic leaders look at Christ and see he was strategic with his use of parables. They note that Paul always started in the synagogue. Jesus and Paul had more than passion. They had a plan. Do we?

In all these strategies, God is also tactical. There were certain objectives in loading Noah's ark (Gen. 6:14–22), and specific instructions for transporting God's other ark (Ex. 37:1–5). Neglecting tactics comes with a price. Just ask Uzzah (2 Samuel 6).

These are the stories that remind leaders to do their task with exactness and care. Carelessness is not a fruit of the Spirit. It is necessary to think through matters of who and when and how. Perceptive leaders understand they will be held accountable for doing their work in the right way—as well as for bringing things to completion (Rom. 14:10; 2 Cor. 5:10). The task of leading is not finished until the mission is accomplished, the vision of faith comes to fruition, and the strategic plan is fulfilled. The parable of the talents underscores that God is not patient with those who play it safe and do it halfheartedly (Luke 19:11–27).[51] He does, however, lavish rewards on those who are faithful, strategic, and tactical.

Jesus made his aims clear. "I have come that they may have life, and have it to the full" (John 10:10). "In fact, for this reason I was born, and for this I came into the world, to testify to the truth" (18:37 NIV 1984). "The reason the Son of God appeared was to destroy the devil's work" (1 John 3:8). These unambiguous statements underscore that we are to be unequivocal in our aims. They tell us what missional, visionary, and strategic leaders—employing the best tactics—should be about. We lead to see lives flourish. We lead to promote the cause of truth. We lead to confront, confuse, and take down the darkness—which has its own schemes (Eph. 6:11).

CONCLUSION

Our intentional God is bringing every purpose and plan of his to completion. Nothing will be left undone. He will usher in a new heaven and a new earth. At a final moment, the Alpha and the Omega, the one who declared in the upper room, "I have overcome the world" (John 16:33), and on the cross, "It is finished" (19:30), will say on his throne, "It is done" (Rev. 21:6).

Leaders in step with him will join the party. In the meantime we are called to be missional, visionary, strategic, and tactical in our leadership calling. This is our task, to guide the teams we lead to collectively answer these core questions: Why do we exist? Where are we going? How will we get there? Who has the responsibility and when must this happen?

---

51. John E. Johnson, *Under an Open Heaven: A New Way of Life Revealed in John's Gospel* (Grand Rapids: Kregel, 2017), 233.

When answered and captured in a plan, these become what Lencioni calls "the playbook."[52]

This is the task of a leader. When each of the answers are rooted in God, this is what starts a revolution. And given the times, God knows we need one. Ross Douthat, in his sobering book *The Decadent Society*, concludes that a religious revolution, rather than a political one, is the likeliest path out of our present decadence. It might come at the level of a Great Awakening, the level of the Reformation or Counter-Reformation, or even at the level of Christianity's beginnings. The story of history is one of unexpected resurrections.[53]

If this is to happen, it will also require a power that goes beyond our own, a subject that we will look at in the next chapter. But first a look at an apostle who understood and fulfilled the tasks associated with leading.

⚜ PAUL ⚜

Paul understood the tasks of a leader. Precise and exacting, he tenaciously laid hold of his plans for leadership. He had his mission and his strategy (destroying the church by incarcerating the followers of Jesus). On his own path forward, he was suddenly and powerfully summoned by God for mission. In a moment his identity shifted from persecutor to apostle. From that day forward, he gave himself fully to his leadership task (Phil. 3:12).

Paul received his missional orders: "This man is my chosen instrument to proclaim my name to the Gentiles and their kings and to the people of Israel" (Acts 9:15; cf. Gal. 1:15–16). "Chosen instrument" literally reads, "vessel of selection" (*skeuos eklogēs*). It would be a new frontier, though Paul's mission was in keeping with promises made as far back as Abraham's day (Gen. 12:3). To bear the name of God was following through with the third commandment: "You shall not misuse the name of the LORD your God" (Ex.

---

52. Lencioni, *The Advantage*, 135.

53. Ross Douthat, *The Decadent Society: How We Became the Victims of Our Own Success* (New York: Simon & Schuster, 2020), 221–27.

20:7). Paul would devote the rest of his life as God's implement, declaring that King Jesus is Lord over all.

From the very beginning of his first journey, Paul announced, "This is what the Lord has commanded us: 'I have made you a light for the Gentiles, that you may bring salvation to the ends of the earth'" (Acts 13:47). Paul saw his mission as one of opening the eyes of the blind (Acts 26:18), a mission whose ultimate goal was the glory of God (Rom. 16:27).

More than this, Paul was a visionary. He was always seeing beyond the horizon to where he should go next (Rom. 15:23–24). His mission compelled him to ever press forward; his faith prompted him to see possibilities. Like any true visionary, he would not be distracted by faithlessness or pushback (Gal. 1–2). The vision God implanted in his heart was offensive for some. It was inconceivable to the Jew that outsiders could become insiders (Eph. 2:19; 3:6). But with a visionary spirit, Paul could see that God is a God of the impossible. In a chapter that reinforced his mission, Paul closed with a doxology that fuels the faith of any visionary: "Now to him who is able to do immeasurably more than all we ask or imagine, according to his power that is at work within us, to him be glory in the church and in Christ Jesus throughout all generations, for ever and ever!" (Eph. 3:20–21).

Paul's vision, however, went beyond the immediate to the ultimate future. As Schreiner notes, "Eschatology pervades Pauline theology."[54] Paul made it his mission to keep the future in front of those he led:

- "... when the times reach their fulfillment—to bring unity to all things in heaven and on earth under Christ" (Eph. 1:10).
- "... that at the name of Jesus every knee should bow" (Phil. 2:10).
- "The day of the Lord will come like a thief in the night" (1 Thess. 5:2).
- "We must all appear before the judgment seat of Christ" (2 Cor. 5:10).

---

54. Thomas R. Schreiner, *Paul: Apostle of God's Glory in Christ: A Pauline Theology* (Downers Grove, IL: InterVarsity Press, 2001), 453.

These are words that move leaders to always think forward, setting whatever vision the organization adopts in an ultimate context.

Paul was also strategic in everything he did. He had to be, for he was called to navigate multiple worlds—Jewish, Roman, and Greek—and each was happy to be rid of Paul. The Romans were threatened by a mission that proclaimed Jesus—not Caesar—was Lord of the world; the Greeks were alienated by a message that declared Yahweh was Lord over all other pagan gods; the Jews were enraged that Paul claimed Jesus was the Messiah and that Paul took the message to the gentiles.[55]

Considering the challenges, Paul set out with multiple strategies. First, Paul determined to go where the gospel had not been preached (Rom. 15:20). Second, he chose to begin in the synagogue (Acts 14:1; 17:2, 17; 18:4). This was his custom, his strategic plan. His credentials gave him immediate access into the synagogue and into the city. Here he took the opportunity to speak and convince the Jews that Jesus was the Messiah and that the gentiles were included in God's saving purposes (Ps. 47:9; Isa. 11:10).

Third, Paul moved outside of his Jewish context and into a pagan one, where he could reach a gentile audience and give an apologetic for a Christian worldview (Acts 17:17–31). Fourth, Paul was willing to adapt his leadership to bring as many as possible to Jesus (1 Cor. 9:22). Fifth, Paul determined to leverage his gentile ministry to arouse his countrymen to jealousy, so they would come to Jesus (Rom. 11:13–15).

In every setting Paul was a disruptor. Strategically, he used the power of Word and Spirit to change hearts. He knew that the gospel is the power of God unto salvation, and prayer is what opens doors and spreads the Word (Rom. 1:16; Col. 4:2–3; 2 Thess. 3:1). He rooted his leadership in the servant leadership model of Jesus. He used the message of the cross and the power of the resurrection and ascension to confound the wise and powerful.[56] He turned common assumptions about title, honor, and power upside down. A strategy of naked love always triumphs over one of naked power.

---

55. N. T. Wright, *Paul* (Minneapolis: Fortress, 2005), 163.

56. Scot McKnight, *Pastor Paul: Nurturing a Culture of Christoformity in the Church* (Grand Rapids: Brazos, 2019), 156.

Finally, Paul was tactical. He avoided micromanaging and getting trapped in the weeds. But he also kept to the details. He urged Timothy to stay in Ephesus (1 Tim. 1:3); he left Titus in Crete to "put in order what was left unfinished" (Titus 1:5). Most of his letters ended with specific instructions that held leaders accountable. It was his intention that, like himself, everyone complete their ministry and finish the race (2 Tim. 4:7). His closing words to Archippus underscored the importance of completing one's operational plan: "See to it that you complete the ministry you have received in the Lord" (Col. 4:17).

In the end, it was not so much about Paul's ministry or mission or vision or strategy or objectives. It was Christ's. Speaking to this outcome, Paul declared, "To this end I strenuously contend with all the energy Christ so powerfully works in me" (Col. 1:29).

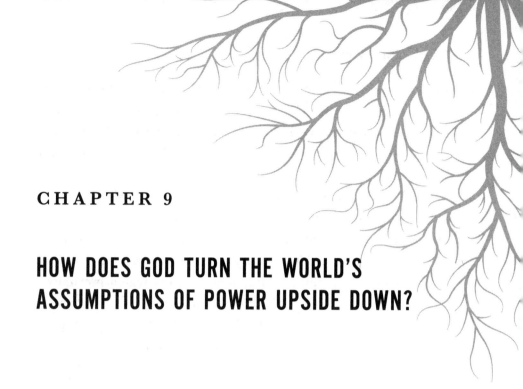

CHAPTER 9

HOW DOES GOD TURN THE WORLD'S ASSUMPTIONS OF POWER UPSIDE DOWN?

Power through weakness, dramatized in the Lamb on the throne or God on the cross, lies at the very heart of ultimate reality, even of the very being of God himself.
—JOHN STOTT

His political career had an impressive trajectory, taking him from the House of Representatives to the Senate, and eventually to the very pinnacle of political leadership, the presidency. As he entered retirement, the stress and worry were behind him. No more hectic fundraising responsibilities, no more energy-draining political campaigns, no more sleepless nights spent making policy decisions, and no more malicious attacks on his leadership. He could finally sit back and enjoy time on his spacious ranch. And why not? There was much to take pleasure in.

He had more money in his portfolio than he could ever spend. His penthouse in nearby Austin was always available, as were the half dozen cars fully equipped with telephones and bars. If he wanted to play on the water, a sailboat and a speedboat were ready to launch. If he wanted to catch a film, the ranch included a movie theater, equipped with servants who catered to his every whim. He could travel anywhere in the world, and if he wanted company, he had the companionship of an extraordinary wife, along with two spirited daughters.

Yet something was missing, and because it was, he found little pleasure in the toys he had accumulated. One could not miss the vacant look on his face, the aimless days, and the emptiness that characterized his soul. As one who experienced leadership at the highest levels, Lyndon Johnson had lost what so gripped and enlivened him—power. In Washington, proximity is power, but now an endless gulf separated him from the levers. He was a master at acquiring it and *the* master in using it, but now that it was gone, life was empty. Retirement became for him a little death.[1]

DEFINING POWER

We use the word often, but what do we mean by *power?* There's no simple definition, especially if one turns to books on leadership. Stanley McChrystal served at the highest levels of military leadership, experiencing power up close. A graduate of the United States Military Academy, he spent thirty-eight years in uniform—from a West Pointer to a commander of all US and NATO forces in Afghanistan. Since his retirement, he has given himself to writing, teaching, and thinking more deeply about leadership and power. "Power," he writes, "is maddingly difficult to describe."[2] It is at once concrete and vaporous, long-lasting and ephemeral. He goes on to say that power has its own rules. It is derived more from reputation than from rank, more from persuasion than from direction, and more from example than from prescription.[3]

---

1. Doris Kearns Goodwin, *Lyndon Johnson, and the American Dream* (New York: Open Road Media, 2015), loc. 389 of 9729, Kindle.

2. Stanley McChrystal, *Leaders: Myth and Reality* (New York: Portfolio/Penguin, 2018), 246.

3. Ibid.

How Does God Turn Assumptions of Power Upside Down?

Janet Hagberg, an artist and writer, notes that some of the struggle in understanding power is related to what she calls "power myopia."[4] There is a complexity to it, and we fail to see power in its multiple stages, which range from "powerlessness" to "power by achievement" to "power by wisdom."[5] Context adds to the difficulty. When times are peaceful, power is hardly felt. In times of crises, power may need to be more coercive and controlling. Power can be as obvious as a list of executive orders signed by a president. It can also be as subtle as silence maintained to make a point.

Other authors writing on leadership attempt some definition of power:

- Power is the ability to make something of the world.[6]
- Power is the ability to affect others' beliefs, attitudes, or course of action.[7]
- Power is the probability one will carry out one's will.[8]
- Power is the capacity to ensure the outcomes one wishes and prevent those one does not wish.[9]
- Power is the capacity to get one to do whatever the leader wants, no matter another's preference—and if necessary, use force.[10]

Together these definitions underscore that power is largely about getting one's way, asserting one's will, and effecting one's plans. Capacity seems to be a running thread, implying that power can be influenced by the size and weight of one's person and leadership.

---

4. Janet O. Hagberg, *Real Power: Stages of Personal Power in Organizations* (Sheffield: Sheffield Press, 2002), xix.

5. Ibid., xxi.

6. Andy Crouch, *Playing God: Redeeming the Gift of Power* (Downers Grove, IL: InterVarsity Press, 2013), 17.

7. Peter G. Northouse, *Introduction to Leadership: Concepts and Practice* (Thousand Oaks: SAGE, 2015), 272.

8. Max Webber, quoted in James MacGregor Burns, *Leadership* (New York: Open Road Media, 2012), 12.

9. John W. Gardner, *On Leadership* (New York: Free Press, 1993), 55.

10. Barbara Kellerman, *The End of Leadership* (New York: Harper Business, 2012), loc. 171 of 4487, Kindle.

GAINING POWER

How does a leader acquire power? In most cases power comes as one assumes a position of leadership. A title and the change of a name on a door begin the transference of authority. Here, power and leadership begin to intersect at many points.[11] Increasing one's power can come through one's proximity to the department head next door. Along the way, leaders increase their authority by developing networks and making all the right connections. They discern that access to power is a form of power all by itself.[12]

It's all part of what David Brooks describes as life on the first mountain. On the first mountain of life, a leader realizes the need to perform, establish an identity, acquire and exercise leadership strength, and make a mark in the world.[13] For most leaders, this first part of their lives is characterized by a fierce ambition and an inordinate drive for influence. There is some innate need to keep score, compare one's strength with others'.[14]

Power also comes through knowledge. The experts in the room often have the power. People turn to them to set the course. Working in the context of Yale University, Volf writes, "To a degree all knowledge is power, and in all disciplines the search for knowledge is also a struggle for some form of power."[15] Those we turn to for answers often command the context.

Power increases as leaders amass wealth and possessions. This gives them the power to buy others and/or gain the leverage to get things done. Some may not have money, but their power is built on their reputational capital (status or prestige). They can be every bit as acquisitive, protective,

---

11. Gardner, *On Leadership*, 55.

12. Peter Baker and Susan Glasser, *The Man Who Ran Washington* (New York: Anchor, 2021), 134.

13. David Brooks, *The Second Mountain: The Quest for a Moral Life* (New York: Random House, 2019), xi.

14. Doris Kearns Goodwin, *Leadership: In Turbulent Times* (New York: Simon & Schuster, 2018), loc. 57 of 11,231, Kindle.

15. Miroslav Volf and Matthew Croasmun, *For the Life of the World: Theology That Makes a Difference* (Grand Rapids: Brazos, 2019), 143.

and ruthless about reputational capital, i.e., symbolic power, as they are about wealth, if not more.[16]

Finally, there are those who simply claw their way to power by coercion, purges, manipulation of information, division of potential rivals, and downright terror. Frank Dikotter has studied the tyrannical rule of dictators like Mussolini, Hitler, Stalin, and Mao. Common for all, he discovered, was the soul-destroying cult of personality. Its power "debased allies and rivals alike, forcing them to collaborate through common subordination."[17]

More alarming is how such types retain their power. In today's world, autocracies are less about one bad guy and more about sophisticated networks. These are composed of kleptocratic financial structures, security services (military, police, paramilitary groups, surveillance), and professional propagandists. Power is preserved and enhanced by what Applebaum refers to as "an agglomeration of companies—call it Autocracy Inc."[18]

THE BENEFITS OF POWER

Power is essential, for without it, leadership is nearly impossible. Because of this, leaders often obsess over it. They cannot help but pause from time to time to assess the state of their power. As Gardner observes, "To say that a leader is preoccupied with power is like saying that a tennis player is preoccupied with making shots his opponent cannot return."[19] Leadership, after all, is about making sure one does not lose the contest.

---

16. James Davison Hunter, *To Change the World: The Irony, Tragedy & Possibility of Christianity In the Late Modern World* (New York: Oxford University Press, 2010), 190.

17. Quoted in Tunku Varadarajan, "A Poetics for Tyrants," *Wall Street Journal* (November 30–December 1, 2019), a review of Frank Dikotter, *How to Be a Dictator: The Cult of Personality in the Twentieth Century* (London: Bloomsbury, 2019), https://www.wsj.com/articles/how-to-be-a-dictator-review-a-poetics-for-tyrants-11575065830.

18. Anne Applebaum, "The Autocrats Are Winning," *The Atlantic* (December 2021), 46.

19. Quoted in McChrystal, *Leaders*, 297.

Power promises a bigger life, the acquisition of wealth and fame, and the ability to accomplish organizational transformation. Acquiring greater authority, leaders gain a different vantage point. Former president Richard Nixon saw power as essential to "standing at the pinnacle, seeing what others do not have the wits to see, confronting the forces of history, and acting unilaterally on behalf of his followers."[20]

With power, a leader can be decisive and get initiatives accomplished. Power enables one to achieve purpose, master one's environment, and take control. It is often the final arbiter, ensuring the outcomes one wishes and prevents those one does not wish.[21] It enables one to bind together diverse segments and bring them in line.

There are also social and symbolic gains that also come with power. Powerful leaders often satisfy a need in followers who want someone to protect and provide for them. Many want someone capable of controlling those otherwise unable or unwilling to control themselves.[22] Some leaders believe that their leadership will be measured by the amount of influence and power they have accumulated over time. Whether this is true or not, it's easy to believe power is the factor determining the outcome of a leader's engagement with the world.[23]

Coupled with credibility (character, wisdom, skills), power can, in the end, be a means for accomplishing great good. Power and authority promote goodwill, build confidence, bring about security, protect followers from adversaries, and create order. This power is more interested in collaboration than in domination. It does not abuse but wisely stewards the gift, leading to an ethos of flourishment. Leaders who come to mind include Joan of Arc, Abraham Lincoln, William Wilberforce, Dietrich Bonhoeffer, and Nelson Mandela.

---

20. David Gergen, *Eyewitness to Power: The Essence of Leadership; Nixon to Clinton* (Boston: GK Hall, 2001), 82.

21. Gardner, *On Leadership*, 55.

22. Kellerman, *The End of Leadership*, 9.

23. Hunter suggests this in his chapter "The Problem of Power," in *To Change the World*, 99.

THE LIABILITIES OF POWER

History reveals that while power has its benefits, coming into power has its dangers. We are, as Burns puts it, both "bewitched and titillated by it."[24] Though attracted to it, leaders and followers need to be wary. Power has the potential to both increase our worlds and corrupt them, and this should give leaders and followers pause.

In his book *Corruptible*, Klaas does numerous case studies, arguing that corrupt people do not become worse with power. Their bad intent remains static, but their effectiveness at corruption increases.[25] In other cases, the data shows that modest and unassuming types can come into leadership and become "drunk with power." They lose their inhibitions, start to feel as if the rules don't apply, act impulsively, and take candy from children.[26] Once at the top, they shift from preservers of justice to instruments of injustice.

Misguided followers often play a part. They can grant leaders too much power. This happens when they assume a leader has the capacity to change the course of history and guarantee their success. This is especially true in the political realm.[27] Devotees increase their expectations and leaders overstep their bounds, not realizing that power can go in many directions.

A sense of entitlement often causes leaders to overstep their bounds and demand what is not theirs. Kellerman and Pittinsky, in their chapter "Lust for Power," write, "Researchers have found that people with power think they can break the rules not only because they can get away with it, but also because they feel at some intuitive level that they are entitled to take what they want."[28] Power and lust become joint travelers on the same road.

Power can also mess with one's perception of reality. Those in high

---

24. Burns, *Leadership*, 9.
25. Klaas, *Corruptible*, 138.
26. Ibid., 157.
27. Note Hunter's helpful discussion in *To Change the World*, 99–196.
28. Barbara Kellerman and Todd L. Pittinsky, *Leaders Who Lust: Power, Money, Sex, Success, Legitimacy, Legacy* (Cambridge: Cambridge University Press, 2020), 16.

positions are prone to worship it. This usually leads to the worst kind of leadership. Leaders become abusive, expecting followers to do their bidding. People become pawns on their giant chessboards. Absent of values like compassion, trust, openness, and responsibility, naked power can be unadulterated, brutal, and arbitrary in its application, eliminating all expressions of nonconformity.[29] As Dikotter affirms, power devolves into coercion, domination, and violence, and good things like technology can be used as tools to confront those who disagree and subvert the freedom of those who challenge.[30]

Just as power corrupts, it also invites destructive forces. The moment leaders gain power, they become fair game, a visible target to take down. Some are escorted out in handcuffs, given a one-way ticket in the dead of night. Others leave in a casket.[31] In his book, *Power: Why Some People Have It—And Others Don't,* Jeffrey Pfeffer warns that people will want your power.[32] One way or another, a leader with power is eventually knocked off the mountain. Others are always there to create an opportunity for themselves through another's downfall or decline.

It might be sabotage. A leader might be released. They might get voted out of office. It might be a sudden tragedy or the gradual dissatisfaction with one's leadership. The fickleness of followers strips one of power as quickly as they give it. As McChrystal observes, "The challenge is that, while the leader is leading, the situation is constantly changing and those constituencies and institutions that endowed the leader with power are always on the lookout for who might do a better job."[33] Just ask almost any president.

In the end, a leader will lose one's grip on power. We can organize and schmooze and network our way to the heights, but soon enough power

---

29. Quoting Vaclav Havel, in Barbara Kellerman, *Leadership: Essential Selections on Power, Authority, and Influence* (New York: McGraw-Hill, 2010), 276–77.

30. Quoted in Tunku Varadarajan, "A Poetics for Tyrants," *Wall Street Journal* (November 30–December 1, 2019), a review of Frank Dikotter, *How to Be a Dictator: The Cult of Personality in the Twentieth Century* (London: Bloomsbury, 2019), https://www.wsj.com/articles/how-to-be-a-dictator-review-a-poetics-for-tyrants-11575065830.

31. Klaas, *Corruptible,* 101.

32. Jeffrey Pfeffer, *Power: Why Some People Have It—And Others Don't* (New York: HarperCollins, 2010), 183–96.

33. McChrystal, *Leaders, 300.*

ebbs and declines. Rank and position have all the staying power of sandcastles at high tide. This often leads to "power withdrawal." As power fades, it becomes much harder to get things done. Leaders morph into caretakers who watch events unfold. Those who refuse to transition end up presiding over rebellious or sclerotic organizations that have moved beyond their power to control. If it is not completely gone before a leader dies, power will be gone when a leader does die.[34]

This explains the emptiness in Lyndon Johnson in the latter years before he died. During his political career, power both elevated and ruined him. His biographer, Robert Caro, writes, "Never has there been a clearer example of the enormous impact—both for good and for ill—that political power has on people's lives than during the presidency of Lyndon Johnson."[35] On one side, his legislative powers led to the Civil Rights Act; on the other, his abuse of power contributed to a war in Vietnam that took fifty-eight thousand lives. Either way, the loss of power left an enormous hole in his soul.

Fear of losing power can so dominate that one loses one's bearings. On inauguration night, when Richard Nixon was about to become the vice president, his mother handed him a note: "To Richard, You have gone far and we are proud of you always—I know that you will keep your relationship with your Maker as it should be for after all that, as you must know, is the most important thing in this life."[36] Nixon put it in his wallet and kept it for the rest of his life. But his paranoia and fear of losing control eclipsed the hopes of a mother and made the note irrelevant.

GOD'S VIEW ON LEADERSHIP AND POWER

The subject of power has to be one of the most perplexing themes in leadership. Given that it is a key factor determining leadership effectiveness

---

34. Peter J. Leithart, *Solomon among the Postmoderns* (Grand Rapids: Brazos, 2008), 127.
35. Robert A. Caro, *Working* (Visalia, CA: Vintage, 2019), 161.
36. Evan Thomas, *Being Nixon: A Man Divided* (New York: Random House, 2015), 84.

and leadership corruption, we have to get it right. This is why we need a theology of power. Theology pierces the complexity and takes us back to the roots, to power's source and design. The biblical stories guide us in this task. Power plays a role in every leadership account, underscoring that to step into leadership is to step into power. What leaders did with power determined their future—as it determines ours. Here are the things we sometimes miss but must give ourselves to see:

God Is the Source of Power

Many of the world's leaders assume that the power they possess is intrinsic to themselves and their actions. They think they own power. But this is a serious misjudgment. All power is inherently rooted in God and his character. This is the clear testimony of Scripture. There is no other source. God does not look beyond himself; he exists by his own energy and is the cause of his own being—and ours.

The essence of God is power (Ps. 147:5). His power and authority reign over all the kingdoms (Isa. 37:16). Paul writes, "In him all things were created: things in heaven and on earth, visible and invisible, whether thrones or powers or rulers or authorities; all things have been created through him and for him. He is before all things, and in him all things hold together" (Col. 1:16–17). Whatever power any pharaoh, emperor, king, prime minister, president, or any leader has, no matter how imposing and expansive, is at best derived. As Oden puts it, "No power has any other empowering source ultimately than God."[37]

In many of the biblical stories, there is a confrontation between the world's powers and God's. Ruthless and efficient regimes, from Egypt to Babylonia to Greece to Rome, seek to impress with their power. Pharaoh does everything he can to intimidate Moses, Nebuchadnezzar struts before Daniel and his compatriots, Pilate lets Jesus know he makes things happen, and King Agrippa pronounces to Paul that his future is in the king's hands.

These rulers assume they have imposing power and act autonomously.

---

37. Thomas C. Oden, *Classic Christianity: A Systematic Theology* (New York: HarperOne, 2009), 51.

But like every leader in Scripture who chooses to bow to other gods, in time they are exposed as decorated irrelevance. It is God who is on the throne, and no power has any other source than God.[38] Pharaoh must eventually yield to Moses's demands, and Nebuchadnezzar's sense of importance is humbled by the power of God's hand. When Pilate informs Jesus, "Don't you realize I have power either to free you or to crucify you?" (John 19:10), Jesus responds, "You would have no power over me if it were not given to you from above" (v. 11). And Paul lets Agrippa know Paul's life is in God's hands. His destiny is for God to control (Acts 26:22). Within God's mighty purposes, those captured by men are actually deployed by God.[39]

Many of the present kings and prime ministers and presidents still assume power is sourced in themselves. They believe it is their prerogative to use power as they wish. Why would they need to start the day on their knees? But it is God who set the world in motion, and it is God who directs its course by his command. It is God who gives dominion and power to leaders (Dan. 2:37). When kings of the earth gather and assert themselves against God, he laughs at their pretentiousness (Ps. 2:1–4). He does not take them as seriously as they take themselves.[40]

God's Power Transcends Human Understanding

Like all God's attributes, God's power cannot be measured by size or weight or anything. It cannot be comprehended. Unlike ours, God's power has no limits, no boundaries, no conditions, and no contingency other than being expressed in accordance with his character.[41] Because of this, he does whatever he pleases (Ps. 115:3). God has the power to work out everything "in conformity with the purpose of his will" (Eph. 1:11). Nothing he conceives and wills to do is beyond his power to accomplish. He has the power required for God to be God.[42]

---

38. Thomas C. Oden, *The Living God* (New York: Harper & Row, 1987), 75.

39. Peter J. Leithart, *1 & 2 Chronicles* (Grand Rapids: Brazos, 2019), 37.

40. John Goldingay, *Psalms* (Grand Rapids: Baker, 2006), 1:99.

41. Michael F. Bird, *Evangelical Theology: A Biblical and Systematic Introduction* (Grand Rapids: Zondervan, 2013), 132.

42. Oden, *The Living God*, 75.

The magnitude of God's power is evidenced in his names. He is El-Shaddai, God Almighty (Gen. 17:1). He is everywhere and over everything. He is also Yahweh Sabaoth, Lord of the armies (Isa. 6:3 NASB). He commands the forces of heaven. God is referred to as the Mighty One (*dynamis*) in Mark 14:62 and the Almighty (*pantokratōr*) in Revelation 1:8. These declare that God's kingdom is not one of many; his throne rules over all (Ps. 103:19). Every human event, every activity, and every headline are under God's rule, penetrated by God's rule, judged by God's rule, and comprised by God's rule. This includes all leader's personal thoughts and feelings and actions.[43] Who can grasp this?

Over and over the point is made in Scripture. God does not seem to tire of telling us of his incomparable and incomprehensible might. Perhaps it is because we are often impressed with our own sense of force, not to mention we are dominated by our own fears of another's power. We become overwhelmed by the constant noise of the daily news. There is this tendency in us to become entranced by human leaders and their claims of power to set the world's agenda.

Our myopia keeps getting in the way. We can't see that God is "the great King above all gods" (Ps. 95:3). He is accountable to no one but himself (Dan. 4:35). He does whatever his hand sets out to do. The one who made the world by his power continues to sustain it by his power. With his outstretched arm he controls every movement in nature (Jer. 10:12; 27:5). He makes the clouds rise and releases the winds from his storehouses (Ps. 135:7). He blows on the rulers of this world, and they wither and are swept away like chaff (Isa. 40:23–24). When God chooses to show the face of his power, humanity cannot but be moved to silence and self-abasement (Job 42:6; Prov. 30:2). God rebukes any suggestion we have any clout on our own or that worry should play any role.

Occasionally God speaks into the seemingly impossible moments with centering questions like, "Is the LORD's arm too short?" (Num. 11:23;

---

43. Eugene H. Peterson, *The Jesus Way: A Conversation on the Ways That Jesus Is the Way* (Grand Rapids: Eerdmans, 2011), 203.

cf. Isa. 50:2; 59:1). In response to Abraham's question about whether God would keep his promises, God asked, "Is anything too hard for the Lord?" (Gen. 18:14). These questions are left open, perhaps because they are the questions that surface throughout history. Speaking to God's question to Abraham, Brueggemann notes it is "the fundamental question every human person must answer. And how it is answered determines everything else."[44] We ask, "Will this job come through?" "Can this pattern end?" "Is there a future?" "Will God save my leadership?" Behind these questions, God is asking, "Is anything too challenging for me?" and asking us, "Do you know how to answer?"

Some, like Jeremiah, had some conception. To the possibility God might extend his mercy in an unbearable moment, the prophet declared, "Ah, Sovereign Lord, you have made the heavens and the earth by your great power and outstretched arm. Nothing is too hard for you" (Jer. 32:17). Those on the inside and in the know, serving next to God in the heavenly court, had the evidence. To a startled Mary, the angel Gabriel said, "Nothing is impossible with God" (Luke 1:37 NIV 1984).

Whatever his goals, God carries them out by his power. None of his plans can be thwarted (Job 42:2). They stand firm forever (Ps. 33:11). No other power can frustrate or overcome God's purposes. As Brueggemann notes, "There is at the center of the historical process a force and a will that cannot be harnessed, domesticated, manipulated, or bought off."[45] God's mission cannot be impeded. He guides everything to its ultimate purpose (Prov. 21:1, 31).

One's mind is overwhelmed by the sheer weight of these verses. Any contemplation of God's power should lead any leader, no matter one's position of authority, to humility—to amazement and wonderand worship. Writes Brueggemann, "The statement of Yahweh's incomparable power— the capacity to assert sovereignty—is the subject of Israel's most sweeping

---

44. Walter Brueggemann, *Genesis: Interpretation; A Bible Commentary for Teachings and Preaching* (Louisville: Westminster John Knox, 1986), 159.

45. Walter Brueggemann, *Like Fire in the Bones: Listening for the Prophetic Word in Jeremiah* (Minneapolis: Fortress, 2006), 79.

doxologies."[46] God's power to lead is beyond impressive. We cannot exaggerate its impact. God's acts of power, as with all his characteristics, are not simply human qualities idealistically pumped up to a superhuman level.[47] His might is not like the world's power, only more awesome. It is unique, astounding, and even bewildering. It points to that "superabundant plenitude whose glory spills over into every corner of created reality."[48] No wonder Pascal wrote, "The greatest single distinguishing feature of the power of God is that our imagination gets lost when thinking about it."[49]

God's Power Is Essential to Our Leadership

From the beginning, leaders have been given divine power and authority to cultivate, preserve, protect, and rule (Gen. 1:28). Without it we go nowhere. If we depend only on ourselves and others, our help is worthless (Ps. 108:12). God alone has the rule and authority, and to grant them is his right. He assigns dominion to whomever he pleases (Jer. 27:5). Power is his gift, and leaders are God's plenipotentiaries (Dan. 2:23).

We tend to talk about how a leader comes to power, but theology reframes our assumptions. *It's not how a leader comes to power but how power comes to a leader.* God bestows his strength on those he chooses (Ps. 89:19). We may wield power, but it is not ours to gain and possess. Power is God's to give, as well as take away. He gives his authority to accomplish his will, and a day is coming when those powers, dominions, and authorities that conflict with his will, will be dethroned and rendered ineffective.

The Spirit of God has a history of unleashing power wherever he goes. The Old and New Testaments are a witness to his work of empowering leaders. In the Old Testament God placed his Spirit on the seventy elders so they could lead (Num. 11:17, 24–25). The force of his Spirit

---

46. Walter Brueggemann, *Theology of the Old Testament: Testimony, Dispute, Advocacy* (Minneapolis: Fortress, 2005), 268.

47. Steven D. Boyer and Christopher A. Hall, *The Mystery of God: Theology for Knowing the Unknowable* (Grand Rapids: Baker, 2012), 186.

48. Ibid.

49. Blaise Pascal in *Pensees* (Open Road Integrated Media, 2011), *ProQuest Ebook Central*, http://ebookcentral.proquest.com/lib/westernseminary-ebooks/detail.action?docID=4353553.

emboldened and energized judges, kings, and prophets to carry out his aims (Judg. 6:34; 16:28; 1 Sam. 11:6; 2 Kings 2:9). Jesus was empowered by the Spirit for his ministry (Luke 4:14). He promised his disciples that they would do extraordinary things when the Spirit showed up (John 14:12). And when the Spirit was poured out at Pentecost, buildings shook and leaders received power to work miracles and fight spiritual battles (Acts 4:31; 6:5; Rom. 15:18–19; Eph. 6:17).

At every turn, God's Word tells us that all our power is derived. Unless a leader is empowered from God, they have no real power. Whatever is done in their own power is fruitless and in vain (Ps. 127:2; John 15:5). But with divine power a leader can do the unimaginable. This is the point of Ephesians 3:20–21. Paul seems to get lost in an attempt to describe it. Think of God's power as infinite immensity—a power that transcends any dam, any weather pattern, any empire, any person.

God's Power Is Unleashed by Our Faith

God is the source of a power way beyond our ability to grasp. We are helpless without it. But how is God's power obtained? Assuming he wants to share it, what's required?

In John 14:12 Jesus makes one of the most radical statements regarding the sharing of his power: "Very truly I tell you, whoever believes in me will do the works I have been doing, and they will do even greater things than these, because I am going to the Father." We're not sure what to do with this verse. Perhaps it is because we are not doing much with the initial words. "Whoever believes" is what drives the passage. If we don't get the first part right, the rest doesn't matter. Whatever power God chooses to give, it will come to those who believe. A leader with such faith will have the same power:

- a power to be indifferent to anything but God's purposes
- a power to fearlessly lead
- a power to say no to sin and its aim to distort our leadership
- a power to trust God in troubled times—no matter what

It is faith that unleashes God's power, and this is an ongoing theme in Scripture. God shows us that power and faith are necessary complements. Just as faith leads to power, faithlessness leads to powerlessness. To the perplexed and powerless disciples who could not heal, Jesus replied, "Because you have so little faith" (Matt. 17:20).

There is a faith available, one that moves mountains (v. 20), but it is a faith informed by the Word. This is Paul's statement: "Faith comes from hearing the message, and the message is heard through the word about Christ" (Rom. 10:17). This faith lays hold of and moves the hand of God and releases the power of God. It is the kind of faith that believes that God will do not whatever we demand but whatever he commands.

The power of God never wears out, leaks out, or dies out. How it is experienced comes back to belief. It is always available to those who take God at his word and seek to be dominated by his force. When God's power was unleashed, this force took matter and made something of it for his glory (Genesis 1–2).[50] The same creative power remains available. In his book *Playing God*, Crouch refers to this as the deepest form of power.[51] Leaders have the potential to take God's power and keep creating new opportunities. With the force of divine power and the working out of faith, we can bring believers to maturity, to the outcome (*teleios*) for which they were created, and leadership to its intended outcome (Col. 1:28–29).

Scripture tells us that faith releases God's power, but faithfulness is required to sustain it. When a leader neglects self-leadership and ignores the disciplines critical to godliness, divine power is removed. There is a loss of gravity in one's voice. Battles are lost. One is forced to depend on one's own power, which is often used to tear down rather than build up. Many of the accounts in Kings and Chronicles testify to this.

The Spirit of God came upon Saul with power, and Saul's early leadership led Israel to victory (1 Sam. 10:10; 11:11). Unfortunately, Saul chose the way of disobedience, and one day Saul had no power other than raw

---

50. Crouch, *Playing God*, 17.
51. Ibid., 54.

power—the kind of power in which the Spirit is absent. And this usually leads to destruction (22:6–19).

At the pinnacle of his power, David lost his spiritual bearings, sacrificed his humanity at the altar of power, and abused power to take what was not his to take—another man's wife and the life of an innocent man. Even more tragic was his son Solomon. God enlarged his boundaries and increased his power, but his character did not keep pace. It failed to extend to the same edges; hence Solomon gave himself increasingly to the practice of "pharaonic power."[52] His power became one of accumulation, taxation, forced labor, arms trafficking, and polygamy. Like so many leaders who abuse power, Solomon began to play God in the lives of others. He schmoozed with the power brokers, the wealthy merchants, and the influential bureaucrats. He built numerous alliances, using marriage to secure more and more diplomatic muscle.

Hollowed out by the acid of his own ego, Solomon's self-serving power eventually led to his undoing. Power, originally intended to create possibilities, steward resources, manage creation, fight injustice, bring peace, and accomplish divine purposes, curdled into selfish ambition and self-advancement. In the end Solomon's house of cards collapsed. God raised up adversaries and tore the kingdom away from him (1 Kings 11:11–14).

It was no different with others. Asa became more enamored with the power that comes from treaties with pagans than with the power that comes from God. Uzziah was marvelously helped by God until he became strong and used his power to cross the line and seek authority that was not his to possess (2 Chron. 26:15). Without exception, loss of character brought loss of power. These leaders lost what power they had hoped to keep, becoming a shell of their former selves. Once leaders make power and authority their god, life eventually crashes.

Look around and listen. Can you hear the air coming out of those who have yielded to their worst impulses? Faith initiates the power of God, but it is fidelity to God that maintains it.

---

52. Walter Brueggemann, *Truth Speaks to Power: The Countercultural Nature of Scripture* (Louisville: Westminster John Knox, 2013), 57.

God's Power Is Counterintuitive to the World's Assumptions about Strength and Authority

This is where a theology plays a most pivotal role. Power, as God sees it, is different than what most assume. Leaders tend to associate power with self-expansion and accumulation, deep voice inflection, high-backed chairs, and imposing desks. We think in terms of territories and numbers and market shares and influence and control. We pray for power to do big things.

I see this with some leaders in ministry. They measure the power of their preaching by the force of their boldness and the positiveness of the response. They seek signs and wonders as evidence that the power of God is moving in their midst. They assess their impact by how many congregants are in their pews, how big their budgets are, and how many hits they are getting on social media.

This is inconsistent with the biblical narrative. In fact, it is contrary. The power of God is less about prideful achievements and more about acts of humility. We sometimes forget, for example, that behind the biblical narrative of Israel's kings is a much greater story. As Brueggemann puts it, "In a daring move, back behind 'the great men,' the narrative locates the origin of Israel's future and the source of its 'great leaders' in the story of a bereft, barren woman named Hannah" (1 Sam. 1:2).[53] This is where the real power was at work.

In the New Testament God takes us to the definitive example. In Christ we see again that the power of God is more about self-emptying than about self-expanding. God's power is manifested not in a list of arbitrary decrees but in sacrificial, other-serving love. Of this kind of power, Oden remarks, "It is a power whose depth is most fully known through self-giving love, as made known on the cross (Col. 2:14–15)."[54] Bloesch adds, "His power is his conquering love."[55] Though he is *the* omnipotent power of God to whom

---

53. Walter Brueggemann, *First and Second Samuel* (Louisville: John Knox, 1990), 11.

54. Oden, *The Living God*, 76.

55. Donald G. Bloesch, *God the Almighty: Power, Wisdom, Holiness, Love* (Downers Grove, IL: InterVarsity Press, 1995), 106.

belongs all authority, Jesus chose to set aside status, reputation, and the privileges that come with them and to give his life for us.

At the summit of the book of Philippians—and maybe the summit of the New Testament—Paul turns poetic. The literary form tells us the text in chapter 2 was composed to be internalized, especially by leaders who think about power. Christ is our perfect model of power. Though coequal with the Father and Spirit, having the same rank, status, and class, he did not consider his equality with God as something to forcibly hold. Rather he set aside the full weight of his attributes and allowed himself to be poured out (vv. 5–11). He refused to use his power to turn stones into bread in the wilderness. He did not exercise his authority to call on the angels at Gethsemane. Instead he took on the form of the powerless, washing the feet of those he led and submitting his will to the Father.

Reflecting on this, Paul wrote these words to a church that was experiencing division and likely some jockeying for power: "Have the same mindset as Christ Jesus" (v. 5). One can hear him saying to leaders, "Your leadership should not be about posturing, asserting oneself, seeking the places of honor, trying to impress, and using your authority to manipulate and exploit others."

In his self-emptying, Jesus was not giving up power but demonstrating it.[56] Out of his suffering, he dethroned the world's kingdoms and established his own, defining leadership for what it is—service (Mark 10:45; Col. 2:13–15). Through his resurrection, he replaced the kingdoms of this world with one whose power is the power of the servant and whose strength is the strength of love.[57]

The lesson for leaders is this: power is a paradoxical mix of strength *and* weakness, holding on and giving up, kingdom and cross, resurrection and suffering. Power proves its might through the act of humble affection. Apart from this, power is "worse than nothing."[58] Leaders who are generous to give

---

56. Crouch, *Playing God*, 164.

57. N. T. Wright, *How God Became King: The Forgotten Story of the Gospels* (New York: HarperOne, 2012), 205.

58. Bloesch, *God the Almighty*, 25.

away their power ironically become more powerful. Leadership in God's kingdom means restraining the full weight of one's power, reorienting one's leadership to serve, knowing that power is easily distorted and misused to play God, exploit the weak, and push around one's weight.

Paul not only wrote it; he lived it. Before he met Christ, Paul thought power was about gaining status and wielding control. He lived in a Roman world, where symbols of power were everywhere. Brutality, emperor worship, and festivals in honor of leaders defined the cultural landscape. All of this reinforced his natural human desire for influence (Phil. 3:4–6). His learnings gave him knowledge, which gave him power, which in turn gave him celebrity status in the synagogue.

When Paul came to Christ, all of this flipped. Paul discovered that the power of God is far greater than anything the world offers. In his letters Paul took the leadership marks of the world and subverted them. He came to the realization that power is perfected not in one's climb up the ladder, not in attending leadership summits and networking with the elite, but in descending and acknowledging one's weakness (2 Cor. 4:7; 12:9). He discovered that it's through broken vessels—not people who have it all together—that power becomes most obvious. Here God's power becomes most visible (4:11). As Schreiner notes, "Paul's commitment to suffer and die for Christ is the means by which the strength of Jesus and his life are revealed through Paul."[59]

CONCLUSION

Theology takes us beyond our nearsightedness and enables us to see a more expansive view of power. We gain a more realistic look at both its potential for good and bad. If we take the message of Scripture seriously, we will avoid the path of destruction so many leaders take. We will turn the world's assumptions of power upside down.

Over and over, God challenges us not to be captivated by the world's

---

59. Thomas R. Schreiner, *Paul: Apostle of God's Glory in Christ: A Pauline Theology* (Downers Grove, IL: InterVarsity Press, 2001), 96.

assumptions. Yet, more than we care to admit, we tend to model our leadership after the world. We are captured by large works and brash personalities, by leaders more interested in power acquisition than in character development. We fall over ourselves to get in the same room with people of rank. We do this even though there are endless stories of leaders who have fallen because they uncritically pursued the dominant ways of life.[60] Too many seek power *over* rather than power *for*. This is the kind of power that keeps a rotted tree propped up, but only for so long. Divine winds have a way of thinning the forest. I have witnessed the work of these storms.

Psychologist Diane Langberg, who has tracked the seduction of power, both individual and institutional, sees a failure of education as part of the problem. In an interview with *Christianity Today*, she noted, "Seminaries give practical knowledge about how to run a church or a ministry, but they aren't doing enough to illuminate the nature of power and the dynamics that cause issues of abuse to arise—and then be covered up."[61]

If we don't come back to a careful theology here, we will chase after power for our own ends, and this will create its own abyss. This is how C. S. Lewis imagined hell—a place where everyone is personally concerned with power and authority, with one's status and rank and advancement, where everyone has a grievance, and where everyone lives out the deadly serious passions of envy, self-importance, and resentment.[62]

For today's leaders every day is an opportunity to exchange false forms and cheap imitations of power for the true power of God. There is a resurrection power to lay hold of and an indwelling Spirit to be filled with (Phil. 3:10; Eph. 5:18). This enables leaders to more than endure—they overcome.[63] But more than overcome, they do the unimaginable. They pray, tapping into God's glorious might (Col. 1:11), and serve, releasing his power to work through their weakness (Mark 10:45). If we are faithful here, ours will be a power that confounds and overwhelms the world. But leaders

60. Hunter, *To Change the World*, 185.

61. Quoted in an interview by Tim Hein, "How Churches Elevate and Protect Abusive Pastors," *Christianity Today*, November 2020, 70.

62. C. S. Lewis, *The Screwtape Letters*, annotated ed. (New York: HarperOne, 2013), xxxv, xxxvii.

63. Bloesch, *The Holy Spirit*, 320.

must also contend with suffering, and this is where we go next. Before leaving, a look at a servant of God well acquainted with divine power.

🌿 ELISHA 🌿

King Jehoram is curious. He wants to know—he pleads to know—all the great things Elisha the prophet has done (2 Kings 8:4). "Great things," a translation of the Hebrew *gedolot*, is an interesting choice of language. It is sometimes used to describe the work of God. The king is awed by the power Elisha possesses. The prophet's activities border on the supernatural, so Jehoram sits spellbound as Elisha's servant recounts the prophet's exploits. If only the king could touch the hem of his garment!

The bulk of 2 Kings 3–9 serves as the working material for a biography of Elisha's life. He is sometimes in the shadows and at other times on center stage. Intermittent explosions shake the text. Elisha is in a class of his own. He was an unknown at work in the fields until Elijah showed up. Elisha burned his bridges (1 Kings 19:21), joined this "troubler of Israel" (1 Kings 18:17), and gave himself to "[pouring] water on the hands of Elijah" (2 Kings 3:11). Elisha must first learn what it is to be powerless. In time he will become the most important—indeed the most powerful person—in the story. He has the ear of God, and this unnerves his world.

Soon enough people discover Elisha is not a leader to be messed with (2 Kings 2:23–25). He has the spirit of Elijah, which is the Spirit of Yahweh, so he can call out bears from the forest as readily as Elijah called out fire from heaven.[64] He can do this because he understands that power, real power, comes from God. Prophetic voices, even if they are on the margins, are those who impact the course of life. They are the true history makers. They are not overly impressed with official forms of power; they believe that the real stuff of history is breaking out underneath in ways the dominant ideology does not even notice.[65] Isn't this what Jesus was saying about the power of his covert kingdom?

---

64. Peter J. Leithart, *1 & 2 Kings* (Grand Rapids: Brazos, 2006), 176.
65. Brueggemann, *Like Fire in the Bones*, 191.

How Does God Turn Assumptions of Power Upside Down?

Elisha has witnessed the hand of God on Elijah, and he wants the same. Clarification: he wants a double portion of the same spirit. The mantle of leadership does not unnerve him. Elisha believes he has the capacity to bear any of and all of the might God wants to give. God brings it on, and with divine strength pulsing through him, Elisha knows he can do whatever God says to do. Nothing is too hard for this Sovereign (2 Kings 3:18). Power's only limitation is our lack of faith.

Elisha is not interested in power for the sake of power. He wants to be a conduit for God; he will use the power of God for the purposes of God. With it he makes the land productive (2:19–22). He provides guidance to the desperate (3:16). Whatever he prays gets accomplished. With the power of word, he enables people to get through their poverty (4:3–7). By his voice there is birth and recovery, food for empty stomachs, and healing to overcome diseases (4:8–42; 5:10–14). With divine sight Elisha can see a world beyond his own, one where donkeys talk, fires burn without stopping, and hills are filled with chariots of fire. Elisha will even use the weight of divine glory to recover lost ax-heads (6:5–7).

Given the divine power Elisha possesses, he is not at all awed by the trappings of earthly authority. He is not interested in getting on the king's schedule, posing for photo ops, getting an imperial autograph, or riding in *Chariot One*. Kings have thrones, armies, and crowns. They like to be seen with other elites—Hollywood A-listers, business moguls, and royals—spending weekends at their one-percenter's paradise, comparing their power trips. They have servants to attend to their needs. They use their muscle to force nations to get in step. But because they for the most part have little regard for God, they are empty suits. They give the impression of might, but their power is pathetic and frail in comparison.

Elisha lives at another level. Filled with the power of God, those who follow his path become a force of healing, redemption, and destabilization. Such a God-anointed presence will continue to unmask and strip the powers of this age of their semidivinity and foreshadow their end.[66]

---

66. Marva J. Dawn, *Powers, Weaknesses, and the Tabernacling of God* (Grand Rapids: Eerdmans, 2001), 29–30.

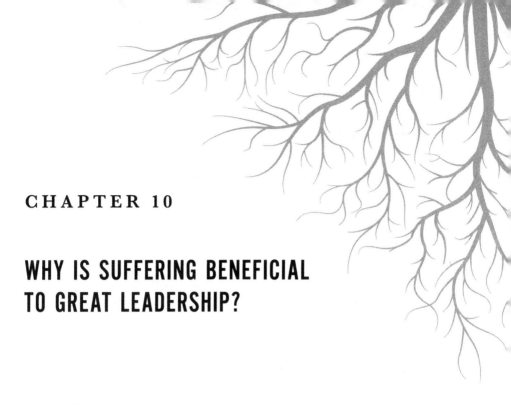

CHAPTER 10

WHY IS SUFFERING BENEFICIAL TO GREAT LEADERSHIP?

*God has shown us, again and again, that things are
not what they seem and that he is always weaving
something wise and good out of the painful, perplexing
threads that look like a tangle in our lives.*
—JOHN PIPER

It was supposed to be a short, uneventful trip from Heathrow Airport to a country estate where we were staying for the night. Once the car was rented, we were on our way. Traveling with others, my wife and I were excited to settle in and have dinner. But things began to come apart.

It began with renting a car too small to hold all of us, searching for the right highway, then missing the exit. The signs were a bit confusing (my excuse), and before we knew it, what should have taken fifteen minutes took hours. We were hopelessly lost. Has this happened to you? After an hour of travel, we pulled into a rest stop. A helpful trucker told us we were headed in the right direction. "Just catch the M-25 and you will be there." It turned out to be a city with a similar name. Turned out that we were pulled over for having too many people in our vehicle. Turned out the police gave us an expensive fine and took one of our passengers. Turned out the M-25 had no exits for miles and miles. All in all, it turned out that what should have been a short trip went late into the night.

Life shouldn't be this hard, but it is. In fact, it is often much harder. Let's face it, we all live arduous lives. Suffering and its aggravation by malevolence are part of living. They are unshakable existential truths.[1] This is especially true of leaders, and many of us in leadership can't help but ask, "Why?"

There's not an abundance of help. Topics like setbacks, trials, conflict, and enemies are not standard subjects. Leadership conferences seldom include the "S—Happens" workshop. Speakers would rather generate enthusiasm, selling the advantages of becoming a leader and laying out the quickest course to money, power, achievement, and success. But after taking the helm of leadership, a leader soon faces reality. Setbacks are part of leadership's landscape.

The leadership task often begins as relatively painless. Most everyone is deferential and supportive. Well-wishers shake your hand and ask about the family. Someone slips a Starbucks gift card into your pocket. Any feedback is signed with, "We're praying for you." People are committed to your success. But these halcyon days of dream casting and team building can begin to turn turbulent. What began as a smooth sail soon encounters stiff winds. Prickly team members and resistance to new ideas surface to slow the journey. One faces obstacles, missteps, criticisms, grievances, embarrassments—even acts of sabotage.

Writing this, I reflect on some of my challenges (there is no room for growth), obstacles (people are not willing to change), sabotage (team members are undermining you behind your back), chaos (whoa, I have just boarded a runaway train!), annoyances (a recalcitrant staff member is not yielding to correction), trials (the deficit continues), crises (one of your

---

1. Jordan B. Peterson, "Be Grateful in Spite of Your Suffering," in *Beyond Order: 12 More Rules for Life* (New York: Portfolio, 2021), 355.

best leaders has morally failed), mistakes (why did I hire this person?), and grievances ("How could you say that from the pulpit?").

No matter the context—political, corporate, religious, athletic—leaders will experience a degree of pain. Andrew Roberts, after studying wartime heroes, writes, "However generous the sprites and fairies are when they gather around the leader's cradle with their gifts, there always seems to be a malicious one present to snatch back one gift from the cornucopia."[2] There's always one.

In this chapter, I will identify the particular challenges that come with leadership, as well as examine some of the ways we can counter them. The greater part will look at what theology has to say, discovering that it again takes us back to the roots and sets things in perspective.

A common metaphor used for leadership trials is a crucible. Once one accepts the call to lead, one will be tested as through fire. Reflecting on his years of teaching, Bennis speaks to the challenges of leading, noting that every leader will undergo at least one intense, transformational experience.[3] It may be a setback, a misunderstanding, alienation, loneliness, personal failure, adversaries, or loss. Let's look at each one.

Setbacks

So much of leadership is about moving forward. Invariably, there will be pushback. Unexpected obstacles that bog things down. Economic meltdowns or world pandemics. Plans and dreams that were pressing ahead begin to slow and shift into neutral, if not reverse. A number of leadership initiatives get put on hold. It can be a financial setback, health issues, defeats, an unexpected shift in growth, followers who have a sudden change of heart, decisions that don't gain traction. There are stories we would just as soon force down the memory hole—deny they ever happened. There are

---

2. Andrew Roberts, *Leadership in War: Essential Lessons from Those Who Made History* (New York: Penguin, 2019), 203.

3. Warren G. Bennis and Robert J. Thomas, *Geeks and Geezers: How Era, Values, and Defining Moments Shape Leaders* (Boston: Harvard Business Review Press, 2002), 14.

some, as Peggy Noonan put it in a column, we would like to shove down before they have a chance to become a memory![4]

Misunderstandings

Communication has to work through many layers. A leader discovers early on that people often choose to hear what they want to hear. They may hear a tone that has nothing to do with your intentions. Such misunderstandings are often birthed out of expectations that are inconsistent with reality.

In his book *Just Listen*, Goulston remarks that we often deal with dissonance. He defines it this way: "Dissonance occurs when you think you're coming across in one way but people see you in a totally different way."[5] A leader steps in and takes an assignment out of a desire to serve, but it is misinterpreted as a lack of confidence in someone else. You think you are demonstrating confidence, while others see it as arrogance; you are attempting to be decisive, while others see you as impulsive; you hope you are exhibiting patience, but others see it as slowness; you have determined to be straightforward, but others interpret it as rudeness.

This leading is becoming as pleasurable as bathing a cat!

Alienation

Leaders come with an agenda. They see themselves as catalysts for change, and this upsets the equilibrium. Leaders tend to, as Tichy says, "stage revolutions."[6] They mobilize resources to bring down the walls of the status quo, splash cold water on people's complacency, disrupt the conventional, and confront risk-averse people.

This is threatening, especially to those who see themselves as preservers of the past or caretakers of the present. Followers who have slighter power and authority often resist the idea that they are expected to fall in

4. Peggy Noonan, "Victory, Sacrifice, and Questions of 'Collusion,'" *Wall Street Journal* (July 13, 2017), https://www.wsj.com/articles/victory-sacrifice-and-questions-of-collusion-1499987057.

5. Mark Goulston, *Just Listen: Discover the Secret to Getting Through to Absolutely Anyone* (New York: AMACOM, 2015), loc. 1375 of 4032, Kindle.

6. Noel Tichy, *The Leadership Engine: How Winning Companies Build Leaders at Every Level* (New York: HarperBusiness Essentials, 2007), 28.

line. This creates what Garry Wills describes as a feud, "a serious meddling in people's lives."[7] While some honor and cherish their leaders, others are prone to oppose and clash. Envy and jealousy also play a role. Leaders begin to establish policies that will impact the organization, and for some this leads to resentment. Plantinga calls it "a posture of againstness."[8]

The irony is that people often choose a leader on the premise that he will bring needed change. It turns out many are fine with change as long as it does not affect them. Leaders often discover, rather painfully, that organizations are not so inclined to reinvent themselves. After some initial proposals, someone is bound to speak for others, declaring, "If it ain't broke, don't fix it." This, however, often ignores the fact that it might be broken, and if it isn't, it will be.

Loneliness

Alienation leads to isolation. There are few places lonelier than leadership. Barton describes it as "a very particular kind of loneliness."[9] Moments come when you take your stand and discover that no one else is standing with you. Have you experienced this? You find yourself working through pain, and no one seems to know or care. You come to a place where you feel abandoned even by God, which is the worst kind of loneliness.

Leaders, by necessity, spend a portion of their time sorting out things alone. Colin Powell warns that every aspiring leader must prepare for this. Before accepting the assignment, one needs to ask oneself, "Can I bear the final responsibility? Can I take the heat when it comes? Can I stand alone?"[10]

Personal Failure

Leaders will make mistakes. Much of a leader's work is on-the-job training, so there are bound to be misjudgments. (This is what I would

---

7. Garry Wills, *Certain Trumpets: The Nature of Leadership* (New York: Simon & Schuster, 1994), 11.

8. Cornelius Plantinga Jr., *Not the Way It's Supposed to Be: A Breviary of Sin* (Grand Rapids: Eerdmans, 1995), 155.

9. Ruth Haley Barton, *Strengthening the Soul of Your Leadership: Seeking God in the Crucible of Ministry* (Downers Grove, IL: InterVarsity Press, 2008), 155.

10. Oren Harari, *The Leadership Secrets of Colin Powell* (New York: McGraw-Hill, 2002), 245.

often tell my teenage kids when I messed up again.) We can initiate too soon or respond too late. There are moments when we fail to decide, and the lost opportunity cannot be retrieved. And much of this is right out there in the open for all to see.

I think of misfires when it came to hires and evaluations. Overlooking rather than confronting performance issues. Failing to hold staff accountable. Not being transparent enough to share my struggles. Overreaching and underselling. It is easy to either spend more dollars than we have in the bank or not seize the opportunity to spend what we have. The problem with malfunctions is that people will remind us. Some have no formal role, but they keep a daily log, ready to give their annual review. Others do not wait, jetting into orbit at our first misjudgment.

Adversaries

No matter how well liked, leaders will face difficult people. Some will be envious and jealous of one's power. It might be chemistry that gets in the way, creating its own antagonism. As Fisher puts it, "No matter who we are or what we accomplish, some people will not like us, won't follow us, and may even reject our ministry. None of us are exceptions to that rule."[11]

Over time, adversaries can create a toxic environment. A leader steps into a room and smells the radioactive gas. These might include bullies (who seek to intimidate), manipulators (who seek to control), and derailers (who seek to disrupt). Most disturbing are those who were once friends. They stood by you and cheered you on, but they have turned on your leadership. They know you better than others, so they use what they know to betray you.

Loss

For all the gains of leadership—the thrill of leading, achieving an objective, and fulfilling a purpose—there are inevitable losses. It's part of the journey. Loss of growth, income, people, and relationships. There is

---

11. David Fisher, *The 21st Century Pastor: A Vision Based on the Ministry of Paul* (Grand Rapids: Zondervan, 1996), 129.

also the loss of joy. Leadership has its gains, for sure, but there will be forfeitures.

Part of loss is the loss of momentum. Things flatten out. You can't put a finger on it, but something is not right. Something has been lost. Leaders are energized by growth, but a season of loss and decline can begin to take its toll. Self-doubt and criticism can creep in. There can be the loss of confidence, even a loss of purpose, and this is most dangerous.[12] When you cannot find the "why" to live for, the will to endure life and leadership can dry up.

One of the more painful losses in leadership is a realization that one is entering personal decline. A leader is at full press and then senses he is losing the thread of his life.[13] There is a loss of energy and enthusiasm. A creeping malaise sets in. In a most transparent way, Barbara Brown Taylor described the day her mind began to coast like a car out of gas.[14] She began to question her desire to lead. She writes, "Drawn to care for hurt things, I had ended up with compassion fatigue. Drawn to a life of servanthood, I had ended up a service provider. Drawn to marry the Divine Presence, I had ended up estranged."[15] There's a good chance some of us will write similar words one day.

Leadership biographies reveal that either leaders handle the challenges or the challenges handle them. Those who fail to handle them well tend to lose their leadership. David Gergen found that Richard Nixon could not handle criticism without giving back as good as he got. Unfortunately, he let his demons have the upper hand. Rather than absorb the punishment, he surrendered his soul.[16] And lost his presidency.

The reality is that we have moments in which we respond in a defensive, horrible way. In other moments, however, we find the strength to

---

12. David Brooks, *The Second Mountain: The Quest for a Moral Life* (New York: Random House, 2019), 28–30.

13. Ibid.

14. Barbara Brown Taylor, *Leaving Church: A Memoir of Faith* (New York: HarperOne, 2012), 4.

15. Ibid., 102.

16. David Gergen, *Eyewitness to Power: The Essence of Leadership; Nixon to Clinton* (Boston: GK Hall, 2001), 81.

handle conflict well. To process hardship effectively, leaders need to know when to press forward, when to pull back, and recognize what it is that must be learned.

Leadership does require tenacity, staying with it, making do with whatever one has at hand.[17] Duckworth calls it grit, a.k.a. ferocious determination.[18] Resilience is another word that fits. Bolsinger devotes a book to the subject (*Tempered Resilience*), noting that leadership requires a capacity to "look the brutal facts square in the eye, to name the mountain of despair, and to keep hammering away with your tempered chisel."[19]

Tenacity means staying the course when you believe it is the right one. Without determination, leaders will give up. The tenacious know who they are, why they have been called, what their mission is, and how they intend to get there. They will not allow fear to take hold. They will not cave to approval. To lead, a leader must be able to disappoint those who follow.[20] Leaders like Harriet Tubman, Winston Churchill, Franklin Roosevelt, Martin Luther King Jr., and Margaret Thatcher come to mind.

There are times to pull back. Sometimes a setback is a signal that it is time to face reality, reorganize, modify, and revise. To borrow from Bolsinger, there are times when you prepare to canoe and then discover the terrain is one of mountains rather than rivers.[21] In these moments adaptive capacity becomes a leader's great skill. Successful adaptation enables a leader to transcend adversity, with all its attendant stress, and emerge even stronger than before.

Sometimes leaders face a perfect storm, in which threats converge all at once. Some years ago I was leading an expansion project on our campus. The economy was at full tilt, leading to surging construction costs.

---

17. Diane Coutu, "How Resilience Works," *Harvard Business Review* (May 2002), https://hbr.org/2002/05/how-resilience-works.

18. Angela Duckworth, *Grit: The Power of Passion and Perseverance* (New York: Scribner, 2016), loc. 198, Kindle.

19. Tod Bolsinger, *Tempered Resilience: How Leaders Are Formed in the Crucible of Change* (Downers Grove, IL: InterVarsity Press, 2020), 156.

20. Tod Bolsinger, *Canoeing the Mountains: Christian Leadership in Uncharted Territory* (Downers Grove, IL: InterVarsity Press, 2018), 172.

21. Ibid., 25.

Urgency to begin was a must. Architectural plans had been drafted and approved, but before we knew it, a twelve-million-dollar estimated cost mushroomed into a twenty-four-million-dollar price tag. And just before we broke ground, the subprime mortgage disaster led to an economic collapse. It was 2008, and I suddenly realized I might be remembered as the pastor who led the church into bankruptcy. It was time to stop, adjust, change course, and move forward.

There are moments to learn. Though leaders seldom enjoy the pain of loss or setbacks or criticism, most acknowledge these can serve as opportunities to deepen their leadership.

Bennis points out that these crucibles, painful as they are, are necessary. They are places where life is stripped of distractions and essential questions are asked: "Who am I? Who could I be? Who should I be?"[22] Trials have a way of ridding one of superficiality. They forge a leader's life, just as storms shape mountains. They are lessons if one is willing to learn. Bennis writes, "The extraction of wisdom from the crucible experience is what distinguishes our successful leaders from those who are broken or burnt out by comparable experiences."[23]

In his book *The Second Mountain*, columnist David Brooks speaks to the benefits of hardship. He writes, "Seasons of suffering kick us in the ass. They are foghorns that blast us out of our complacency. They shatter the illusion of self-sufficiency and warn us we are heading for the wrong life."[24] This is true. Setbacks and disappointments are wake-up calls that compel us to look deep within and make the necessary course correction. We suffer our way to wisdom—the kind that cannot be found any other way.

Though we don't want to go through the same fire again, we are grateful for the results. Writer Mark Buchanan, retracing his own path, acknowledges the same: "My bent, maybe yours, is to find the easy way . . . the shortest distance . . . the safest course. . . . Yet the times I've stumbled

---

22. Warren G. Bennis and Robert J. Thomas, *Geeks and Geezers: How Era, Values, and Defining Moments Shape Leaders* (Boston: Harvard Business School Press, 2002), 99.

23. Ibid., 94.

24. Brooks, *The Second Mountain*, 36.

upon the hard way—the long stretch, the costly journey, the twisted path, the route that doubles back, circles around, crisscrosses, detours, skirts the precipice—those have been the best."[25] He adds, "The easy route rarely transforms anyone."[26] When answering the question, "What experiences have made you the leader you are?" no one answers, "I really was a shallow, dysfunctional leader until I spent a week snorkeling in Hawaii and gorging at luaus."

We have seen that leadership challenges cannot be avoided. If we are to prepare future leaders, we need to be transparent about the trials and hurts that come with leading. It's important to share our journeys in the hopes that they will learn and avoid some of our errors of judgment, our bouts with impatience, and our dead ends with resentment. If these lessons are ignored, leaders will remain stuck in leadership adolescence. But no one gains full maturity until they look at suffering through the lens of God.

GOD'S VIEW ON LEADERSHIP AND SUFFERING

From the broad narrative of Scripture, it is obvious that becoming a leader is to step into a high seas environment, where winds and ocean swells can easily capsize the unprepared. Without exception, there will be challenges and there will be suffering. Self-help books get us only so far. Only a sound theology will get us through the night.

If we read his Word and listen to his Spirit, God will help us see some of the underlying reasons for our trials and sufferings. On the surface, we might see our leadership challenges as difficult people, a convergence of grueling circumstances, an unexplainable setback, or simply fate. Our troubles, however, often go much deeper. Behind many of our misunderstandings, personal failures, and losses are distorted desires, and behind them is sin (James 4:1). No matter how much we prepare, how careful we

---

25. Mark Buchanan, *God Walk: Moving at the Speed of Your Soul* (Grand Rapids: Zondervan, 2020), 146.

26. Ibid., 148.

develop a compelling vision, and how disciplined we work at collaboration, we can't escape that there is something wrong in humanity's wiring. Our human condition is fallen, ravaged by a certain depravity. Gradually, as the makeup wears off, we see this in our leadership.

As we have seen in chapter 5, a radical self-centeredness is at work in all of us to hinder and compromise our leadership. Daily we experience its appalling force to pervert, adulterate, and destroy good things.[27] Many of our difficulties come as a result of our own doing—our determination to take our own course.

A lack of training or experience might play a role in our missteps, but as noted, leaders are this mix of creatureliness and goodness and fallenness. This is what creates so much confusion and pain. It explains why leaders are at times unable to do what they want to do (Rom. 7:15). Difficulties do arise because of personality differences, unfortunate circumstances, divisive people, heartless competitors, and unbearable colleagues. These bring their own hurt and pain and suffering. But it is a leader's internal dysfunction, the dysfunction in others, the spiritual war, and the mystery of God that leads to much of the angst. Let's unpack each one.

The Leader's Dysfunction

For leaders one of the most common expressions of sin is pride. We see it in many of the biblical stories. We start to move ahead of God. Almost every leadership failure comes back to this. We can become enamored with power, start believing the press that tells us we are really good. If we are not careful, we might begin to assume privileges that are not ours, take what is not ours, and cover up our misdeeds. We tend to become moody, demanding, and abrasive. If we don't watch ourselves, we loosen the restraints we once put on our language. And then suddenly we fall from the heights to the depths.

Scripture warns us, "Pride goes before destruction, a haughty spirit before a fall" (Prov. 16:18). Paul also speaks of consequences, of a wrath that

---

27. Plantinga, *Not the Way It's Supposed to Be*, 27.

comes to those who give themselves to their egoistic earthly nature (Col. 3:5–6). Some recover from the shattering, but others only harden their hearts.

Leaders have a choice: to say no to sin or proceed with their folly. Some leaders in Scripture started well, but then they failed. Think of Moses, Saul, David, Solomon, Asa, Uzziah, Jonah, and Peter. Their breakdowns involved pride, revealing itself in mistrust, disobedience, lust, abuse of power, overreach, hardness of heart, disregard for calling, denial, and betrayal. Each led to their undoing.

What we come to painfully realize is that we can choose our sin, but we cannot choose the consequences. When we commit ourselves to what Plantinga calls "jackassery," we are in danger of self-destructing.[28] We can forfeit our greatest hopes (Num. 20:8–12; Deut. 3:23–28).

Uzziah's judgment signals what happens when one moves outside of reality and becomes enamored with self-importance. The end of Solomon's life shows what happens when one becomes infatuated with objects that one has no business loving. The historian reveals what happens when an effectual leader like David ignores his family obligations (2 Samuel 13), as well as the sourness that can overtake a man like Jonah when he runs from God (Jonah 4).

The Dysfunction in Others

Sometimes our challenges are less about our sin and more about the sins of others. The state of organizational sickness may be due to a divisiveness within the people we lead. We may have to contend with mean-spirited people bent on having more control, inert souls that slow the growth, or people in opposition who wish to do us harm. Consider this brief survey:

- Moses faced Miriam and Aaron, as well as the darker enemies of Korah and Dathan.
- David fought Goliath, Doeg, Saul, the sons of Zeruiah, and his own son Absalom.

---

28. Ibid., 126.

- Solomon contended with Hadad.
- Elijah fled for his life from Jezebel.
- Mordecai and Esther encountered the evil of Haman.
- Nehemiah was threatened by Sanballat and Tobiah.
- Jeremiah was attacked by Pashhur.
- Jesus was betrayed by Judas.
- Peter was intimidated by a servant girl.
- Paul was harmed by Alexander.

Behind it all is the same corrupt and twisted nature.

The Work of an Unseen Enemy

This requires spiritual eyesight. Some are able to see beyond the circumstances to a corrupt heart in themselves and others. But theology takes us further, deeper. Behind many of a leader's hardships is a spiritual war. There are forces devoted to bringing chaos and determined to use leaders to carry out evil's agenda. If a leader chooses to lead with integrity and righteousness and gospel, these forces of darkness will do everything they can to undo all that the leader has accomplished. As Bloesch notes, "Faith does not lead us beyond conflict but right into conflict, for the devil fights for our souls as we try to remain steadfast in our determination to give glory to Christ."[29]

While it is important that a leader not immediately blame his difficulties on unseen powers (sometimes they are the result of foolish behavior), it is also important to realize that adversaries of the unseen sort—this triad of world, flesh, and devil—unite to wreak havoc on a leader's soul, disrupt her leadership, and incite opposition (Eph. 6:12). They work to destroy our peace and are often behind the painful and unfair criticism, the setbacks, the loss of personal confidence, as well as those dark nights of the soul.

Jesus told his emerging leaders that when one chooses to align with the King of kings, there will be war. There will be a cost, so prepare for alienation. Just as Christ was persecuted, so his followers will be (John 15:20).

---

29. Donald G. Bloesch, *The Holy Spirit: Works & Gifts* (Downers Grove, IL: InterVarsity Press, 2000), 321.

When one aligns with Jesus, one is declaring that he is Lord of the world, not Caesar. One is affirming that there is one God, not many gods. Paul gave the same warning to those he led. Anyone who chooses to live a godly life in Christ is a marked person (2 Tim. 3:12). We should not be surprised if we are despised.

The Ways of God

Sometimes conflict and suffering will mystify us. The assurance that no harm befalls the righteous (Prov. 12:21) will conflict with reality. We are confident that we are doing all the right things—but our world is collapsing. Like Job, we have examined ourselves and cannot see why we are facing such opposition, why growth has suddenly stopped, or why we have been released from our responsibilities of leadership. Scripture tells us God is often doing things we cannot see (1 Cor. 13:12). If we try to figure them out, we find that his ways are unsearchable (Rom. 11:33).

We come to understand that the Hebrew proverbs we sometimes claim as promises are intended to be little more than observations. In the main, leaders who align their lives with divine realities will face fewer pitfalls. But Scripture also directs us to the lives of godly leaders like Job, who wrote his own proverb: "Man is born to trouble as surely as sparks fly upward" (Job 5:7). Trouble ('amal) includes the experiences of mischief, sorrow, travail, pain, grievance, and wickedness. Job knew them all. A man who once sat in the gates, who walked with such gravitas that the chief men would cover their mouths (29:9), was now a local joke. His "comforters" built their misguided theology on rigid misinterpretations of common proverbs like we see in Proverbs 12:21, suggesting that godliness prevents tragedies like Job's, but it doesn't.

Behind so many of our trials are personal sin, the sins of others, an unseen spiritual war led by the demonic, and divine mystery. There is wisdom in making sure we are looking at the right source. But theology does more than help us see the underlying reasons.

Theology guides us through our trials and sufferings. It reminds us we are never alone, no matter what we face. In a world under the sovereign presence and incomparable grace of God, God shepherds us through. He gives us examples to warn us and for us to reflect on and learn from. He provides what we need to handle the challenges. And he enables us to endure.

These God-given examples tell us that we are in good company. Though trials can lead to periods of loneliness, and dark nights of the soul can overwhelm us, the biblical narrative tells us that we stand in a long line with others. Their stories serve as reference points, preserved to guide us on the way.

We notice early on that following God's call does not give one a pass when it comes to difficulty. It leads to the opposite—suffering. Abraham was summoned to lead a nation, but he spent years facing one delay after another. Joseph received a vision to lead but was promptly hurled into a pit. Moses prepared to lead his people into the promised land, only to face a forty-year reversal. David set out to build his dream temple for God but then was told he couldn't. Jeremiah became a mouthpiece for God and was thrown into a pit.

In the New Testament one thinks of the apostle Paul. Summoned for a divine mission, he faced one test after another. The list is unnerving: left for dead in Lystra, imprisoned in Philippi, chased out of Thessalonica, mocked in Athens, and scorned by churches he planted. There were times when he was in advance mode, but then things would turn sideways (Acts 16:6–7).

Jesus foretold the coming days, telling his disciples they would face severe adversity, though not alone. "If the world hates you, keep in mind that it hated me first" (John 15:18). From the beginning to the end of his earthly leading, the Son of God was misunderstood. His family observed his missional leadership, as well as those who followed him, and thought he was out of his mind (Mark 3:21). The religious accused him of being raving mad, sending him to the cross.

If we still believe that what we are facing is unique, we need to go back and read the early church fathers. Many were solid theologians with a passion for obedience, but almost all experienced loss as a result of their leadership. In recounting their lives, Purves notes that Gregory of Nazianzus died in lonely retirement, thinking himself a failure; John Chrysostom died in exile in a rain ditch; Gregory the Great was dragged to the papacy on his sickbed and could get up only a few hours a day thereafter; and Martin Bucer died in exile in England, thrown out by the people among whom he had so faithfully ministered.[30]

No matter what leaders face, God equips us to handle the challenges. It is never the intention of God that we face leadership problems on our own. If we think we're alone, we need to realize that in our darkest moments he stands with us as one "[able] to empathize with our weaknesses" (Heb. 4:15). More than empathize, he equips.

The church in Ephesus was a dangerous leadership post, where "wild beasts" were part of the flock (1 Cor. 15:32). Among the imperatives, Paul urged Timothy to "keep . . . the pattern of sound teaching" (2 Tim. 1:13), "guard the good deposit" (v. 14), and "continue in what you have learned" (3:14). Like every leader who hopes to survive, Timothy will need to saturate his mind with the Word. The revelation of God will help leaders develop the necessary strength for dealing with trials. It will tell you things about you and your leadership that one is incapable of knowing on one's own. It will enable you to keep your head in every situation, endure the hardship that comes with leading, and prepare for the difficult days to come (2 Tim. 3:1; 4:5).

God also enables us through the power of prayer. Prayer got Moses through some of his most difficult leadership moments. Rather than lashing out at those who attacked his leadership, he got alone and battled things out with God (Ex. 17:3–4). He prayed over his soul, as well as for those who mercilessly attacked him (Ex. 32:11, 14; Num. 11:2; 12:13; 14:19).

There are times in this war when leaders must fight the unseen enemy with the unseen power of praying through the psalms. A leader who prays through the psalms will find himself aligning with the emotions of the

---

30. Andrew Purves, *The Crucifixion of Ministry: Surrendering Our Ambitions to the Service of Christ* (Downers Grove, IL: InterVarsity Press, 2010), 91.

psalmist, even praying an occasional imprecatory prayer, calling for God to renounce and confront (Pss. 22:19–21; 44:23–26; 60:5–12; 74:10–11; 79:5–13; 80:2–19). Some of the psalms are volcanic eruptions of outrage, and this is okay. Evil can do great damage to divide and destroy, and there are times when a leader must ascend to the throne of God, fall down, and pray against those who violate justice. Some of our most effective prayers are personalized psalms in which evil is named, confronted, and shamed.[31]

A leader can ill afford to ignore the evil that underlies much of the suffering. Moses took on the sons of Korah, David defied Goliath, Esther exposed Haman, and Nehemiah stared down Sanballat and Tobiah. Leadership will be a fight, and sometimes it is a good fight (1 Tim. 6:12; 2 Tim. 1:7). Word and prayer are the weapons God provides. When the attacks are sourced in the spiritual realm—and many are—God has also given us a spiritual authority to exert with full force (Mark 3:15). Under his sovereign rule, we have no reason to fear (Col. 1:13). We have the power to say no to the flesh (Rom. 6:1–2; 1 Cor. 9:27), not conform to the world (Rom. 12:2), and resist the devil (James 4:7). Theology teaches that there are instances in which the Spirit will say that a leader does not have permission to remain neutral and sit still. One must fight.

God's power enables us to endure, grow, and trust. We can whine and squeal and run from our troubles, but our theology won't allow us. God is at work, and as the stories of Scripture indicate, he never wastes a crisis. Difficulties are some of the best means of our development. Obedience is learned through suffering (Heb. 5:8). Paul writes, "We know that suffering produces perseverance; perseverance, character" (Rom. 5:3–4). Opposition and persecution have a way of forging the soul (2 Cor. 11:23–29). In weakness we become strong (12:10).

God allowed Abraham to face setback after setback to fashion his faith. Behind the story of Joseph's crucibles was a loving God refining an arrogant, spoiled teenager who needed to become a man.[32] It's in the barren and

---

31. N. T. Wright, *Evil and the Justice of God* (London: SPCK, 2012), 133.

32. Timothy Keller, *The Prodigal Prophet: Jonah and the Mystery of God's Mercy* (New York: Viking, 2018), 28.

the quiet that Moses developed a shepherd's heart. Here David's character was also shaped to lead.

Like the psalmists, we discover that this shaping comes from unexpected sources, ones we would not choose. People we thought to be our friends betray us (Pss. 41:9; 55:12–13). Maintain the daily discipline of reading and praying the psalms, and you discover the writers were "criticized, teased, avoided, attacked, shot at, abandoned, stoned, cursed, hunted down, snubbed, stabbed in the back, treated like a doormat, and damned with faint praise."[33] And out of these trials, faith germinated and grew. Sometimes sufferings come in the ordinary, inglorious sides of leading, where we are not called to rise above but find the holiness of Christ in them.[34] And in this holiness, we find that God is developing faith and moral excellence in us for even greater, more effective service.

Afflictions have a way of opening our eyes to things we would otherwise miss in ourselves—a growing autocratic spirit, an assumption that we are irreplaceable, an aloofness to the pain of others. It is in the desert that God stripped away some of the illusions that Moses and David and Paul must have carried. There were habits that needed to be shaved. Alone and free of distractions, a leader sees in a mirror certain painful realities. Trials often provide the necessary space to discern what is true. We become more attuned to the presence of God and how life actually works. We become more aware of what has to change in us, especially if we are to influence others.

We find that narcissistic behaviors amount to suicide. It's like pulling the plug on your own resuscitation.[35] It's sawing off the branch that supports your leadership. Hurt and loss can help us see whether we have brought on these consequences by our actions. Divine purgation clears the decks for action.[36]

---

33. Eugene H. Peterson, *Leap Over a Wall: Earthy Spirituality for Everyday Christians* (New York: HarperCollins, 1997), 48.

34. M. Craig Barnes, *Diary of a Pastor's Soul: The Holy Moments in the Life of Ministry* (Grand Rapids: Brazos, 2020), 31.

35. Plantinga, *Not the Way It's Supposed to Be*, 126.

36. Barton, *Strengthening the Soul of Your Leadership*, 53.

There will be nights of the soul when we will have to decide if we will give up or hold firmly to God. Trials can take us into some dark valleys where there are no happy endings (at least immediately). We might identify with the words of Heman, leader of the Korahite guild, who wrote, "Darkness is my closest friend" (Ps. 88:18). We will come to the end of ourselves and scream, only to find that our situation—like Jonah in the whale and Jeremiah in the pit—has not changed. Will it be faith or faithlessness that responds?

Trusting God through the hardships of leading means

- knowing we are not alone—God suffers with us (2 Cor. 1:3–4);
- anticipating a glorious ending that transcends the present pain (Rom. 8:18); and
- holding on to the fact that God is more than able to draw good out of whatever setback or loss or attack we face (Rom. 8:28).

CONCLUSION

In his memoir *The Pastor,* Eugene Peterson talks about the annual pilgrimage he and his family would take, driving from his Maryland parish to their family cabin in Montana. It would begin in a green landscape of growth and fertility, eventually shifting to a featureless aridity, a.k.a. the Dakota Badlands. It became a metaphor for his leadership.

Every leader at some point crosses into the badlands. We've identified a number of them and looked at how leaders survive. Seeing them through a theological frame, we find that these stretches of barrenness aren't entered by chance or by accident or without purpose. Behind the setbacks, the seasons in the wilderness, and the losses is the hand of God. Scriptural accounts reveal that suffering is understood "within the orbit of God's power and purpose."[37] He is never caught unawares by our pain, and

---

37. Michael F. Bird, *Evangelical Theology: A Biblical and Systematic Introduction* (Grand Rapids: Zondervan, 2013), 690.

what he is doing is ultimately good (Gen. 50:20). Goodness is his nature. This is why all things will work together for the good of those who love him (Rom. 8:28).

In almost every case, there will be the purging of illusion, indulgence, and self-importance. There will be the expelling of idolatries, inordinate desires, self-aggrandizement, ungodly ambitions, and disingenuousness. At the same time, there will be the working in of the necessary leadership virtues of fortitude and perseverance. The value of the benefits that come out of our God-designed suffering will be invaluable, far greater and longer lasting than the temporary cost.

What matters is how we handle the griefs that come with leading. Tucked away in one of my leadership journals is a remark made by a theologian who said, "Tell me how you suffer. This reveals your character." God alone shows us how.

The good news is that the difficulties and griefs that come with leading are temporal. Leadership, as we will see in the next and final chapter, is eternal. But first, a look at a leader who lived a life of lament.

✺ JEREMIAH ✺

Few leaders have faced the pain that Jeremiah the prophet encountered. Setbacks, misunderstandings, loneliness, failure, enemies, and loss all intersected with his life. It's in the nature of a prophet to be the voice of God, which is a hazardous calling. Such an act of leadership presses the flesh to its limits. Prophets upset the equilibrium. They speak words that destabilize, and these often incur the wrath of those who hear.

Born in a town on the brink of the Judean wilderness, Jeremiah was acquainted with life on the edge. But Jeremiah would soon be in the center, the place of exposure where leaders often live. It all started years earlier. Jeremiah was summoned for a divine purpose while still in the womb (Jer. 1:4–5).

As God's prophetic leader, Jeremiah must hear, receive, and speak whatever God tells him. Like every leader, he will have to step out and live with the consequences. Because he is a threat, Jeremiah will have more than his share of adversaries. This is his lot. He has been appointed over the nations to fulfill the will of God. His words are given by God to bring change—to uproot, tear down, destroy, and replant (v. 10). As with any prophet of God, his words are intended to confront the evils in a world where evil is normalized. Like bombshells, they will impact and blast apart present behaviors, policies, and ways. People will be offended and ask, "Who gave you the right?"

Jeremiah will complain, of course, feeling pushed into all this by God. He has to tell his world

- that the alleged power of the dominant culture is fraudulent;
- that God, not nations or kings or presidents, rules the world; and
- that living for one's appetites is a quick way to eat yourself to death.

Jeremiah will speak against the political establishment and eventually get arrested. He will speak against the false pastors, including those in his hometown, and have everyone turn on him (11:21). He will "face the crushing storms of hostility and furies of bitter doubt . . . every muscle in his body stretched to the limits by fatigue, every thought in his mind subjected to rejection, every feeling in his heart put through fires of ridicule."[38] Jeremiah will be derided and isolated for the forty years he speaks out. The deepest pain of all is that no one will listen, so loneliness will stalk his life.

Nonetheless, leaders have to step up and rise to the occasion. When life feels unfair, there will be the temptation to find a way out, to seek a release from divine obligation, and to demand answers. Jeremiah will scream, "Why should I pay the price for the disobedience of others?" Like Job, he will get so angry that he will curse the day he was born (20:14). He will also hope God will console him and soften the assignment. What leader, during

---

38. Eugene H. Peterson, *Running with the Horses: The Quest for Life at Its Best* (Downers Grove: InterVarsity Press, 2019), loc. 113, Kindle.

harsh times, doesn't wish for this? But as the narrative reveals, God will not put up with our hesitancies. He will overrule our protests, for God has an overriding and tenacious commitment to his own purposes.[39]

There will be moments in our whining when God will ask the same question he asked Jeremiah: "If you have raced with men on foot and they have worn you out, how can you compete with horses? If you stumble in safe country, how will you manage in the thickets by the Jordan?" (12:5). Peterson paraphrases: "If you are fatigued by the run-of-the-mill crowd of apathetic mediocrities, what will you do when the real race starts, the race with the swift and determined horses of excellence?"[40]

A leader will have to decide whether she will step up and fulfill the summons she has received or play it safe and live a life of incrementalism (small changes to small things). Will we live cautiously or courageously? Choosing to live courageously, to run with the horses, would look like this:

- standing in God's presence, stretched to live at our best
- holding out hope when everything appears hopeless
- standing our ground no matter what
- living a life of purpose rather than a life of comfort
- being mobilized rather than paralyzed
- living life at God's level rather than self-level
- living maximally rather than minimally
- living intentionally rather than aimlessly
- living authentically rather than vicariously
- changing the world rather than conforming to it
- living as a victor rather than a victim

This is leading that typifies Jeremiah's, that leads to large changes to large things. Anything less is a waste of time. But it may cost one's relationships, one's comforts, one's status, and even one's life.

---

39. Walter Brueggemann, *Like Fire in the Bones: Listening for the Prophetic Word in Jeremiah* (Minneapolis: Fortress, 2006), 6.

40. Peterson, *Running with the Horses*, loc. 155 of 1984, Kindle.

CHAPTER 11

IS THERE A FUTURE FOR LEADERSHIP?

*I'm not given to waxing romantic about aging and
dying. I simply know that the first is a privilege and the
second is not up for negotiation.*
—Parker J. Palmer

Endings are inevitable for leaders. Or so it seems. Health. Uprising. Revolt. End of term. Voted off the island. Ascension to the highest rung of the ladder begins a clock ticking down toward the leader's inevitable departure.[1]

Winston Churchill was eventually cast out of office. The nation's war leader had run at full tilt, but then the war ended. His Conservative Party lost its authority to rule, and Churchill was haunted with the question, "What now?" Churchill's daughter, Mary, gives an account of his final night in power: "It was an agonizing spectacle to watch this giant among men—equipped with every faculty of mind and spirit wound to the tightest

---

1. An observation made by Stanley McChrystal while sitting at the table of the Joint Chiefs of Staff. *Leaders: Myth and Reality* (New York: Portfolio/Penguin, 2018), 246.

pitch—walking unhappily round and round unable to employ his great energy and boundless gifts—nursing in his heart a grief and disillusion I can only guess at."[2] As the evening came to an end, she and the family went to bed both tired and dead inside.

As we come to the end of this book, it is fitting to talk about leadership's transition, its end, as well as its future. We know there is an end point, but is there a future? Just as we saw with power, leadership does end unceremoniously for most. But is this the finale? Is there a leadership beyond leadership? This is the eleventh question leaders inevitably face.

What we know for sure is that every leader faces a transition, and often it is difficult. As the story of Churchill reveals, the shift from a leader who is regarded as the future to one who represents the past can be incredibly painful. Especially for those who have wielded great power, managing influence as though it were a tangible commodity.[3] The pain is exacerbated when one is only looking backward.

For three decades, James Baker III had his hand in nearly every major event in the nation's capital. With such titles as chief of staff and secretary of state, he shaped events that shaped the world. But time and decline take their toll. As his biographers put it, "He was one more former, one more voice from the past, dismissed as out of date and out of touch . . ."[4] Eventually, he was shunned as a relic of the past with seemingly little to look forward to.

Robert Caro, in his book *Working*, tells another story of another painful transition, one he saw up close. There was a season when Robert Moses was one of New York's most powerful men. He was a twentieth-century power broker whose influence diminished over time. Witnessing this, Caro writes, "I realized that Robert Moses' days of power were over, and to the complex mixture of my feelings about him was added a wholly new one: pity. For as one of his secretaries told me, 'He had just as much energy

---

2. Quoted in Erik Larson, *The Splendid and the Vile: A Saga of Churchill, Family, and Defiance during the Blitz* (New York: Penguin, 2020), 503.

3. McChrystal, *Leaders*, 298.

4. Peter Baker and Susan Glasser, *The Man Who Ran Washington* (New York: Anchor, 2021), 838.

as ever. And what was he going to do with it now?' An architect who knew him said, 'The idea of this great mind having nothing to do—that's the most awful thing.' And his wife, who knew him best, added, 'It's horrible. For him, that would be hell.'"[5]

I have witnessed something of this in a number of leaders I have known. Their identity, the perks, the power, and the full schedule are suddenly things of the past. Life becomes unsettling. Especially if one has given no thought to tomorrow.

This temporal hell is also captured in the film *About Schmidt*. It's one more story about endings, told through a character by the name of Warren Schmidt. He is an insurance actuary played by Jack Nicholson. It begins with Schmidt sitting at a desk, much like a prisoner, staring at a clock and waiting for his sentence to begin. Retirement will be his prison. Once the second hand hits twelve, Warren takes his briefcase and exits the firm. There are the customary goodbyes, the retirement dinner, and the invitation to visit when in the neighborhood. It's all smiles, except for Warren. He is sad and lost. He wakes up to a life with no identity, no real meaning, and no clear purpose. He visits his young successor to offer his help, but it is clear his experience and counsel are of no value. To make matters worse, he leaves the building only to see that the contents and files of his life's work have been thrown into a dumpster awaiting the garbage collectors.

Eventually, we all become a part of the past. In time, both mind and body will collapse under the weight of mortality, and reality sets in. As writer Parker Palmer puts it, "Age gives us a chance to outgrow what William Butler Yeats called 'the lying days of our youth' and wither into what Oliver Wendell Holmes called 'the simplicity that lies on the other side of complexity.'"[6] But many of us tend to hang on to the notion that both the end of leadership and death are for someone else.

The result is that few leaders prepare for a smooth changeover. Jeffrey Sonnenfeld studied the succession process in American culture,

---

5. Robert A. Caro, *Working* (New York: Knopf, 2019), 61.
6. Parker J. Palmer, *On the Brink of Everything: Grace, Gravity & Getting Old* (Oakland: Berrett-Koehler, 2018), 23.

and after years of research and interviews, he concluded that many leaders must be forcibly extracted.[7] In some of these cases the organization has no transition plan because leaders do not have one for themselves. They are unprepared intellectually, emotionally, and spiritually for what comes next.

Compounding this, few leadership books give much advice for those leaders heading into the last chapters of their lives. One exception is Christopher Wright's *The Third Third of Life*.[8] The subject of a leader's passage from one season to the next is often avoided or at best left for one's memoir. Like most, leaders are tempted to live in denial. They keep revising upward the number of years left to lead. It's notable that at the end of his book *Still Surprised*, Warren Bennis referred to his end date of work as "hypothetical" rather than what it is—actual.[9]

Some books, like *A Leader's Legacy* by Kouzes and Posner, are the exception. The authors look at leadership from a larger context and deal with closure. They define legacy as the life you lead, focusing on the core areas of leadership you want to be remembered for: significance, relationships, aspiration, and courage.[10] Another book speaking to transition is Noel Tichy's *The Leadership Engine, though he devotes only eight pages at the end*. His main advice is that a leader must develop other leaders and know when it is time to leave.[11]

Ultimately a leader must work through basic questions like, "Have I fulfilled my objectives? Have I lost my passion to lead? Has the organization outgrown me? Is it time to pass the baton?" "What is next?"[12] Seeking advice from other leaders, we tend to receive a sort of, "Figure it out" and

---

7. Jeffrey Sonnenfeld, *The Hero's Farewell: What Happens When CEOs Retire* (New York: Oxford University Press, 1988), 81–215.

8. Walter C. Wright, *The Third Third of Life: Preparing for Your Future* (Downers Grove, IL: InterVarsity Press, 2012).

9. Warren G. Bennis and Patricia Ward Biederman, *Still Surprised: A Memoir of a Life in Leadership* (San Francisco: Jossey-Bass, 2010), 212.

10. James M. Kouzes and Barry Z. Posner, *A Leader's Legacy* (San Francisco: Jossey-Bass, 2006), 180.

11. Noel Tichy, *The Leadership Engine: How Winning Companies Build Leaders at Every Level* (New York: HarperBusiness Essentials, 2007), 189–96.

12. I devote a chapter to leadership and transitions in my book *Missing Voices: Learning to Lead beyond Our Horizons* (London: Langham, 2019), chap. 11.

"Good luck with that." Maybe it is part of the denial. What's needed is a better structure. One that not only faces the realities of transition and mortality but is curious and courageous enough to look at leadership beyond this thing called time. We will need theology for this.

GOD'S VIEW ON THE FUTURE OF LEADERSHIP

Theology speaks to the obvious present as well as introduces us to the less recognizable future. We can see only so far, though some theologians claim the kind of foresight that can see further out. To them Bloesch warns, "It is always a temptation to claim to know too much about heaven and hell. We tend to forget that these are mysteries beyond human comprehension."[13]

The doctrine of last things (a.k.a. eschatology) includes subjects like the kingdom of God, the intermediate and final states, heaven and hell, Christ's return, and future judgment. Most theologies give a substantive part of their works to discussing the future. Typically, this subject is the last volume or the final chapter of a theology, though Bird's *Evangelical Theology* places the subject toward the front. As he explains it, eschatology provides the framework for Christian theology as well as comprises the nucleus of the Christian gospel.[14] Any theology that is not "colored, flavored, saturated, and pervaded by eschatology" is deficient.[15]

Could it be that any leadership study that is not "colored" by eschatology is also incomplete? This chapter will make the case that an analysis of leadership is less than comprehensive if it has not grappled with leadership's inevitable decline and leadership's certain future in eternity. Four truths stand out.

---

13. Donald G. Bloesch, *The Last Things: Resurrection, Judgment, Glory* (Downers Grove, IL: InterVarsity Press, 2004), 229.

14. Michael F. Bird, *Evangelical Theology: A Biblical and Systematic Introduction* (Grand Rapids: Zondervan, 2013), 236.

15. Ibid.

Leadership Comes to a Conclusion in Time

Let's begin with the obvious. Some may live with the illusion of leadership continuing in perpetuity, but life—and theology—remind us that leadership on this present earth has a terminus. With few exceptions (Enoch and Elijah), the biblical narrative records that every leader experienced death. Their deaths foreshadow our own.

The patriarchs were summoned to lead and eventually were buried in ceremonial fashion. We read that Joshua replaced Moses, but not before we are given a careful account of how Moses's life ended. Moses's impulsive action and mistrust led to an early, forced retirement. As with every leader, God will allow Moses to go only so far (Deut. 34:4). Like him, some may or may not make it across the Jordan.

David followed Israel's first king, and like David, each succeeding king and his dynasty followed the one before. The transitions weren't always smooth. Some kings departed in dramatic fashion (Amaziah). Others took their own lives (Saul). Some were short-lived (Absalom). Others hung on too long (Hezekiah). Some transitions were less turbulent and more of a graduation. Elijah passed the mantle to Elisha. Jesus sent his disciples out as the Father sent him. Paul handed leadership to Timothy, declaring, "I have finished the race" (2 Tim. 4:7).

In every case, we find that leadership has its cycles. As we saw in Ecclesiastes 4:13–16, leadership has a painfully short shelf life. Nonetheless, Scripture hints at the human tendency to live in denial and perceive death as hypothetical. The psalmist writes with a hope that the faithful will still bear fruit in old age, staying "fresh and green" (Ps. 92:14). But even with facial creams and a high-fiber diet, we don't stay green. Frailty and death are the great intruders, and theology does not suggest otherwise.

Leadership's Course Is Not Ours to Define

Theology deconstructs the notion that we have leadership under control. It is not up to us to determine our destiny and the parameters of our leading. As another wisdom passage underscores, most of our leadership endeavors are unforeseen and beyond our command (Eccl. 9:11–12). The swift may run the race, but they may not make it to the end. Skillful leading matters, but time and events will rule the outcome—and no one knows when and how it ends. The fish may swim merrily, and the birds may fly effortlessly, but in a moment, they might be entrapped. Our plans go only so far. In a world conceited about itself and its achievements, success is not ours to command. It's not in man to direct his steps (Jer. 10:23). The only thing we can hold on to is God's providence. The wise give him all they have today, for they will have less tomorrow.

Leadership Has a Future in Eternity

This is one of the stunning statements in Scripture. Scripture reveals that although earthly leadership has a terminus, leadership continues on the other side. Jesus made this clear to his time-bound disciples. Toward the end of Jesus's time on earth, his disciples began to wonder if the sacrifice of their lives would pay off in the future. Speaking for the others, Peter asked, "What then will there be for us?" (Matt. 19:27). Jesus announced both a present kingdom and a future kingdom and summoned them to lead in both. With the passing of time, they would have positions of leadership in heaven, sitting on twelve thrones, judging the twelve tribes of Israel (v. 28). Jesus repeated this truth again at the Last Supper (Luke 22:30). Seat assignments, however, will be determined by the Father (Mark 10:40).

John fills out the picture. In Revelation we are given a vision of a new heaven and a new earth as the final eschatological reality (21:1–3). There will be a corporate merger of sorts between heaven and earth, with the former being the change agent and the latter being changed.[16] Any previous sense of God's absence will be replaced by his eternal presence (v. 3). The last words of the book of Ezekiel tell us that the name of the eschatological city will be *Yahweh Shammah*, "THE LORD IS THERE" (48:35).

In this context, we are told, the disciples will sit in the realm of Jesus's throne (Rev. 3:21). The city will be surrounded by a great and high wall having twelve gates. On these will be the names of the twelve tribes (21:12).

---

16. Ben Witherington III, *Biblical Theology: The Convergence of the Canon* (New York: Cambridge University Press, 2019), 416.

These will provide entrance for those outside the city, and it may be that here is where the disciples will sit. They will eat and drink with those coming from the east and the west (Matt. 8:11; Luke 22:30).

Important to note is that the promise of a future leadership role made to the disciples has also been extended to a broader core of saints—in particular to those who have sacrificed and endured. Paul stated, "If we endure, we will also reign with him" (2 Tim. 2:12). Anticipating possible doubt, Paul declared to Timothy *pistos ho logos*—count on it! He informed others of the same truth, telling the Romans that all who have received God's saving grace will reign through the one man, Jesus Christ (Rom. 5:17–19).

Jude envisioned the same (vv. 14–15). Toward the end of Revelation, John again connects future rule to those who have suffered. Heaven will include a tribunal of leaders made up of victorious martyrs (20:4).

The idea of a future in which saints are leading others is a common apocalyptic theme that goes back to Daniel 7:18 and 27: "The holy people of the Most High will receive the kingdom. . . . Then the sovereignty, power and greatness of all the kingdoms under heaven will be handed over to the holy people of the Most High." The saints will have a dominion that extends over the kingdoms, but who are they? Revelation 21:22–27 foresees the ongoing existence of nations, even though their authority and power are gone (1 Cor. 15:24). Will the sacred and secular unite in an enduring synthesis?[17] Scripture seems to shade into mystery.

In another vision, John hears Jesus promise, "To the one who is victorious and does my will to the end, I will give authority over the nations" (Rev. 2:26). The leadership described here is anything but that of benign caretakers. John adds, "That one 'will rule them with an iron scepter and will dash them to pieces like pottery'" (v. 27). The words come from Psalm 2:8–9. The psalmist envisioned this day, but the context remains a mystery, as does the nature of judging.

The word *judging* is used often to describe the leadership role, but what the full work of judging entails is unclear. *Krinō* speaks to the work of

---

17. Something suggested by Bloesch in *The Last Things*, 230.

upholding God's justice and bringing humanity's injustice to light. The Septuagint influence broadens the meaning of the term to include the authority to rule.[18] We are not told much more than this. Since hell does not eclipse heaven but is made to serve heaven, this may give some insight to this more severe side of judging.

Millard Erickson acknowledges, "It is not clear just what is involved in this judging, but apparently it is service or work done on behalf of the king."[19] While we tend to view the role of judging from a negative standpoint, it also has the positive role of establishing a divine order that shall persist forever.[20] Could this be because perfection in heaven might mean unending progress, a never-ceasing advance? Quoting from Irenaeus, Bloesch writes, "God will always have something more to teach man, and man will always have more to learn from God."[21] This may require continual adjudicating .

Leadership as God Intended Will Be Restored

It's astounding to consider that leadership has an eternal dimension. But in some sense, it is not a surprise. It could be that this future vision of leading serves to bring together God's original intent for leadership. From the beginning humanity was created to lead. God made humanity in his own image and said, "Be fruitful and increase in number; fill the earth and subdue it. Rule over the fish in the sea and the birds in the sky and over every living creature that moves on the ground" (Gen. 1:28; cf. Ps. 8:6–8). Stewardship and care are part of it (Gen. 2:15).

As noted in earlier chapters, humanity was placed in a garden temple to rule, as well as give praise and adoration to the King. People were created not only to serve as vice-regents but to function as priests, in charge of honoring the presence of God and keeping the temple holy. In his helpful chapter "Priests and Rulers," N. T. Wright gives this summary: "The royal

---

18. Walter Schneider, "judgment," *The New International Dictionary of New Testament Theology* (Grand Rapids: Zondervan, 1978), 2:365.

19. Millard J. Erickson, *Readings in Christian Theology* (Grand Rapids: Baker, 1987), 3:1230.

20. Bloesch discusses this in *The Last Things*, 66.

21. Ibid., 232.

and priestly vocation of all human beings, it seems, consists in this: to stand at the interface between God and his creation, bringing God's wise and generous order to the world and giving articulate voice to creation's glad and grateful praise to its maker."[22]

Like two threads that run from Genesis to Revelation, this dual identity of ruler and priest surfaces from time to time. God called Moses (leader) and Aaron (priest) to work as one to guide God's people out of Egypt. Once his people were liberated from Pharaoh, God told them, "Although the whole earth is mine, you will be for me a kingdom of priests" (Ex. 19:5–6). In similar fashion, Peter, in his first letter to the church, refers to the church as "a royal priesthood" (1 Peter 2:9).

Passages of Scripture pointing to eternity confirm that this dual vocation will come to perfect expression. The eschatological promises of Daniel 7:27 and Revelation 1:5–6; 5:9–10; and 20:4 will be fulfilled. An eternity is coming when humanity will no longer be royal priests in waiting. They will rule as God intended from the beginning. Revelation 22:3–5 reveals saints serving as royal priests before his throne, "and they will reign for ever and ever" (v. 5).

These threads help to explain why eternal rewards are royal by definition. We will receive crowns, but unlike earthly crowns, these will last forever (1 Cor. 9:25). They go by various names: the crown of righteousness (2 Tim. 4:8), the crown of life (James 1:12), and the crown of glory (1 Peter 5:4). They are to be held on to, as well as cast before the King (Rev. 3:11; 4:10–11). It may be that part of the motivation to be faithful in the present is the promise of crowns, and the more one possesses, the greater the opportunity to serve as a ruler-priest.

Theologian Michael Bird gives this summary: "God has delegated a special authority to humanity to reign on the earth as kings and priests in a *penultimate* stage of the kingdom in the context of the present world, and then God has also intended for humanity to rule over the world in the

---

22. N. T. Wright, *After You Believe: Why Christian Character Matters* (New York: HarperOne, 2010), 80–81.

ultimate stage of the kingdom characterized by everlasting glory."[23] We will participate in the rule of Christ over the eternal kingdom and perhaps exercise sovereignty over the new creation in a way similar to how Adam was to rule over every living thing.[24]

Just as we should think not in terms of the end of God's creation but in terms of the end of creation in its current condition, so we should think not in terms of the end of leadership but in terms of the end of leadership in its current state. Such hope reinforces the conviction that Christianity is not exclusively theocentric but "theoanthropocentric."[25] In heaven, God will be exalted, and leadership as God intended will be restored and transfigured, all to the glory of God.

CONCLUSION

For those of us fascinated with leadership, the good news is that leadership will not end. Our eventual loss of a leadership role in the present may not be anything more than a transition. A postponement. Could it be that our most significant leadership lies ahead? The leadership we have carried out is simply preparatory. This life and leadership is a prelude to a future story without end.

Think of a future leadership in which there will be no more setbacks, misunderstandings, failures, and adversaries. No more criticism. No more sense of loneliness. No more battles with the unseen enemy. No more preparation. *No more leadership books!* Leaders will be perfectly prepared to lead for the love of leading. We will lead as God initially intended, as servant leaders whose power is in our humility.

This does, however, have present implications. The promise that we will rule in heaven should impact how we lead in the present. If we will

---

23. Bird, *Evangelical Theology*, 287, italics in the original.
24. Grant R. Osborne, *Revelation* (Grand Rapids: Baker, 1999), 776.
25. Donald G. Bloesch, *The Holy Spirit: Works & Gifts* (Downers Grove, IL: InterVarsity Press, 2000), 332.

be given such extraordinary authority in the future, we should be able to handle the earth-size things we face in the present. Paul illustrates this in his letter to the Corinthians. Here God tells us that the church will rule with him over a dominion that one day will include the angels (1 Cor. 6:2–4). Given this, the church should be able to settle earthly matters. Looking to secular judges to pass judgment on issues we are equipped to work out on our own is an admission of failure. We fail to understand our future role—as well as our present power and ability to carry out our leadership as God intended.

Back to his book *On the Brink of Everything*, Parker Palmer reflects on his life experience. He notes, "I can't imagine a sadder way to die than with the sense that I never showed up here on earth as my God-given self."[26] God has summoned us to pursue a vocation as royal priests with the mission of serving God and bringing glory to him. This is a leader's God-given identity, one that will continue well beyond the end of time. It is time to show up as our God-given selves and start practicing for the future. Our final character study serves as a great example.

SAMUEL

There's something promising about the young man. There he is, all dressed in his linen ephod, whatever that was. We know it was associated with divine presence and guidance, though it was nothing like the special garment worn by the high priest, one decked out with its gemstones and onyx clasps. That would come later.

Samuel is emerging, but he is coming onto the stage of leadership as someone more than a priest. It will not be long before Israel will recognize his as "a manhood of enormous authority," destined by God.[27] His words begin to have such force that God will "let none of Samuel's words fall to the

---

26. Palmer, *On the Brink of Everything*, 59.
27. Walter Brueggemann, *First and Second Samuel* (Louisville: John Knox, 1990), 22.

ground" (1 Sam. 3:19). His occasional posts go viral. Everyone can see he is both priest and prophet. Scripture says his words "came to all Israel" (4:1).

Everything was coming together for Samuel, and then everything went dark.

For twenty years Samuel disappeared from the scene. It was a horrific time, worse even than the period of the judges. At least then there was still Shiloh, a place known for its tranquility and security and as a place for Israel's worship. But Shiloh was no longer. The ark of the covenant was stolen, Samuel was displaced, Eli died a tragic death, and the glory of God departed (4:10–22). It's hard to find a more shattering chapter in Scripture. It marked the end of the Mosaic period.[28]

Marginalized, politically weak, economically wrecked, and morally decayed—this was the state of the nation. What life that remained in Israel was gradually sucked out. It was like one long funeral (7:2). Everyone was hunkered down in their own little bubble. Meanwhile the Philistines were not faring so well either. After their big victory and the stealing of the ark, things began to come apart. It started with the pagan gods mysteriously falling over and breaking into pieces. And then came the rats. But when a whole city was afflicted with hemorrhoids, that was it (5:9). It was a tipping point for everyone.

Samuel's words broke Israel's long silence: "Rid yourselves of the foreign gods . . . and commit yourselves to the LORD" (7:3). The sheer force of Samuel's gravitas awakened Israel out of its stupor. Everyone gathered at Mizpah, and Scripture notes Samuel became more than priest and prophet. Samuel became the leader of Israel (v. 6). He fleshed out the role of royal priest, what God intended for leaders to be from the beginning (Gen. 1:28). For a season Samuel spoke prophetic words, led as Israel's judge, and served as the nation's priest. He did this within the context of a theocracy, in which the lines of authority and the patterns for well-being were clear, effective, and accepted as valid.[29] *This was rooted leadership!*

---

28. Peter J. Leithart, *A Son to Me: An Exposition of 1 & 2 Samuel* (Moscow: Canon, 2003), loc. 575, Kindle.

29. Brueggemann, *First and Second Samuel*, 48.

Samuel is a fitting model to end on. He points back to Genesis and ahead to Revelation. He was a leader's leader, a priestly king. The small boy wearing the robe his mother made him grew to rule and worship. He combined these into extraordinary leadership. He prayed the kind of prayers that set armies to flight. The savor of his offerings and intercessions lifted skyward, coursing their way to heaven. And God—as he is prone to do with leaders with whom he is well pleased—hurled them back to earth in the form of answered prayers. Inspired by Revelation 8:5, Peterson refers to such prayers as "reversed thunder," where petitions ascend and reenter history with incalculable effects.[30]

Receiving Samuel's worship and acting through one called to serve the purposes of God, God threw Israel's enemies into a panic (1 Sam. 7:10). From that point on, and throughout Samuel's lifetime, the hand of the Lord was against the Philistines. As the narrator notes, "So the Philistines were subdued and they stopped invading Israelite territory" (v. 13).

Like all leaders, Samuel dies, but we receive a glimpse of Samuel's future leadership in eternity. Called up by a desperate Saul, Samuel reemerged back into time still wearing the robe marking him as a royal priest (28:14). Verse 15 tells us he was "disturbed," but could it be that it was not as one out of a deep sleep but one interrupted from greater leadership responsibilities, those fitted for leaders of the future in eternity?

---

30. Eugene H. Peterson, *Reversed Thunder: The Revelation of John & the Praying Imagination* (New York: HarperOne, 1991), 88.

CONCLUSION

It is possible.

We can bring leadership to another level—and we need to. We can raise the bar and lead over it. But this effort will require a different leadership mindset. One that recognizes that in leadership discussions, theology not only has a place at the table; it sits at the head, showing us how to lead in a profoundly better way. One that is rooted in God. That's the argument of this book.

Working my way through a vast amount of what has already been written on leadership, I have gained a renewed respect for the many who have contributed to leadership theory—be they a Harvard professor, a retired military general, a political historian, a corporate authority, or a ministry consultant. There's so much to learn and keep learning from them. But I have discovered that the best wisdom for leading is found in going back to the original source—God—to study the subject of leadership. God's leadership takes us to a higher plane of understanding and providing practical advice for day-to-day activities. Even the best parts of so much that is taught by other disciplines originated in the Bible.

Sound theology finds its source and authority in God's revealed Word. This is why much of the leadership theory discussed in this book goes back to biblical passages. Ultimately, all human beings turn to some theory to guide their lives and turn to models to follow. It is in God's authoritative Word and in the biblical models, however, that we find some of our best leadership material. A more substantive understanding of leadership develops on that basis, which goes beyond many of the thin, pragmatic models popular today.

Many of the greatest lessons for leadership come from God. He answers the core questions every leader faces. It's to be expected. He is the one who invented leadership and created it for his purposes. He teaches us through the likes of Abraham, Moses, Samuel, Joshua, David, Solomon, Nehemiah, Esther, Paul—and others. None are perfect. Sometimes we learn as much from their misbehavior as from their godly conduct. Only one person serves as the polestar, the essence of leadership, and that is Jesus. The Son of God is the leader par excellence.

From these examples, we discovered that there is no mystery to leadership's definition: leadership is the ability to use the authority and power of God to serve the purposes of God. That's it. Every leadership theme is built on this. God summons leaders to be servants. That's one of the paradoxes of theological leadership.

Though we might find it offensive to our notion of self-importance, God does not need leaders. Yet it is clear that God has chosen to use leaders to help achieve his purposes. Little is accomplished without leaders. Leaders are "dispensably indispensable." They bring order and direction and stem the chaos. So God summons leaders as part of his grand plan.

Theology enables us to delineate leadership credibility. There are three essential components: moral character, wisdom, and competence. Principled leaders build their values on the character of God. They admit that any sense of a true north is beyond them. The only redemptive answer is Jesus. The wisdom to be gained is from God; hence it's a wisdom that goes beyond personal experience. True wisdom is sourced in God, its distinguishing mark being a leader's fear of God. Turning to skills, there are at least seven competencies to develop, and each is referenced and illustrated in the revelation of God. It's here where theory and practice come together.

Credible leaders are equipped to carry out the leadership task. Leaders are called to help the institution they lead answer these central questions: Why are we here? Where are we going? How can we get there? This implies missional, visionary, strategic, and tactical leadership. In the process, the very best leaders realize that their task is not complete until there is implementation and execution.

To carry out the task, leaders will need to be empowered. So much of leadership is about power, but power is elusive, easily abused, and often misunderstood. Only theology can help us gain our bearings. It is here where we find another counterintuitive truth. Power's greatest expression is not in our self-expanding but in our self-emptying. Hard as it is to comprehend and accept, power is perfected in our weakness.

It's in the nature of leaders to get into trouble. A leader's flawed nature explains many of the reasons for trials and enemies—an abusive use of power being one. Other reasons exist for the pain and suffering leaders experience, however. There's enough rebelliousness in all of us to bring grief to even the best of leaders. And there's also an unseen war none of us escape this side of eternity. God nonetheless uses these challenges for his purposes, and those leaders who understand this, submit to this process, and get in step with God become far stronger.

Unlike some things that will end with time (death, taxes, and dental appointments), leadership is different. It is eternal. It's inherent in our identity that God has made us to rule as royal priests (Gen. 1:28), and Scripture informs us that we will do this for all eternity.

In the meantime, this can be our moment. I do believe God is still looking for leaders who will stand in the gap. The God who summoned Abraham is still calling. Are you ready and willing? He has provided the means to a new life, a map that shows the way to leadership as he sees it, answers the critical questions leaders face, and provides the power to carry out the leadership task. It can extend far beyond our imagination (Eph. 3:20–21).

ACKNOWLEDGMENTS

Somewhere, in one of Eugene Peterson's "Prayers at the Writing Desk," he wrote a prayer that he must have prayed nearly every time he sat down to write. It goes like this:

> *Lord Jesus Christ*
> *Word from the beginning*
> *Word made flesh*
> *Shape words also into speech*
> *and bring them to print*
> *that tell the truth*
> *and speak your glory. Amen.[1]*

Peterson was devoted to shaping sentences and words out of his soul. He accepted the ascetic appropriate to it. Over my years as a pastor and professor and writer, I have borrowed many things from Peterson. I have also copied this prayer and made it my own. It is this I must first acknowledge.

I have also drawn from nearly forty years of service in various leadership roles. Much of what I have written I owe to these contexts in which I have labored. There are leadership and theological insights I have

1. Winn Collier, *A Burning in My Bones: The Authorized Biography of Eugene H. Peterson* (Colorado Springs: Waterbrook, 2021), 169.

discovered in numerous books, what Proust refers to as "the noblest of distractions."[2] They are too numerous to note here, but they are found in the bibliography.

I am grateful for the leadership insights gained from a small group of consultants and friends that include Bud Lindstrand, Steve Reinhart, Alex Kulpecz, and Clayton Lewis. I am particularly indebted to Brad Kerr, who edited my work, taking it on as if it was his own. Given his corporate experience with Shell Oil, and his deep passion for God and his church, he has been an invaluable resource.

The idea behind this book was birthed in a library at Arab Baptist Theological Seminary, Beirut, Lebanon, where I was teaching leadership to students from regions including Sudan and Egypt and Syria. Seeing their desperate condition, as well as the decline of leadership in my own culture, I became convinced that a book bringing both leadership and theology together is an urgent need. Submitting a proposal to Zondervan, I am grateful God led me to Ryan Pazdur, vice president and publisher. I owe much to him for his guidance and encouragement. I am also appreciative of the superb editors whose work of reshaping and refining—and refining— have helped bring this together. I am also grateful to Chuck Conriry, president of Western Seminary, for his initial counsel and support, as well as my colleagues.

Writing is, as author Mark Buchanan put it, "a relentlessly tedious and solitary act . . . a bit like being under house arrest."[3] Yet I must confess that nearly every morning I have escaped in my kayak to paddle the Pend Oreille River, closing the day by making another break to bike a nearby loop. In such moments, I have gained some of my best insights. Ultimately, I have God to thank for all of this.

---

2. Quoted in Epstein, *Gallimaufry*, 16.
3. Buchanan, *God Walk*, 227.

SELECT BIBLIOGRAPHY

Applebaum, Anne. "The Autocrats are Winning." *The Atlantic*, December 2021.

Ayers, Michale. "Toward a Theology of Leadership." *Journal of Biblical Perspectives in Leadership* 1, no. 1 (Fall 2006): 3–27.

Bailey, Sarah Pulliam. "Newly Leaked Letter Details Allegations that Southern Baptist Leaders Mishandled Sex Abuse Claims." *Washington Post*, June 5, 2021.

Baime, A. J. *The Accidental President: Harry S. Truman and the Four Months That Changed the World.* New York: Mariner, 2017.

Baker, Peter, and Susan Glasser. *The Man Who Ran Washington.* New York: Anchor, 2021.

Baldwin, Joyce G. *1 and 2 Samuel: An Introduction and Commentary.* Downers Grove, IL: InterVarsity Press, 1988.

Bardwick, Judith M. "Peacetime Management and Wartime Leadership." In *The Leader of the Future: New Visions, Strategies and Practices for the Next Era,* edited by Frances Hesselbein et al., 131–40. San Francisco: Jossey-Bass, 1996.

Barna, George. *Leaders on Leadership: Wisdom, Advice, Encouragement on the Act of Leading God's People.* Grand Rapids: Baker, 1998.

Barnes, M. Craig. *Diary of a Pastor's Soul: The Holy Moments in the Life of Ministry.* Grand Rapids: Brazos, 2020.

Bartholmew, Craig G. *Ecclesiastes.* Grand Rapids: Baker, 2009.

Barton, Ruth Haley. "The Old Testament Tells All." *Christianity Today,* July/August 2020.

———. *Pursuing God's Will Together.* Downers Grove, IL: InterVarsity Press, 2008.

———. *Strengthening the Soul of Your Leadership: Seeking God in the Crucible of Ministry.* Downers Grove, IL: InterVarsity Press, 2008.

Bauckham, Richard. *Who Is God? Key Moments of Biblical Revelation.* Grand Rapids: Baker, 2020.

Baxter, Richard. *The Reformed Pastor: A Pattern for Personal Growth and Ministry*. Portland: Multnomah, 1982.

Belsky, Scott. *Making Ideas Happen: Overcoming the Obstacles Between Vision and Reality*. New York: Penguin, 2010.

Bennis, Warren G. *On Becoming a Leader*. New York: Addison-Wesley, 1989.

Bennis, Warren G., and Patricia Ward Biederman. *Still Surprised: A Memoir of a Life in Leadership*. San Francisco: Jossey-Bass, 2010.

Bennis, Warren G. and Robert J. Thomas. *Geeks and Geezers: How Era, Values, and Defining Moments Shape Leaders*. Boston: Harvard Business School Press, 2002.

Bird, Michael F. *Evangelical Theology: A Biblical and Systematic Introduction*. Grand Rapids: Zondervan, 2013.

Bloesch, Donald G. *God the Almighty: Power, Wisdom, Holiness, Love*. Downers Grove, IL: InterVarsity Press, 1995.

———. *The Last Things: Resurrection, Judgment, Glory*. Downers Grove, IL: InterVarsity Press, 2004.

———. *The Holy Spirit: Works & Gifts*. Downers Grove, IL: InterVarsity Press, 2000.

———. *The Paradox of Holiness: Faith in Search of Obedience*. Peabody, MA: Hendrickson, 2016.

———. *A Theology of Word & Spirit*. Downers Grove, IL: InterVarsity Press, 1992.

Bolman, Leo G., and Terrance E. Deal. *Reframing Organizations: Artistry, Choice, and Leadership*. San Francisco: Jossey-Bass, 1996.

Bolsinger, Tod. *Canoeing the Mountains: Christian Leadership in Uncharted Territory*. Downers Grove, IL: InterVarsity Press, 2018.

———. *Tempered Resilience: How Leaders Are Formed in the Crucible of Change*. Downers Grove, IL: InterVarsity Press, 2020.

Bossidy, Larry, and Ram Charan. *Execution: The Discipline of Getting Things Done*. New York: Random House, 2011.

Boyer, Steven D., and Christopher A Hall. *The Mystery of God: Theology for Knowing the Unknowable*. Grand Rapids: Baker, 2012.

Brafman, Ori, and Rod A. Beckstrom. *The Starfish and the Spider: The Unstoppable Power of Leaderless Organizations*. New York: Portfolio, 2006.

Brooks, David. *The Road to Character*. New York: Penguin, 2015.

———. *The Second Mountain: The Quest for a Moral Life*. New York: Random House, 2019.

Brown, Archie. *The Myth of the Strong Leader: Political Leadership in the Modern Age*. New York: Basic, 2014.

Brown, Colin, ed. *The New International Dictionary of New Testament Theology.* 3 vols. Translated by Lothar Coenen, Erich Beyreuther, and Hans Bietenhard. Grand Rapids: Zondervan, 1975.

Brueggemann, Walter. *1 & 2 Kings.* Smyth & Helwys Bible Commentary. Macon: Smyth Helwys, 2018.

———. *First and Second Samuel.* Louisville: John Knox, 1990.

———. *Genesis: Interpretation; A Bible Commentary for Teachings and Preaching.* Louisville: Westminster John Knox, 1986.

———. *Like Fire in the Bones: Listening for the Prophetic Word in Jeremiah.* Minneapolis: Fortress, 2006.

———. *The Prophetic Imagination,* 2nd ed. Minneapolis: Fortress, 2001.

———. *Theology of the Old Testament: Testimony, Dispute, Advocacy.* Minneapolis: Fortress, 2005.

———. *Truth Speaks to Power: The Countercultural Nature of Scripture.* Louisville: Westminster John Knox, 2013.

Bryson, Bill. *The Body: A Guide for Occupants.* Prescott, AZ: Anchor, 2019.

Buchanan, Mark. *God Walk: Moving at the Speed of Your Soul.* Grand Rapids: Zondervan, 2020.

Burns, Daniel E. "Our Post-Pandemic Decadence," a review of *The Decadent Society: America Before and After the Pandemic* by Ross Douthat. *National Review,* July 12, 2021.

Burns, James MacGregor. *Leadership.* New York: Open Road Media, 2012.

Burns, John S., John R. Shoup, and Donald C. Simmons, Jr., eds. *Organizational Leadership: Foundations and Practices for Christians.* Downers Grove, IL: InterVarsity Press, 2014.

Burton, Tara Isabella. *Strange Rites: New Religions for a Godless World.* New York: PublicAffairs, 2020.

Busch, Eberhard. *The Great Passion: An Introduction to Karl Barth's Theology.* Grand Rapids: Eerdmans, 2004.

Carlyle, Thomas. *On Heroes, Hero-Worship, and the Heroic in History.* 1840. Reprint, University of California Press, 1993.

Caro, Robert A. *Working: Researching, Interviewing, Writing.* Visalia, CA: Vintage, 2019.

———. *The Years of Lyndon Johnson: The Passage of Power.* New York: Knopf, 2012.

Charnock, Stephen. *The Existence and Attributes of God.* Grand Rapids: Baker, 1979.

Charry, Ellen. *By the Renewing of Your Minds: The Pastoral Function of Christian Doctrine.* Oxford University Press, 1993.

Ciulla, Joanne B. *The Nature of Leadership*. Los Angeles: Sage, 2004.

Clinton, J. Robert. *The Making of a Leader: Recognizing the Lessons and Stages of Leadership Development*. Colorado Springs: NavPress, 2012.

Cole, R. Alan. *Exodus: An Introduction and Commentary*. Downers Grove, IL: InterVarsity Press, 1984.

Collier, Winn. *A Burning in My Bones: The Authorized Biography of Eugene H. Peterson*. Colorado Springs: Waterbrook, 2021.

Collins, Jim. *Good to Great: Why Some Companies Make the Leap . . . And Others Don't*. New York: Harper Business, 2001.

———. *Good to Great and the Social Sectors: Why Business Thinking Is Not the Answer*. New York: Harper Business, 2001.

———. *Turning the Flywheel: A Monograph to Accompany Good to Great*. New York: HarperCollins, 2019.

Copan, Paul. *Is God a Moral Monster? Making Sense of the Old Testament God*. Grand Rapids: Baker, 2011.

Coutu, Diane. "How Resilience Works." *Harper Business Review*, May 2002.

Crenshaw, James L. *Old Testament Wisdom: An Introduction*. Louisville: Westminster John Knox, 1998.

Crouch, Andy. *Playing God: Redeeming the Gift of Power*. Downers Grove, IL: InterVarsity Press, 2013.

Cundall, Arthur E., and Leon Morris. *Judges & Ruth*. Downers Grove, IL: InterVarsity Press, 1968.

Dawn, Marva. *Powers, Weakness, and the Tabernacling of God*. Grand Rapids: Eerdmans, 2001.

DePree, Max. *Leadership Is an Art*. New York: Dell, 1989.

———. *Leadership Jazz*. New York: Dell, 1992.

Dolan, Timothy G. "Called to Lead." In *Organizational Leadership: Foundations and Practices for Christians*, edited by Burns et al., 15–34. Downers Grove, IL: InterVarsity Press, 2014.

Douthat, Ross. *The Decadent Society: How We Became the Victims of Our Own Success*. New York: Simon & Schuster, 2020.

Drucker, Peter. "Not Enough Generals Were Killed." In *The Leader of the Future: New Visions, Strategies and Practices for the Next Era*, edited by Frances Hesselbein et al., xi–xvi. San Francisco: Jossey-Bass, 1996.

Dryden, J. de Waal. *A Hermeneutic of Wisdom*. Grand Rapids: Baker, 2018.

Duckworth, Angela. *Grit: The Power of Passion and Perseverance*. New York: Scribner, 2016.

Eaton, Michael A. *Ecclesiastes: An Introduction and Commentary.* Downers Grove, IL: InterVarsity Press: 1983.

Eikhonon, Goldberg. *The Wisdom Paradox: How Your Mind Can Grow Stronger as Your Brain Grows Older.* New York: Gotham, 2005.

Epstein, Joseph. *Gallimaufry: A Collection of Essays, Reviews, Bits.* Edinburg: Axios, 2020.

———. "The Perfect Critic." Review of *The Complete Prose of T.S. Eliot* by Ronald Schuchard et al., *Wall Street Journal*, November 27–28, 2021. https://www .wsj.com/articles/the-collected-prose-of-t-s-eliot-review-tradition-keeper-of -the-flame-joseph-epstein-11637943045.

———. "Where the Self Meets the World," review of *Character: The History of a Cultural Obsession* by Marjorie Garber. *Wall Street Journal*, July 18–19, 2020. https://www.wsj.com/articles/character-review-where-the-self-meets-the -world-11594998822.

Erickson, Millard J. *Readings in Christian Theology.* Grand Rapids: Baker, 1987.

Eva, Nathan, et al. "Servant Leadership: A Systematic Review and Call for Future Research," *Leadership Quarterly* 30, no. 1 (February 2019): 111–32.

Ferguson, Niall. *The Square and the Tower: Networks and Power from the Freemasons to Facebook.* New York: Penguin, 2017.

Fisk, Robert. "11 August 2020: How Do You Save a Truly Corrupt Country Like Lebanon?" *Independent*, November 10, 2020. https://www.independent .co.uk/news/long_reads/robert-fisk-lebanon-beirut-explosion-corruption -government-resign-hezbollah-assad-sisi-b1642016.html.

Fisher, David. *The 21st Century Pastor: A Vision Based on the Ministry of Paul.* Grand Rapids: Zondervan, 1996.

Fleming, Dave. *Leadership Wisdom from Unlikely Voices: People of Yesterday Speak to Leaders of Today.* El Cajon, CA: EmergentYS, 2004.

Fox, Michael V. *Proverbs 1–9.* New Haven: Yale University Press, 2000.

France, R. T. *The Gospel of Matthew.* Grand Rapids: Eerdmans, 2007.

Franke, John R. *The Character of Theology: An Introduction to Its Nature, Task, and Purpose.* Grand Rapids: Baker, 2005.

———. *Missional Theology: An Introduction.* Grand Rapids: Baker, 2020.

Friedman, Edwin H. *A Failure of Nerve: Leadership in the Age of the Quick Fix.* New York: Seabury, 1999.

Galli, Mark. *Karl Barth: An Introductory Biography for Evangelicals.* Grand Rapids: Eerdmans, 2017.

Gardner, John W. *On Leadership.* New York: Free Press, 1993.

Garrett, James Leo. *Systematic Theology*. 2nd ed. Eugene, OR: Wipf & Stock, 2014.

Gentry, Peter J., and Stephen J. Wellum. *Kingdom through Covenant: A Biblical-Theological Understanding of the Covenants*. Wheaton, IL: Crossway, 2012.

George, Bill. *Discover Your True North: Becoming an Authentic Leader*. San Francisco: Jossey-Bass, 2007.

Gergen, David. *Eyewitness to Power: The Essence of Leadership; Nixon to Clinton*. Boston: GK Hall, 2001.

Gerth, H. H. and C. Wright Mills. *From Max Weber: Essays in Sociology*. New York: Oxford University Press, 1958.

Goldberg, Jonah. *Suicide of the West: How the Rebirth of Tribalism, Populism, Nationalism, and Identity Politics Is Destroying American Democracy*. New York: Crown Forum, 2018.

Goldingay, John. *Psalms*. 3 vols. Grand Rapids: Baker, 2006.

Goleman, Daniel, Richard Boyatzis, and Annie McKee. *Primal Leadership: Learning to Lead with Emotional Intelligence*. 2nd ed. Boston: Harvard Business School Press, 2013.

Gomez, Doris. "The Leader as Learner." *International Journal of Leadership Studies* 2, no. 3 (2007).

Goodwin, Doris Kearns. *Leadership: In Turbulent Times*. New York: Simon & Schuster, 2018.

———. *Lyndon Johnson and the American Dream*. New York: Open Road Media, 2015.

Goulston, Mark. *Just Listen: Discover the Secret to Getting Through to Absolutely Anyone*. New York: AMACOM, 2015.

Graham, Ruth. "The Rise and Fall of Carl Lentz, the Celebrity Pastor of Hillsong Church." *New York Times*, December 5, 2020. https://www.nytimes.com/2020/12/05/us/carl-lentz-hillsong-pastor.html.

Green, Andy. *The Office: The Untold Story of the Greatest Sitcom of the 2000s; An Oral History*. Hialeah: Dutton, 2020.

Greenleaf, Robert K. *On Becoming a Servant Leader: The Private Writings of Robert K. Greenleaf*. Edited by Don M. Frick and Larry C. Spears. San Francisco: Jossey-Bass, 1996.

———. *Servant Leadership: A Journey into the Nature of Legitimate Power and Greatness*. New York: Paulist, 1977.

Grint, Keith. *Leadership: A Very Short Introduction*. Oxford: Oxford University Press, 2010.

Grudem, Wayne. *Systematic Theology: An Introduction to Biblical Doctrine*. Grand Rapids: Zondervan, 2009.

Guinness, Os. *The Call: Finding and Fulfilling God's Purpose for Your Life*. Nashville: Nelson, 2003.

———. *Character Counts: Leadership Qualities in Washington, Wilberforce, Lincoln, and Solzhenitsyn*. Grand Rapids: Baker, 1999.

———. *Prophetic Untimeliness: A Challenge to the Idol of Relevance*. Grand Rapids: Baker, 2005.

Gushee, David P., and Colin Holtz. *Moral Leadership for a Divided Age: Fourteen People Who Dared to Change Our World*. Grand Rapids: Brazos, 2018.

Hagberg, Janet O. *Real Power: Stages of Personal Power in Organizations*. Sheffield: Sheffield Press, 2002.

Hamilton, Nigel. *The Mantle of Command: FDR at War, 1941–1942*. Boston: Mariner, 2014.

Harari, Oren. *The Leadership Secrets of Colin Powell*. New York: McGraw-Hill, 2002.

Harris, Brian. "What Do Theologians Do?" January 8, 2019.

Harris, R. Laird, Gleason L. Archer Jr., and Bruce K. Waltke, eds. *Theological Wordbook of the Old Testament*. 2 vols. Chicago: Moody, 1980.

Heath, Chip, and Dan Heath. *Decisive: How to Make Better Choices in Life and Work*. New York: Crown Business, 2013.

Hein, Tim. "How Churches Elevate and Protect Abusive Pastors." *Christianity Today*, November 2020.

Hersey, Paul. *The Situational Leader*. New York: Warner, 1985.

Hesselbein, Frances. "The 'How to Be' Leader." In *The Leader of the Future: New Visions, Strategies and Practices for the Next Era*, edited by Frances Hesselbein Marshall Goldsmith, and Richard Beckhard, 121–24. San Francisco: Jossey-Bass, 1996.

Higginbotham, Adam. *Midnight in Chernobyl: The Untold Story of the World's Greatest Nuclear Disaster*. New York: Simon & Schuster, 2019.

Horton, Michael. *The Christian Faith: A Systematic Theology for Pilgrims on the Way*. Grand Rapids: Zondervan, 2011.

Hunter, James Davison. *To Change the World: The Irony, Tragedy & Possibility of Christianity in the Late Modern World*. New York: Oxford University Press, 2010.

Hutchison, John. "Servanthood: Jesus' Countercultural Call to Christian Leaders." *Bibliotheca Sacra* 166 (January–March 2009).

Irving, Justin A., and Mark L. Strauss. *Leadership in Christian Perspective: Biblical Foundations and Contemporary Practices for Servant Leaders*. Grand Rapids: Baker, 2019.

Isaacson, Walter. *Steve Jobs*. New York: Simon & Schuster, 2011.

Johnson, John E. "Is Apostolic Leadership the Key to the Missional Church?" Unpublished paper presented at the meeting of the Evangelical Theological Society, November, 2009.

———. *Missing Voices: Learning to Lead beyond Our Horizons*. London: Langham, 2019.

———. *Under an Open Heaven: A New Way of Life Revealed in John's Gospel*. Grand Rapids: Kregel, 2017.

Johnson, Keith L. *Theology as Discipleship*. Downers Grove, IL: InterVarsity Press, 2015.

Kapic, Kelly. *A Little Book for New Theologians: Why and How to Study Theology*. Downers Grove, IL: InterVarsity Press, 2012.

Kaplan, Robert S., and David P. Norton. *The Strategy Focused Organization: How Balanced Scorecard Companies Thrive in the New Business Environment*. Boston: Harvard Business School Press, 2001.

Keller, Timothy. *The Prodigal Prophet: Jonah and the Mystery of God's Mercy*. New York: Viking, 2018.

Kellerman, Barbara. *The End of Leadership*. New York: Harper Business, 2012.

———. *Followership: How Followers Are Creating Change and Changing Leaders*. Boston: Harvard Business Press, 2008.

———. *Leadership: Essential Selections on Power, Authority, and Influence*. New York: McGraw-Hill, 2010.

Kellerman, Barbara, and Todd L. Pittinsky. *Leaders Who Lust: Power, Money, Sex, Success, Legitimacy, Legacy*. Cambridge: Cambridge University Press, 2020.

Keltner, Dacher. *The Power Paradox: How We Gain and Lose Influence*. New York: Penguin, 2016.

Kidner, Derek. *A Time to Mourn, and a Time to Dance*. Downers Grove, IL: InterVarsity Press, 1976.

———. *Ezra & Nehemiah*. Downers Grove, IL: InterVarsity Press, 1979.

———. *Proverbs: An Introduction and Commentary*. Downers Grove, IL: InterVarsity Press, 1984.

———. *Psalms 1–72*. Downers Grove, IL: InterVarsity Press, 1973.

———. *Psalms 73–150*. Downers Grove, IL: InterVarsity Press, 1975.

Klaas, Brian. *Corruptible: Who Gets Power and How It Changes Us.* New York: Scribners, 2021.

Kohler, Ludwig. *Old Testament Theology.* Philadelphia: Westminster, 1957.

Kotter, John P. *Leading Change.* Boston: Harvard Business Review Press, 1996.

———. *A Sense of Urgency.* Boston: Harvard Business Press, 2008.

Kouzes, James M., and Barry Z. Posner. *Christian Reflections on the Leadership Challenge.* San Francisco. Jossey-Bass, 2006.

———. *Credibility: How Leaders Gain and Lose It, Why People Demand It.* San Francisco: Jossey-Bass, 2003.

———. *A Leader's Legacy.* San Francisco: Jossey-Bass, 2006.

———. *The Leadership Challenge.* San Francisco: Jossey-Bass, 2007.

———. *The Truth about Leadership: The No-Fads, Heart-of-the-Matter Facts You Need to Know.* San Francisco: Jossey-Bass, 2010.

Kruse, Peter. "What Is Leadership?" *Forbes*, April 9, 2013. https://www.forbes.com/sites/kevinkruse/2013/04/09/what-is-leadership/#7fba219a5b90.

Langer, Rick. "Toward a Biblical Theology of Leadership." In *Organizational Leadership: Foundations and Practices for Christians*, edited by John S. Burns, John R. Shoup, and Donald C. Simmons Jr., 65–90. Downers Grove, IL: InterVarsity Press, 2014.

Laniak, Timothy S. *Shepherds After My Own Heart: Pastoral Traditions and Leadership in the Bible.* Downers Grove, IL: InterVarsity Press, 2006.

Larson, Erik. *The Splendid and the Vile: A Saga of Churchill, Family, and Defiance during the Blitz.* New York: Penguin, 2020.

Ledbetter, Bernice M., Robert J. Banks, and David C. Greenhalgh. *Reviewing Leadership: A Christian Evaluation of Current Approaches.* 2nd ed. Grand Rapids: Baker, 2016.

Leithart, Peter J. *1 & 2 Chronicles.* Grand Rapids: Brazos, 2019.

———. *1 & 2 Kings.* Grand Rapids: Brazos, 2006.

———. *Solomon among the Postmoderns.* Grand Rapids: Brazos, 2008.

———. *A Son to Me: An Exposition of 1 & 2 Samuel.* Moscow: Canon, 2003.

———. *The Ten Commandments: A Guide to the Perfect Law of Liberty (Christian Essentials).* Bellingham: Lexham, 2020.

Lencioni, Patrick M. *The Advantage: Why Organizational Health Trumps Everything Else in Business.* San Francisco: Jossey-Bass, 2012.

Lewis. C. S. *Screwtape Letters.* New York: HarperOne, 2013.

Lingenfelter, Sherwood G. *Leading Cross-Culturally: Covenant Relationships for Effective Christian Leadership.* Grand Rapids: Baker, 2008.

Longman, Tremper, III. *The Fear of the Lord Is Wisdom: A Theological Introduction to Wisdom in Israel*. Grand Rapids: Baker, 2017.

Lonsdale, Joe. "America's Leadership Culture is Rotten. That's Why We Need the University of Austin," *Washington Post*, November 22, 2021.

Lowney, Chris. *Heroic Leadership: Best Practices from a 450-Year-Old Company That Changed the World*. Chicago: Loyola, 2003.

Loy, Dan. "The Divine Sabotage: An Exegetical and Theological Study of Ecclesiastes 3." *Conspectus* 5, no. 1, March 2008.

Mancini, Will. *God Dreams: 12 Vision Templates for Finding and Focusing Your Church's Future*. Nashville: B&H, 2016.

Martin, Thomas R. *Ancient Greece: From Prehistoric to Hellenistic Times*. New Haven: Yale University Press, 2013.

Mattis, James. *Call Sign Chaos: Learning to Lead*. New York: Random House, 2019.

Maxwell, John C. *The 21 Irrefutable Laws of Leadership*. Nashville: Nelson, 1998.

McChesney, Chris, Sean Covey, and Jim Huling. *The Four Disciplines of Execution: Achieving Your Wildly Important Goals*. New York: Free Press, 2012.

McChrystal, Stanley. *Leaders: Myth and Reality*. New York: Portfolio/Penguin, 2018.

McCrimmon, Mitch. "Why Servant Leadership Is a Bad Idea." *Management Issues*, August 16, 2010.

McKane, William. *Proverbs: A New Approach*. *Philadelphia*: Westminster, 1970.

McKnight Scot. Five Things Biblical Scholars Wish Theologians Knew. Downers Grove: InterVarsity Press, 2021.

———. *Kingdom Conspiracy: Returning to the Radical Mission of the Local Church*. Grand Rapids: Brazos, 2014.

———. *Pastor Paul: Nurturing a Culture of Christoformity in the Church*. Grand Rapids: Brazos, 2019.

McTague, Tom. "What Joe Biden's Global Legacy Might Be," *The Atlantic*, November 2, 2021. Millard, Candice. *Hero of the Empire: The Boer War, a Daring Escape, and the Making of Winston Churchill*. New York: Anchor, 2016.

Moreland, J. P. "How Christian Philosophers Can Serve Systematic Theologians and Biblical Scholars." *JETS* 63, no. 2 (2020).

Morrow, Lance. "The Gravitas Factor." *Time*, March 14, 1988.

———. "You Are Living in the Golden Age of Stupidity." *Wall Street Journal*, August 29, 2021.

Murphy, Roland. *Ecclesiastes*. WBC. Dallas: Word, 2015.

Nichols, Tom. *The Death of Expertise: The Campaign against Established Knowledge and Why It Matters.* London: Oxford University Press, 2017.

Noonan, Peggy. "Andrew Coumo Plots His Survival." *Wall Street Journal,* March 18, 2021.

———. "Victory, Sacrifice, and Questions of 'Collusion.'" *Wall Street Journal,* July 13, 2017.

Northouse, Peter G. *Introduction to Leadership: Concepts and Practice.* Thousand Oaks: SAGE, 2015.

Nouwen, Henri. *In the Name of Jesus: Reflections on Christian Leadership.* New York: Crossroad, 2000.

Oden, Thomas. *Classic Christianity: A Systematic Theology.* New York: HarperOne, 2009.

———. *Pastoral Theology: Essentials of Ministry.* New York: HarperOne, 1993.

Osborne, Grant R. *Revelation.* Grand Rapids: Baker, 1999.

Owens, Mackubin Thomas. "The Enigma of Robert E. Lee." *National Review,* October 4, 2021. https://www.nationalreview.com/magazine/2021/10/04/the -enigma-of-robert-e-lee/#slide-1.

Packer, J. I. *Knowing God.* London: Hodder & Stoughton, 1973.

Palmer, Parker J. *On the Brink of Everything: Grace, Gravity & Getting Old.* Oakland: Berrett-Koehler, 2018.

Pennington, Jonathan T. *Jesus the Great Philosopher: Rediscovering the Wisdom Needed for the Good Life.* Grand Rapids: Brazos, 2020.

Peterson, Eugene H. *Christ Plays in Ten Thousand Places: A Conversation in Spiritual Theology.* Grand Rapids: Eerdmans, 2005.

———. *Eat This Book.* Grand Rapids: Eerdmans, 2005.

———. *The Jesus Way: A Conversation on the Ways That Jesus Is the Way.* Grand Rapids: Eerdmans, 2011.

———. *Leap Over a Wall: Earthy Spirituality for Everyday Christians.* New York: HarperSanFrancisco, 1997.

———. *The Pastor: A Memoir.* New York: HarperOne, 2011.

———. *Reversed Thunder: The Revelation of John & the Praying Imagination.* New York: HarperOne, 1991.

———. *Running with the Horses: The Quest for Life at Its Best.* Downers Grove: InterVarsity Press, 2019.

———. *Tell It Slant: A Conversation on the Language of Jesus in His Stories and Prayers.* Grand Rapids: Eerdmans, 2008.

———. *Under the Unpredictable Plant: An Exploration in Vocational Holiness.* Leominster, UK: Gracewing, 1992.

———. *The Unnecessary Pastor.* Grand Rapids: Eerdmans, 1999.

———. *Working the Angles.* Grand Rapids: Eerdmans, 1989.

Peterson, Jordan. *Beyond Order: 12 More Rules for Life.* New York: Portfolio, 2021.

———. *12 Rules for Life: An Antidote to Chaos.* Toronto: Random House, 2018.

Pfeffer, Jeffrey. *Leadership BS: Fixing Workplaces and Careers One Truth at a Time.* New York: Harper Business, 2015.

———. *Power: Why Some People Have It—And Others Don't.* New York: HarperCollins, 2010.

Piper, John. *Providence.* Wheaton, IL: Crossway, 2020.

———. *Think: The Life of the Mind and the Love of God.* Wheaton, IL: Crossway, 2011.

Plantinga, Cornelius, Jr. *Not the Way It's Supposed to Be: A Breviary of Sin.* Grand Rapids: Eerdmans, 1995.

———. *Reading for Preaching: The Preacher in Conversation with Storytellers, Biographers, Poets, and Journalists.* Grand Rapids: Eerdmans, 2013.

Pollard, William. "The Leader Who Serves." In *The Leader of the Future: New Visions, Strategies and Practices for the Next Era*, edited by Frances Hesselbein et al., 241–48. San Francisco: Jossey-Bass, 1996.

Ponnuru, Ramesh. "Character Effects," *National Review*, November 7, 2019, https://www.nationalreview.com/magazine/2019/11/25/character-effects.

Prior, Karen Swallow. *On Reading Well: Finding the Good Life through Great Books.* Grand Rapids: Brazos, 2018.

Purves, Andrew. *The Crucifixion of Ministry: Surrendering Our Ambitions to the Service of Christ.* Downers Grove, IL: InterVarsity Press, 2010.

———. *Pastoral Theology in the Classical Tradition.* Louisville: Westminster John Knox, 2001.

Roberts, Andrew. *Leadership in War: Essential Lessons from Those Who Made History.* New York: Penguin, 2019.

Robinson, Marilyn. *What Are We Doing Here? Essays.* New York: Farrar, Straus, and Giroux, 2018.

Rohr, Richard. *Falling Upward.* San Francisco: Jossey-Bass, 2011.

Rubenstein, David. *How to Lead.* New York: Simon & Schuster, 2020.

Rumelt, Richard. *Good Strategy/Bad Strategy: The Difference and Why It Matters.* New York: Crown Business, 2011.

Rumsfeld, Donald. *Rumsfeld's Rules: Leadership Lessons in Business, Politics, War, and Life*. New York: Broadside, 2013.

Ryan, Liz. "Five Signs Your Boss Is Incompetent." *Forbes*, December 12, 2016.

Sanders, J. Oswald. *Spiritual Leadership: Principles of Excellence for Every Believer*. Chicago: Moody, 1967.

Schreiner, Thomas R. *Paul: Apostle of God's Glory in Christ: A Pauline Theology*. Downers Grove, IL: InterVarsity Press, 2001.

Schroeder, Bernard. "To Be a Great Leader Learn How to Be a Great Follower: The Four Rules of Following." *Forbes*, December 5, 2019.

Schwartz, Barry. *Practical Wisdom*. New York: Riverhead, 2010.

Schwartz, Peter. *The Art of the Long View*. New York: Currency Doubleday, 1991.

———. *Learnings from the Long View*. Scotts Valley, CA: Create Space.

Serhan, Yasmeen. "The Common Element Uniting Worldwide Protests." *Atlantic*, November 19, 2019.

Shoup, John R., and Chris McHorney. "Decision Making." In *Organizational Leadership: Foundations and Practices for Christians*, edited by John S. Burns, John R. Shoup, and Donald C. Simmons, Jr., 197–228. Downers Grove, IL: InterVarsity Press, 2014.

Shuster, Marguerite. *The Fall and Sin: What We Have Become as Sinners*. Grand Rapids: Eerdmans, 2003.

Sides, Hampton. *In the Kingdom of Ice: The Grand and Terrible Polar Voyage of the USS Jeannette*. New York: Anchor, 2014.

Smith, Gary V. "The Concept of God/the Gods as King in the Ancient Near East and the Bible." *Trinity Journal* 3, n.s. (1982), 18–38.

Smith, James K. A. *On the Road with Saint Augustine: A Real-World Spirituality for Restless Hearts*. Grand Rapids: Brazos, 2019.

Sonnenfeld, Jeffrey. *The Hero's Farewell: What Happens When CEOs Retire*. New York: Oxford University Press, 1988.

Stackhouse, John G. *Making the Best of It: Following Christ in the Real World*. London: Oxford University Press, 2011.

Stanley, Andy. *Next Generation Leader: 5 Essentials for Those Who Will Shape the Future*. Colorado Springs: Multnomah, 2003.

———. *Visioneering: Your Guide for Discovering and Maintaining Personal Vision*. Colorado Springs: Multnomah, 2005.

Strom, Mark. *Lead with Wisdom: How Wisdom Transforms Good Leaders into Great Leaders*. Milton: Wiley, 2013.

Swaim, Barton. *The Speechwriter: A Brief Education in Politics*. New York: Simon & Schuster, 2015.

———. "Why Read the Bible?" *Wall Street Journal*, March 17, 2021.

Sweet, Leonard. *Summoned to Lead*. Grand Rapids: Zondervan, 2004.

Taylor, Barbara Brown. *Leaving Church: A Memoir of Faith*. New York: HarperOne, 2012.

Templer, Klaus J. "Why Do Toxic People Get Promoted?" *Harvard Business Review*, July 10, 2018. https://hbr.org/2018/07/why-do-toxic-people-get -promoted-for-the-same-reason-humble-people-do-political-skill.

Thielicke, Helmut. *A Little Exercise for Young Theologians*. Grand Rapids: Eerdmans, 2016.

Thomas, Evan. *Being Nixon: A Man Divided*. New York: Random House, 2015.

Tichy, Noel. *The Leadership Engine: How Winning Companies Build Leaders at Every Level*. New York: HarperBusiness Essentials, 2002.

Tichy, Noel M., and Warren G. Bennis. *Judgment: How Winning Leaders Make Great Calls*. New York: Portfolio, 2007.

Tozer, A. W. *The Knowledge of the Holy*. New York: HarperCollins, 1961.

Trueman, Carl R. "The Failure of Evangelical Elites." *First Things, November 2021*.

Tupper, Helen and Sarah Ellis, "Make Learning a Daily Part of Your Routine, *Harvard Business Review*, November 4, 2021. https://hbr.org/2021/11/make-learning-a-part-of -your-daily-routine.

Ulrich, Dave. "Credibility x Capability." In *The Leader of the Future: New Visions, Strategies and Practices for the Next Era*, edited by Frances Hesselbein, Marshall Goldsmith, and Richard Beckhard, 209–20. San Francisco: Jossey-Bass, 1996.

Useem, Jerry. "Power Causes Brain Damage." *Atlantic*, July/August 2017. https://www.theatlantic.com/magazine/archive/2017/07/power-causes -braindamage/528711/.

Useem, Michael. *The Go Point: When It's Time to Decide—Knowing What to Do and When to Do It*. New York: Three Rivers, 2006.

———. *The Leadership Moment: Nine True Stories of Triumph and Disaster and Their Lessons for Us All*. New York: Times Business, 1998.

Van Gelder, Craig, and Dwight J. Zscheile. *The Missional Church in Perspective: Mapping Trends and Shaping the Conversation*. Grand Rapids: Baker, 2011.

Vanhoozer, Kevin J. "Letter to an Aspiring Theologian." *First Things*, August 2018.

———. *The Pastor as Public Theologian: Reclaiming a Lost Vision*. Grand Rapids: Baker, 2020.

Varadarajan, Tunku. "A Poetics for Tyrants," *Wall Street Journal*, November 30–December 1, 2019, a review of Frank Dikotter, *How to Be a Dictator: The Cult of Personality in the Twentieth Century*. London: Bloomsbury, 2019.

Volf, Miroslav. *Captive to the Word of God: Engaging the Scriptures for Contemporary Theological Reflection*. Grand Rapids: Eerdmans, 2010.

Volf, Miroslav, and Matthew Croasmun, *For the Life of the World: Theology That Makes a Difference*. Grand Rapids: Brazos, 2019.

Von Balthasar, Hans. *Prayer*. San Francisco: Ignatius, 1986.

Von Rad, Gerhard. *Wisdom in Israel*. Nashville: Abingdon, 1972.

Wageman, Ruth, Debra A. Nunes, James A. Burruss, and J. Richard Hackman. *Senior Leadership Teams: What It Takes to Make Them Great*. Boston: Harvard Business Review Press, 2008.

Walker, Sam. *The Captain Class: A New Theory of Leadership*. New York: Random House, 2017.

———. "Michael Jordan Didn't Manage People, He Lit Them on Fire." *Wall Street Journal*, May 16, 2020. https://www.wsj.com/articles/michael-jordan -didnt-manage-people-he-lit-them-on-fire-11589601602.

Waltke, Bruce K. *The Book of Proverbs: Chapters 1–15*. Grand Rapids: Eerdmans, 2004.

———. *The Book of Proverbs: Chapters 15–31*. Grand Rapids: Eerdmans, 2015.

———. *An Old Testament Theology: An Exegetical, Canonical, and Thematic Approach*. Grand Rapids: Zondervan, 2007.

Webster, John. *Holiness*. Grand Rapids: Eerdmans, 2003.

Weiner, Eric. *The Socrates Express*. New York: Simon & Schuster, 2020.

Willard, Dallas. *Renovation of the Heart: Putting On the Character of Christ*. Colorado Springs: NavPress, 2002.

Williamson, H. G. M. *Ezra-Nehemiah*. Grand Rapids: Zondervan, 2015.

Willimon, William H. *Pastor: The Theology and Practice of Ordained Ministry*. Nashville: Abingdon, 2016.

Wills, Garry. *Certain Trumpets: The Nature of Leadership*. New York: Touchstone, 1994.

Wilson, Thomas Carlyle. *On Heroes, Hero-Worship, and the Heroic in History*. 1840. Reprint, University of California Press, 1993.

Winters, Bradford. "A Conversation with Walter Brueggemann." *Image 55*. https://imagejournal.org/article/conversation-walter-brueggemann/.

Witherington, Ben, III. *Biblical Theology: The Convergence of the Canon*. New York: Cambridge University Press, 2019.

————. *Who God Is: Meditations on the Character of Our God*. Bellingham: Lexham, 2020.

Woolfe, Lorin. *Leadership Secrets from the Bible: Management Lessons for Contemporary Leaders*. New York: MJF, 2002.

Wright, Christopher J. H. *The Mission of God: Unlocking the Bible's Grand Narrative*. Downers Grove, IL: InterVarsity Press, 2006.

Wright, N. T. *After You Believe: Why Christian Character Matters*. New York: HarperOne, 2010.

————. *Evil and the Justice of God*. London: SPCK, 2012.

————. *How God Became King: The Forgotten Story of the Gospels*. New York: HarperOne, 2012.

————. *Paul*. Minneapolis: Fortress, 2005.

————. *Simply Jesus: A New Vision of Who He Was, What He Did, and Why He Matters*. New York: HarperOne, 2011.

Wright, Walter C., Jr. *Relational Leadership: A Biblical Model for Influence and Service*. Downers Grove, IL: InterVarsity Press, 2009.

————. *The Third Third of Life: Preparing for Your Future*. Downers Grove, IL: InterVarsity Press, 2012.

SUBJECT INDEX

SCRIPTURE INDEX

PROVERBS

ECCLESIASTES

ISAIAH

ROMANS

1 CORINTHIANS

2 CORINTHIANS